TEACHER CERTIFICA▮▮▮▮▮▮▮ ALL FIFTY STATES

The contents of this manual re▮▮▮▮▮▮▮btaining a teaching certificate i▮ The District of Columbia and the fifty states effective July 1ˢᵗ 2008 or as stated in the information u▮ each state. Our references are ▮▮▮▮▮▮▮ certification office in each state. Much of the information ▮▮▮▮▮▮▮ *n and Certification of Educational P*▮▮43 ▮▮▮▮▮▮▮ciation of State Directors of Teacher Ed▮ 26th ed. ▮▮▮▮▮▮▮ *g/*. This online resource is another exc▮▮▮▮▮▮▮ sonnel certifications not presented in ▮▮▮▮▮▮▮

This manual is designed as an accessible quick reference guide for teachers, librarians, administrators, counselors, and psychologists who may be applying for certification or recertification in their own or other states; for college advisors counseling pupils; for library reference; or as an educational reference guide for the classroom or placement office. Many states are revising their requirements for certification, and significant changes occur each year. This year alone, more than 23 states have provided important revisions to their requirements. There is an important movement towards the adoption of performance-based standards rather than the lock-step prerequisite coursework used historically. The use of testing prior to acceptance in an education program at a college or university is becoming much more common as is recognition of National Board for Professional Teaching Standards (NBPTS) certification. Please visit **http://www.nbpts.org/** for more information. Many states have their own certification tests while the majority now expect scores from either NTE or the PRAXIS Pre-Professional and/or Subject Area tests prior to issuing a teaching certificate. For further testing information visit the Educational Testing Service web site at: **http://www.ets.org/teachingandlearning/index.htm**.

With growing shortages of qualified, college and university trained instructors, most states have begun offering various *Alternate Path* certification programs enabling a candidate without the requisite four, five, or six years of teacher/educator training to qualify for initial or provisional certification. Although each state offers admission differences, it is common for the candidate meeting Alternate Path requirements to agree to complete the formal certification requirements of the state within a period of from one to five years after receiving a *provisional* certificate. There is also a successful *Troops to Teachers* program sponsored by the U.S. Department of Education and Department of Defense that helps eligible military personnel begin a new career as teachers in public schools where their skills, knowledge and experience are most needed. For more information, visit **http://www.proudtoserveagain.com/**. Another federal initiative, the No Child Left Behind (NCLB) Act of 2001 requires, among other funding incentives, that every state define and regulate Highly Qualified Teachers. These new standards require that the states define and establish criteria with rubrics to determine both initial and subsequent qualifications to teach in their schools.

All 50 states now have accessible web sites on the World Wide Web. Most include both their requirements and application information. However, it has been our experience that often their complexity and link-depth can still make finding even a single, simple answer daunting. For this reason, this guide continues to serve its original purpose, that of simplifying and clarifying the basic information needs of teachers, support personnel, and administrators who seek to certify or re-certify in their own or other states. *New since the Twenty-First Edition:* Each state entry now includes a special *Recertification* brief for your convenience.

As you use this manual, please contact us if you find an error, omission, or an undocumented change. We diligently strive for accuracy in our certification guide for all fifty states and D.C.

JOEL E. BOYDSTON

Teacher Certification Publications
PO Box 7756
Sebring, Florida 33872-0113

Phone: 863-453-4791
Fax: 863-453-7351

E-Mail: **teachercertification@earthlink.net**
Please visit our web site for current contact information & pricing:
http://home.earthlink.net/~teachercertification/

Dedication

This book is dedicated to my children Amanda and Jeremy. During all the myriad adventures and challenges we've faced together, you two have steadfastly maintained your love and support. No man with children could be any more blessed than I. Thank you.

Special thanks deserve to be given to the creator of <u>Teacher Certification Requirements in All Fifty States</u>, my predecessor in this publication, Dr. Roger E. Goddard. It was you, Roger, who first aroused my interest in certification regulations. For that introduction, I am deeply indebted to you.

"Teaching is an instinctual art, mindful of potential, craving of realizations,
a pausing, seamless process."
- A Bartlett Giamatti -

ITEMS REQUIRED FOR APPLICATIONS
(Found in the "Requirements At A Glance" section for each state)

A.   A completed (and, in some cases, notarized) application form available from the state.

B.   Official transcripts (with seal and signature) of all college credits earned.

C.   Recommendation of the college or university certifying successful completion of a teacher training program.

D.   NCATE program validation for program completed.

E.   Photocopies of certificates held in any state. Some states require the copies be notarized.

F.   Original instructional or staff certificate/license held in another state (if applicable)

G.   Letters from employing superintendents verifying past teaching experience.

H.   Oath of Allegiance to the United States of America.

I.   Proof of United States citizenship.

J.   Criminal Background Check and/or fingerprint identification validation.

K.   Chest X-Ray or TB test within past twelve months.

L.   Basic Skills Competency Test results.

M.   Passing scores on the PRAXIS I: Pre-Professional Skills Tests (PPST) of Reading, Writing, and Mathematics.

N.   Official notice of National Teacher Examination (NTE) **OR** PRAXIS II: Specialty Area Tests including Principles of Learning and Teaching (PLT) scores.

O.   Requirement for beginning instructors to complete the Praxis III: Classroom Performance Assessment.

P.   State Sponsored Testing Program (SSTP) - A multi-state consortium formed to develop tests for initial certification in content areas not covered by existing NTE or Praxis II specialty Area tests. Member states are Arkansas, Connecticut, Indiana, Mississippi, , New York, North Carolina, Ohio, Oregon, Pennsylvania, South Carolina, Tennessee, and Virginia.

Q.   Passing scores on the School Leaders Licensure Assessment (SLLA), or the School Superintendent Assessment (SSA) for school administrators and superintendents.

NOTE: Current fees are stated in the requirements under each state heading and range from *none* to $300.00. Many states also charge an additional fee for fingerprinting and/or background checks.

TABLE OF CONTENTS

STATE OF ALABAMA

State Department of Education
Teacher Education and Certification Office
Gordon Persons Building, Room 5215
P.O. Box 302101
Montgomery, Alabama 36130-2101
Phone: 334-242-9977 / Fax: 334-242-9998
Web Site: **http://www.alsde.edu/html/home.asp**

INITIAL REQUIREMENTS AT A GLANCE:

Also needed will be items: A, B, C, D, F, G, J, K, and M (See page 2). Supplemental application forms are required for many types of certificates. The fee for Initial licensure and renewal is $20.00 (and a $49.00 non-refundable background review) for initial certificates and renewals. Scores on the Praxis II Specialty Area Test ARE required. All professional educator and renewable Career/Technical Certificates are valid for 5 years. Alabama DOES accept candidates with certification from NCATE accredited institutions or from states participating in the NASDTEC Interstate Agreement (Teachers, Support Professionals and Administrators). Individuals who are applying on or after January 1, 2003, for the issuance of a Professional Educator Certificate or for alternative certificates (i.e., Alternative Baccalaureate-Level Certificate, Special Alternative Certificate, or Preliminary Certificate) must meet the requirements of the Alabama Prospective Teacher Testing Program (APTTP) as a precondition for issuance of Alabama certification. The APTTP consists of basic skills assessments, effective for applicants on or after January 1, 2003, and subject assessments, effective for applicants on or after April 14, 2005. Applicants who apply between April 14, 2005, and April 13, 2006, will be required to have passed the basic skills assessments and have taken the appropriate subject assessment of the APTTP. Applicants who apply on or after April 14, 2006, will be required to have passed the basic skills assessments and passed the appropriate subject assessment of the APTTP. Alabama does NOT belong to the Interstate New Teacher Assessment and Support Consortium (INTASC).

Renewal Requirements:
Certificate Continuation - Three years of satisfactory educational experience and five Continuing Education Units (CEUs), equaling 50 clock hours of professional development; **OR** three years of satisfactory educational experience and three (3) semester hours of allowable credit; **OR** five CEUs and three semester credit hours; **OR** six semester credit hours; **OR** initial issuance of NBPTS certification.
Certificate Reinstatement - By verifying nine semester hours of allowable credit earned within five years prior to the beginning date of the reinstated certificate. A maximum of five allowable CEUs, equaling three semester hours, may be applied to this requirement; **OR** if, within the ten years immediately preceding the renewal application, the individual verifies having met the requirements as listed for each of the two five-year periods.

Alabama Certification - The approved approaches for meeting the curriculum requirements for Alabama professional certification are as follows:

Alabama Approved Program Approach - Candidate completes curriculum requirements by completing a state-approved teacher education program with an Alabama institution of higher education in the area certification is desired.
Reciprocal Agreements - Candidates who have graduated from an out-of-state institution and/or have been certified in other states may meet curriculum requirements for Alabama professional certification through of the two following methods:
- A.   Completion of a teacher education program at an out-of-state, regionally accredited, senior institution accredited by NCATE.
- B.   Compliance with the requirements of the National Association of State Directors of Teacher Education and Certification Interstate Agreement (NASDTEC Interstate Agreement).

Other Approaches -

A. Recognition of state-approved programs may be extended to states which are not members of the NASDTEC Interstate Agreement. Verification of completion of such a program must be provided by the institution's certification officer on a specified supplement to the Application.

B. Certificate and experience recognition may be available to candidates who hold valid professional certification in other states. The experience requirement is based on that of the NASDTEC Interstate Agreement in effect at the time of application.

C. Certification based on foreign credentials requires that candidates submit an evaluation of their foreign credits from an approved evaluation agency.

Alternative Approaches to Alabama Certification - Alabama offers a variety of alternative methods to attain certification. There are available provisions for applicants with foreign credentials. Please contact the Alabama Teacher Education and Certification Office for complete information.

A. Alternative Baccalaureate Level (valid one year, renewable twice, in consecutive years) - for grades 6-8 or 9-12 in specific fields and physical education. They may also be issued for grades K-8 in art, dance, instrumental music, vocal/choral music, theater, foreign languages, and physical education.

B. Special Alternative Fifth Year Level (valid one year, renewable twice) - for candidates who have earned a bachelor's degree and been admitted to an Alabama Fifth-Year Program. Areas available include single or comprehensive teaching fields in some middle grades 4-8, or secondary grades 6-12 programs; Elementary Education (K-6); Early Childhood Education (P-3); special education; and other specific Elementary-Secondary (P-12) teaching fields.

C. Speech and Language Impaired Approach (valid five years) - candidates holding a master's or higher degree in speech-language pathology and a valid speech-language pathology license issued by any state's board of examiners in speech pathology and audiology may be eligible for the appropriate professional certificate endorsed in speech-language impaired.

D. Preliminary Certificate (valid two years, renewable once for one year) - applies to School Counselors, Library-Media and Speech/Language Impaired certificate candidates.

E. Nationally Certified School Psychologist Approach - applies to nationally certified school psychologists.

F. National Board for Professional Teaching Standards Approach - applies to national board certified personnel.

TYPES OF CERTIFICATES[1]

Professional Certificates (Teachers)

Early Childhood Special Education . . . . (P-3)
Early Childhood . . . . (P-3)
Elementary . . . . (K-6)
Elementary-Secondary[2] . . . . (P-12)
Middle School . . . . (4-8)
Secondary[3] . . . . (6-12)

Including: Driver and Traffic Safety Education, English Language Arts, Foreign Languages (Modern and Latin), Health Education, Mathematics, General Science, Biology, Chemistry, Physics, General Social Science, Geography, History, Career/Technical Education: Agriscience

Education, Business/Marketing Education, Family and Consumer Sciences[3], Education, Technical Education, and Career Technologies
Collaborative Special Education . . (K-6 and 6-12)
Special Education[2] . . . . (P-12)

Master's and Sixth-Year Level Certificates (Instructional Support)

Educational Administrator . . . . (P-12)
School Counselor . . . . (P-12)
School Library-Media Specialist . . . . (P-12)
School Psychologist . . . . (P-12)
School Psychometrist . . . . (P-12)

---

[1] Alternative and Career/Technical certificates are also available. Contact the Department for a complete listing.

[2] P-12 programs include art, dance, music, physical education, theatre, foreign language, and gifted, hearing impaired, speech and language impaired, and visually impaired in special education.

[3] Secondary level candidates may select one of three field options: (a) a comprehensive teaching field in English language arts, general science, or general social science; (b) one or more single teaching fields in secondary subject area(s); or (c) a single teaching field in an area of career/technical education.

TEACHER EDUCATION PROGRAMS

The teacher certification program consists of two stages: Basic (Class B) and Advanced (Fifth Year - Class A, and Sixth Year - Class AA). Advanced programs differ from basic programs in competencies, not in purpose. Teacher education programs must ensure that candidates have completed general studies which include courses and/or components in humanities, social sciences, mathematics, and science. All education preparation programs must meet or exceed the standards for accreditation of the Southern Association of Colleges and Schools (SACS).

Class B (Baccalaureate) and Alternative Class A (fifth-year) Initial Teacher Certification

A. **General Studies and Teaching Field** - Candidates for the Class B and Alternate Class A Year programs in Early Childhood, Elementary Education, Early Childhood Special Education, and Collaborative Teacher K-6 and 6-12 must complete at least 12 semester hours of credit in each of the following: English language arts, math, science, and social science. Teacher training must meet Alabama State Board of Education knowledge and ability rules in their area(s) in the content area where they plan to teach, NCATE-affiliated specialty guidelines, or the guidelines of other national teaching field specific accrediting agencies. Additional requirements include:
1. Satisfactory completion of state-approved teacher education program; and
2. GPA of at least 2.5 overall in the teaching field, and in professional studies with no grade below a "C" in professional studies.
3. Earn a passing score on a comprehensive written exam.

B. **Field experiences** - The Class B and Alternate Class A programs shall include full time internships with participation for a full semester and preferably including more than one classroom or grade level and have allowed candidates full instructional responsibilities for at least twenty days, ten of which were consecutive. Internships for middle and secondary levels, P-12, and Elementary programs may require experiences in more than one grade level.

C. **Professional Studies** - Teacher preparation shall include an internship and curriculum preparation designed to develop candidates' *knowledge and abilities* in learning and motivation, student diversity, curriculum and instructional delivery, classroom management, assessment, professional development and responsibilities, and integrating technology.

Class A Certifications (Fifth Year).
A. Teaching Fields:

Candidates must have a Class B certificate in the same or broader field of study for which the Class A certificate is sought, except in special education. The purpose of the Class A certificate is to help the teacher develop higher levels of competence, knowledge, and abilities. Additional requirements for teachers include:
1. A survey of special education coursework, unless previously completed;
2. At least one third of the coursework shall consist of teaching field courses;
3. English language arts, general science, and general social science programs shall require at least one course in two areas of the composite field;
4. A GPA of 3.0;
5. Completion of an internship is required for candidates in Adult Education, English as a Second Language, Speech and Language Impaired and Reading Specialist;
6. A practicum will be required for initial certification in a special education field; and
7. Passing score on a final, comprehensive written exam.

B. Educational Administration (P-12):

The study of educational administration begins at the fifth year level. Admission to this program requires one of two options: Option 1, endorsement in educational administration which requires an earned master's level professional educator certificate in a teaching field or instructional support area; or Option 2, master's degree program which requires an earned baccalaureate-level professional educator certification in a teaching field. Program competencies must include: P-12 curriculum, instruction, professional and staff development, student services, leadership skills, school and community relations, management skills, legal responsibilities, and integration of technology. Additional requirements include:

1.   A survey of special education coursework, unless previously completed;
2.   A GPA of 3.25 in an approved educational administration program;
3.   A 300 hour supervised internship with 50 hours in each of the various grade levels and 100 hours at the level chosen;
4.   Passing score on a comprehensive written educational administration test; and
5.   Two years of satisfactory educational experience, including at least one year of P-12 classroom teaching experience.

C. Library-Media (P-12):

The study of Library-Media begins at the fifth-year level. Candidates must have at least a baccalaureate level professional educator certificate in a teaching field. Additional requirements include:

A.   A survey of special education course work, unless previously completed;
B.   A GPA of 3.0 in an approved library-media program;
C.   A 300 hour clinical experience with at least half of them in a P-12 school library;
D.   Passing score on a comprehensive written test; and
E.   Two years of satisfactory educational experience.

D. School Counseling (P-12)

The study of school counseling begins at the fifth-year level. Candidates must have at least a baccalaureate level professional educator certificate in a teaching field. Additional requirements include:

1.   A survey of special education course work, unless previously completed;
2.   A GPA of 3.0 in an Alabama State Board of Education approved school counseling program;
3.   A practicum which includes a minimum of 30 supervised clock hours with direct service work in individual and group counseling with early childhood/elementary and secondary school students;
4.   A supervised P-12 school-based internship of at least 300 clock hours begun subsequent to the completion of the practicum which includes all the activities of a school counselor;
5.   Passing score on a comprehensive written test; and
6.   Two years of satisfactory educational experience.

E. School Psychometry (P-12):

The study of school psychometry begins at the fifth-year level. Candidates must have at least a baccalaureate level professional educator certificate in a teaching field. Additional requirements include:

1.   A survey of special education course work, unless previously completed;
2.   A GPA of 3.0 in an Alabama State Board of Education approved school psychometry program;
3.   A P-12 school-based internship of at least 300 clock hours and supervised by a qualified school psychometrist or school psychologist;
4.   Passing score on a comprehensive written test; and
5.   Two years of satisfactory educational experience.

Class AA (Sixth Year) -
A. Teaching Fields:

Candidates must have a master's level (Class A) professional educator certificate in the same field in which the Class AA certificate is sought, except in special education. Additional requirements for teachers include:

A.   A survey of special education coursework, unless previously completed;
B.   At least one third of coursework must include teaching field courses;
C.   English language arts, general science, and general social science programs shall require at least one course in two areas of the composite field;
D.   A GPA of 3.25 in an approved teacher education program;
E.   A practicum will be required for initial certification in a special education field; and
F.   Passing score on a final, comprehensive written exam covering the content.

B. School Psychology (P-12):

The certification for school psychology is at the sixth-year level. Candidates must have at least a baccalaureate level professional educator certificate in a teaching field and master's level certification as a school psychometrist. Additional requirements include:

1. A GPA of 3.25 on all courses in the approved program;
2. Survey coursework in Special Education unless previously completed;
3. A supervised P-12 school-based internship of at least 300 clock hours; and
4. Passing score on a comprehensive written test.

C. **Other Instructional Support Areas:**

Admission to this program requires a master's level professional educator certificate in the instructional support field in which Class AA certification is sought. Candidates for Class AA certification in educational administration shall hold a master's level professional educator certification as a superintendent/principal, superintendent, principal, supervisor, vocational administrator, or educational administrator. Additional requirements include:

1. A GPA of 3.25 on all courses in the approved program;
2. Programs in Education Administration shall require mentor training and a problem analysis project, thesis, or dissertation;
3. Survey coursework in special education unless previously completed; and
4. Passing score on a comprehensive written test.

STATE OF ALASKA

Alaska Department of Education & Early Development
Teacher Education and Certification
801 West 10th Street, Suite 200
P.O. Box 110500
Juneau, Alaska 99811-0500
Phone: 907-465-2831 / Fax: 907-465-2441
Web Site: **http://www.eed.state.ak.us/TeacherCertification/home.html**

INITIAL REQUIREMENTS AT A GLANCE:

Also needed are items A, B, C, F (only for Type Q, preliminary certificate), J, K, M, and N - See page 2. Fee for all initial certificates is $125.00, and a $66.00 background check fee. Submit all required documents in a single packet. Renewal fee is $125.00 per certificate. Updated background check for renewals. Passing test scores ARE required of *all* initial applicants (see complete list below). Alaska DOES NOT belong to the Interstate Certification Contract and the NASDTEC Interstate Agreement. Alaska does NOT belong the New Teacher Assessment and Support Consortium (INTASC). Alaska does NOT require courses or competencies in Special Education. Major revisions became effective on 9/29/2005.

Renewal Requirements: 6 semester hours within 5 years, with 3 being at the 300 level or above. Verification of current employment in an Alaska public school district in a position requiring a certificate. If an applicant is not employed in this capacity at the time of renewal, fingerprint cards will be required. Complete application and fees.

TEACHING CERTIFICATES

As of 7/15/2008, passing scores from any of the following exams may be submitted to meet the testing requirement for teacher certification in Alaska. Scores from different exams may not be combined to form a set of passing scores. You must have passing scores from all sections of ONE of the approved exams:

Praxis I, CBEST, WEST-B, Alabama Work Keys, Florida Teacher Certification, Georgia Assessment for the Certification of Educators, Illinois Certification Testing, Michigan Test for Teacher Certification, New Mexico Assessment of Teacher Basic Skills, New York State Teacher Certification Liberal Arts and Sciences Test, or the Oklahoma General Education Test. Please check the Department's web site for an updated list.

Initial Certificate: valid for up to three (3) years, NON-RENEWABLE. To qualify for an Initial certificate, an applicant must meet the following requirements:

A. Bachelor's degree or higher

B.   Completion of a teacher preparation program
OR
Current enrollment in a teacher preparation program. Program enrollment cannot be used for individuals enrolled in special education programs. Those individuals must complete their program prior to applying for the Initial certificate.
C.   Passing scores on an approved basic competency exam (see list above)
D.   Fingerprint cards submitted with application for background check
E.   Complete application and fees.
*   Although the Initial Certificate is valid for a period of up to three years, candidates must complete the Alaska studies and Alaska multicultural requirement within two years from the issuance of your Initial Certificate. The requirements for the Professional or Master certificate must be met during the life of the Initial certificate.

Professional Certificate: valid for five (5) years, renewable. To qualify for a Professional certificate, an applicant must meet the following requirements:
A.   Held an Initial Tier I certificate
B.   Completion of a teacher preparation program
C.   Passing scores on two performance reviews
D.   Approved Alaska Studies coursework
E.   Approved Multicultural/Cross-Cultural Communications coursework
F.   Recency credit (six semester hours of credit in the previous five years)
G.   Passing scores on a content area exam
H.   Fingerprint cards submitted with application for background check
I.   Complete application and fees

Master Teacher Certificate: valid for ten (10) years, renewable. To qualify for a Master certificate, an applicant must meet the following requirements:
A.   Meet all requirements for the Professional certificate
B.   Hold a current Initial or Professional certificate
C.   Hold current National Board certification issued by NBPTS
D.   Complete application and fees

To renew a Master certificate, an applicant must meet the following requirements:
A.   Current, renewed National Board certification
B.   Recency credit (Six semester hours of credit taken during the life of the Professional certificate being renewed. A minimum of three semester hours must be upper division or graduate credit.)
C.   Verification of employment in an Alaska public school district in a position requiring a certificate. If an applicant is not employed in this capacity at the time of renewal, fingerprint cards will be required.
D.   Complete application and fees

If the requirements to renew a Master certificate have not been met, an applicant must meet all current renewal requirements for the Professional certificate.

TYPE B ADMINISTRATIVE CERTIFICATES

Requirements:
A.   At least three (3) years experience as a certificated teacher
B.   Completion of an approved teacher education program in school administration
C.   Master's degree or higher from a regionally accredited institution
D.   Recommendation of the preparing institution
E.   Six (6) semester hours or nine quarter hours of credit earned during the five-year period preceding the date of application (See below.)
F.   Three (3) semester hours of approved Alaska studies and three semester hours of approved multicultural education/cross-cultural communications (See below.)
G.   Complete application packet, which includes a signed and notarized application, the institutional recommendation form, official transcripts, two sets of completed fingerprint cards, and all processing fees (All fees are non-refundable).

SUPERINTENDENT

A completed Institutional Recommendation showing completion of an approved superintendency program from a regionally accredited university and verification of at least 5 years of employment as a classroom teacher or administrator. (At least three years must have been satisfactory employment as a teacher with a Type A certificate or comparable certificate issued by another state. At least one year must have been satisfactory employment as an administrator with a Type B certificate or comparable certificate from another state.)

TYPE C SPECIAL SERVICES CERTIFICATE

A. Completion of a program in a special service area
B. Bachelor's or higher degree
C. Recommendation of the preparing institution
D. Six semester hours or nine (9) quarter hours of credit taken within the past five years
E. Three semester hours of approved Alaska studies and three (3) semester hours of multicultural education/cross-cultural communications

Endorsements under a Type C certificate include audiology, occupational therapy, physical therapy, recreation, school nursing, school psychology, school psychometry, social work, speech pathology, school counselor, and library science-media.

School Psychology
For an endorsement in school psychology, you must also hold a master's or higher degree in school psychology; be recommended by an institution whose school psychology program has been approved by NCATE, the National Association of School Psychologists, or the American Psychological Association; and have completed a 1200 hour internship (with 600 of the hours in a school setting); or be certified under the certification system of the National Association of School Psychologists.

Speech, Language, or Hearing
For endorsement in speech, language, or hearing, you must hold either a master's or higher degree with a major emphasis in speech-language pathology, audiology, or speech-language and hearing science; or possess certification of clinical competence from the American Speech Language-Hearing Association. In addition, you must be recommended for endorsement by an institution with a program approved by NCATE or the American Speech-Language-Hearing Association.

STATE OF ARIZONA

Department of Education
Certification Unit
PO Box 6490
Phoenix, Arizona 85005-6490
Phone: 602-542-4367 / Fax: 602-542-1141
Web Site: **http://www.ade.state.az.us/certification**

INITIAL REQUIREMENTS AT A GLANCE:

Also needed will be items: A, B, E, J (1 copy) and K - See page 2. The fee is $60.00 for most certificates (conversion costs may apply). One set of fingerprints ($32.00 processing charge) on their card for new applicants. Arizona Educator Proficiency Assessments–AEPA (Professional and Subject Knowledge) ARE required. Courses or competencies in Special Education ARE required. Arizona DOES belong to Interstate Certification Compact, and may issue *like-kind* certificates. Candidates applying for certification to become a teacher or school administrator are required to pass an examination on the provisions and principles of the Constitutions of the United States and Arizona. Candidates who have successfully completed ADE-approved course work in this area are exempt from this requirement.

PROVISIONAL CERTIFICATION REQUIREMENTS* (ALL CERTIFICATES)

Applies to all Early Childhood, Elementary, Secondary, Special Education Certificates, as well as principal and superintendent certification.

A. Bachelor's degree from an accredited institution;

B. Passing score on the professional *and* subject knowledge portion of the AEPA; and

C. U.S. Constitution test; Arizona Constitution test (within 1 year of issuance).

* A certificate may be issued for one year with these deficiencies.

EARLY CHILDHOOD CERTIFICATE
(Birth - Age 8)

PROVISIONAL CERTIFICATE (Valid 2 years, 2 yr. extension allowed once)

A. A Bachelor's or more advanced degree from an accredited institution. Official transcript(s) must be submitted.

B. Option 1, 2, or 3:

    1. Completion of a teacher preparation program in early childhood education from an accredited institution or a Board-approved teacher preparation program.

    - OR -

    2. Thirty seven (37) semester hours of early childhood education courses from an accredited institution to include all of the following areas of study and a minimum of 8 semester hours of practicum. Practicum must include a minimum of 4 semester hours in supervised field experience, practicum, internship or student teaching setting serving children birth through preschool or one year of full-time verified teaching experience birth through preschool and a minimum of 4 semester hours in a supervised student teaching setting serving children in kindergarten through grade 3 or one year of full-time verified teaching experience kindergarten through grade 3.

        Early childhood education courses shall include all of the following areas of study (a) foundations of early childhood education, (b) child guidance and classroom management, (c) characteristics and quality practices for typical and atypical behaviors of young children, (d) child growth and development, including, health, safety and nutrition, (e) child, family, cultural and community relationships, (f) developmentally appropriate instructional methodologies for teaching language, math, science, social studies and the arts, (g) early language and literacy development, (h) assessing, monitoring and reporting progress of young children.

        One (1) year of verified full-time teaching experience with children in birth through preschool may substitute for 4 semester hours in supervised field experience, practicum, internship or student teaching setting serving children birth through preschool. (Please submit a letter on official letterhead from District Superintendent or Program Director of a school-based education program or center-based program licensed by the Department of Health Services or regulated by tribal or military authorities to verify teaching experience.)

        One (1) year of verified full-time teaching experience with children in kindergarten through grade 3 in an accredited school may substitute for 4 semester hours in a supervised student teaching setting serving children in kindergarten through grade 3. (Please submit a letter on official letterhead from District Superintendent or Personnel Director to verify teaching experience.)

    - OR -

    3. A valid early childhood education certificate from another state.

C. A passing score on the Professional Knowledge Early Childhood portion of the Arizona Educator Proficiency Assessment. The Professional Knowledge assessment shall be waived for applicants who submit verification of one of the following:

    1. A passing score on a comparable Professional Knowledge Early Childhood examination from another state or agency taken within the past 7 years. Submit the original score report at

time of application; or

2.   A passing score on a comparable Professional Knowledge Early Childhood examination from another state or agency taken more than 7 years ago AND 5 years of full-time teaching experience within the past 7 years. Submit the original score report AND a letter on official letterhead from the District Superintendent or Personnel Director to verify teaching experience at time of application; or

3.   A current certificate from the National Board for Professional Teaching Standards. Submit a notarized copy of the certificate.

D.   A passing score on the Subject Knowledge Early Childhood portion of the Arizona Educator Proficiency Assessment. The Subject Knowledge assessment shall be waived for applicants who submit verification of one of the following:

1.   A passing score on a comparable Subject Knowledge Early Childhood examination from another state or agency taken within the past 7 years. Submit the original score report at time of application; or

2.   A passing score on a comparable Subject Knowledge Early Childhood examination from another state or agency taken more than 7 years ago AND 5 years of full-time teaching experience within the past 7 years. Submit the original score report AND a letter on official letterhead from the District Superintendent or Personnel Director to verify teaching experience at time of application; or

3.   A current certificate from the National Board for Professional Teaching Standards. Submit a notarized copy of the certificate.

STANDARD EARLY CHILDHOOD CERTIFICATE (Valid 6 years, renewable)

A.   Option 1 or 2:

    1. Both of the following:

        a. Qualify for the Provisional Early Childhood certificate; and

        b. Two years of verified full-time teaching experience during the valid period of the Provisional certificate may be used to convert the Provisional certificate to a Standard certificate. (Please submit a conversion form signed by the District Superintendent or Personnel Director verifying two years of full-time teaching experience during the valid period of the Provisional certificate being converted.)

  - OR -

  2.   Hold current National Board Certification in Early Childhood

ELEMENTARY CERTIFICATION
(K - 8)

PROVISIONAL CERTIFICATE (Valid 2 years, non-renewable)

A.   See Provisional Certification Requirements (All Certificates) A, B, and C; and

B.   Completion of a teacher preparation program in elementary education from an accredited institution **(OR)** completion of 45 Semester hours from an accredited institution to include at least 8 sem. hrs. of practicum in grades K - 8 **(OR)** A valid elementary certificate from another state.

STANDARD ELEMENTARY (Valid 6 years; renewable).

A.   Qualify for the Provisional Elementary Certificate; and

B.   Passing score on the performance portion of the AEPA;

45 clock hours or 3 sem. hrs. of instruction in research-based systematic phonics; and

An original valid class 1 or class 2 fingerprint clearance card.

SECONDARY CERTIFICATION
(7 - 12)

PROVISIONAL CERTIFICATE (Valid 2 years, non-renewable)

A.   See Provisional Certification Requirements (All Certificates A, B, and C); and

B.   Completion of a teacher preparation program in secondary education from an accredited institution **(OR)** Completion of 30 Sem. hrs. from an accredited institution to include at least 8 sem. hrs. of practicum in grades 7 - 12 **(OR)** a valid secondary certificate from another state.

STANDARD SECONDARY CERTIFICATE (Valid 6 years; renewable).

A. Qualify for the Provisional Secondary Certificate; and
B. Passing score on the performance portion of the AEPA.
Approved Areas: Agriculture; Art; Biology; Business; Chemistry; Communication Arts; Computers; Dance; Drama; Earth Science; Economics; English; Family and Consumer Science; French; General Science; Geography; German; Health; Health Occupations; History; Industrial Technology; Journalism; Marketing; Mathematics; Music; Physical Education; Physics; Political Science; Social Studies; Spanish; and Speech.

SPECIAL EDUCATION CERTIFICATION
(K - 12)

Areas*: Cross-Categorical; Early Childhood (birth to age 5); Emotional Disability; Hearing Impaired; Learning Disabled; Mental Retardation; Orthopedic/Health Impaired; Severely and Profoundly Disabled; Specialized; Speech and Language Impaired and Visually Impaired.

PROVISIONAL CROSS-CATEGORICAL CERTIFICATE (Valid 2 years, non-renewable)
A. See Provisional Certification Requirements (All Certificates A, B, and C); and
B. Completion of a teacher preparation program in special education from an accredited institution which included courses in mental retardation, emotional disability, learning disability, and orthopedic/health impairment **(OR)** completion of 45 Sem. hrs. from an accredited institution to include at least 21 sem. hrs. of special education and 8 sem. hrs. of practicum with students in at least three of the five disability areas **(OR)** a valid cross-categorical Special Ed. certificate from another state.

STANDARD CROSS-CATEGORICAL CERTIFICATE (Valid for 6 years; renewable).
A. Qualify for the Provisional Cross-Categorical Special Education Certificate;
B. Passing score on the performance portion of the AEPA.

* For complete requirements in all Arizona Special Education areas contact the Department.

GUIDANCE COUNSELOR CERTIFICATE (PK-12)
(Valid 6 years; renewable)

A. Master's degree or higher from an accredited institution;
B. Completion of a graduate program in guidance and counseling; and
C. One of the following: Completion of a supervised counseling practicum **(OR)** 2 years of verified, full-time experience as a school guidance counselor **(OR)** 3 years of verified teaching experience.

SCHOOL PSYCHOLOGIST CERTIFICATE (PK-12)
(Valid 6 years; renewable)

A. Master's degree or higher from an accredited institution;
Completion of a graduate program in school psychology having at least 60 graduate sem. hrs. in school psychology from an accredited institution **(OR)** a valid School Psychologist Certificate from another state;
C. Practicum of at least 1000 clock hours in school psychology; and
An original valid class 1 or class 2 fingerprint clearance card.

ADMINISTRATIVE CERTIFICATES (PK - 12)
ADMINISTRATIVE SUPERVISOR

A. Applicant must hold a Standard Certificate;
B. A Master's or more advanced degree from an accredited institution;
A valid supervisor certificate from another state; **(OR)** 3 years of verified teaching experience in PK - 12 **(AND)** completion of a program in educational administration from an accredited institution with a minimum of 18 graduate sem. hrs. of educational administration courses **(AND)** practicum in educational administration from an accredited institution; and
D. Arizona Constitution and U.S. Constitution (a college course or the appropriate exams.)

PRINCIPAL CERTIFICATE
(Valid 6 years; renewable)

A.   See B - D for Administrative Supervisor (except that the Program--with **30** graduate sem. hrs.-- and Practicum must have been for Principals.)

SUPERINTENDENT CERTIFICATE
(Valid 6 years; renewable)

A.   See B - D for Administrative Supervisor (except that the program--with 36 graduate credit hrs.-- and Practicum must have been for superintendents);
Passing score on both the professional knowledge and performance portions of the Arizona Administrator Proficiency Assessment; and
C.   At least 60 graduate semester hours from an accredited institution.

STATE OF ARKANSAS

Department of Education
Professional Licensure
#4 State Capitol Mall, Room 106B or 107B
Little Rock, Arkansas 72201
Phone: 501-682-4342 / Fax: 501-682-4898
Web Site: http://arkansased.org/teachers/teachers.html

INITIAL REQUIREMENTS AT A GLANCE:

Also needed are items A, B, E, G, K, P (if holding an Initial Teaching license), and Q (see Initial Licensure below) - See page 2. There are NO fees. All applicants must successfully complete the required criminal background check. Arkansas DOES belong to the NASDTEC Interstate Contract (Teachers). Arkansas DOES belong to the New Teacher Assessment and Support Consortium (INTASC). Out of State applicants must hold a valid teaching license from another state and, either (a) hold a degree from an NCATE or regionally accredited institution, or (b) hold a certificate from the National Board of Professional Teaching Standards. Out-of-state candidates may have Arkansas testing requirements waived by either verifying 3 years of teaching experience or proof of meeting testing requirements in their originally licensed state. Course(s) in Special Education ARE required. Revisions for administrators are anticipated in 2008.

Renewal Requirements: Licensure renewal is based upon a five-year cycle, and requires the applicant provide evidence of: at least two years (240 work days) of teaching experience out of the past five years, **OR** official transcripts documenting six hours of college coursework within the licensure area during the past six years, **AND** 60 hours of professional development coursework annually over the course of five years. Fee: $48.00 for background check.

INITIAL LICENSURE[1]

Effective January 1, 2002, Arkansas moved to a performance based licensure system. New beginning teachers (novice teachers with less than one year of teaching experience) will follow the following track:

A minimum of a bachelor's level degree is required for all teaching licenses.
All teachers must have successfully completed the following testing:
Praxis I, reading, writing, math
Praxis II, content test for all parts required
Praxis II, Principles of Learning and Teaching

Note: the Praxis III is required to convert an Arkansas Initial Teaching License to a Standard Teaching License

Persons who complete the above requirements through an approved Arkansas teacher education program are eligible for an *Initial Teaching License*. An alternative track, known as the *Arkansas Non-Traditional Licensure Program* is also available. See their web site for further details. An initial teaching license is valid for not less than one year, and no more than three years. During the initial licensure time, novice teachers are considered to be in a time of Induction. During induction, novice teachers will have a site-based, trained mentor assigned to support their practice and professional growth. When novice teachers and their mentors decide that their teaching meets the mentoring requirements, the capstone experience of induction, which is Praxis III performance assessment, will be scheduled. Upon successful completion of the performance assessment a *Standard Teaching License* will be issued.

LEVELS AND AREAS OF LICENSURE
(Standard certificates, valid 5 years)

Levels and Grades:

Early Childhood	Pre-K - 4	Middle Childhood / Early Adolescence	4 - 8
Preschool / Early Adolescence	Pre-K - 8	Adolescence / Young Adulthood	7 - 12
Preschool / Young Adulthood	Pre-K - 12	Post Secondary (PS)	Above Grade 12

Areas of Licensure:

English Language Arts/Social Studies	4-8	Adult Education	PS
Foreign Language	P-8, 7-12	**Special Education:**	
English Language Arts	7-12	Instructional Specialist	4-12
Journalism	7-12	E.C. Instructional Specialist	P-4
Social Studies	7-12	Visual Specialist	P-4, 4-12
Science / Math	4-8	Hearing Specialist	P-4, 4-12
Physical / Earth Science	7-12	Library / Media Science	P-8, 7-12
Life / Earth Science	7-12	Reading	P-8, 7-12
Mathematics	7-12	Guidance and Counseling	P-8, 7-12
Art	P-8, 7-12	Gifted and Talented	P-8, 7-12
Vocal Music	P-8, 7-12	English as a Second Language	P-8, 7-12
Instrumental Music	P-8, 7-12	Educational Examiner	P-8, 7-12
Drama / Speech	P-8, 7-12	Coaching	7-12
Industrial Technology Education	4-8, 7-12, PS	District Administrator	P-12
Family and Consumer Sciences	4-8, 7-12, PS	Building Administrator	P-8, 7-12
Agriculture Sciences and Tech.	4-8, 7-12, PS	Program / Curriculum Administrator	P-8, 7-12
Market Technology	4-8, 7-12, PS	School Psychology Specialist	P-12
Business Technology	4-8, 7-12, PS	Speech Language Pathologist	P-12
Physical Education / Wellness	P-8, 7-12		

ADMINISTRATIVE LICENSURE[1]

Arkansas employs the Administrator Licensure Completion Program (ALCP) to assist candidates who have been offered employment in administrative positions prior to completion of state Building Level Licensure requirements.

Administrative Areas:
Program / Curriculum Administrator: Including Special Education, Gifted / Talented Education, Vocational Education, Content Area Specialist, Curriculum Specialist (P-8, 7-12, or P-12); and
Building Administrator: Including Principal and Assistant Principal
District Administrator: Including Superintendent, Deputy Superintendent, and Assistant Superintendent

Candidates for the *Initial License* must meet the following requirements:
Hold a Standard Teaching License;
4 years of teaching experience with not less than 3 of the 4 years at the level of licensure sought;

Hold a graduate degree which includes an internship;
Portfolio development; and
The Arkansas DOE will review graduate degrees in any area other than educational leadership to determine any individual needs.

Candidates for the **Standard License*** must meet the following requirements:
Participate in a mentoring experience during the period of initial licensure;
Successfully complete the School Leaders Licensure Assessment (SLLA) with a minimum score of 158.

* Candidates for the *District Administrator **Standard License*** must meet the following requirements:
Hold a Standard Teaching License and a Building-Level Administrator license; OR Curriculum Program Administrator License;
4 years of teaching experience with Building-Level experience preferred;
Hold an advanced degree or complete and advanced program based on the Standards for Administrator licensure; and
Successfully complete the School Superintendent Assessment (SSA).

[1] Contact the Teacher Education and Licensure Department for complete details.

STATE OF CALIFORNIA

California Commission on Teaching Credentialing
P.O. Box 944270
Sacramento, California 94244-2700
Phone: 916-445-7254 / 888-921-2682 / Fax: 916-445-7255
Web Site: **http://www.ctc.ca.gov**

INITIAL REQUIREMENTS AT A GLANCE:

Also needed will be items A, B, C, E, G, H, J (or, *Livescan* receipt), K, and Q - see page 2. First time and renewal fees are $55.00. A $56.00 fingerprint processing fee is required for the initial application. Scores on the California Subject Examinations for Teachers (CSET), may be required where subject-matter competence is a requirement. California DOES participate in the Interstate Certification Compact for teachers and administrators and the NASDTEC Interstate Contract (Teachers only). Major changes took effect on 9/28/2006 which affected out-of-state applicant credentialing and the criteria for meeting California's basic skills requirements. California no longer issues Professional Clear Credentials.

Renewal Requirements: A Clear Credential may be renewed upon submission of an application and fee every five year renewal cycle. Fee: $55.00. Add $2.00 service fee for online renewals.

California offers two basic teaching credentials. The Multiple Subject that is generally designed for the elementary self-contained classroom and the Single Subject that is for middle, secondary or departmentalized classrooms. The requirements to be met are similar with the exception of subject matter competence and teacher preparation. The application process does differ for out-of-state candidates and California prepared candidates.

Out-of-state candidates having graduated from an approved program including student teaching may be issued a five (5) year **Preliminary Teaching Credential** prior to meeting the basic skills requirement if employed in California. For those not employed in California, the basic skills requirement must be met before the preliminary credential will be issued.

Within the five year period of the Preliminary Teaching Credential, the holder must meet renewal requirements as listed on the preliminary credential. These may include the verification of subject matter competence, verification of having earned an authorization to teach English learners, and the completion of a Commission-approved professional teacher induction program or a fifth year of study beyond the bachelor's degree(depending by which route the candidate qualified for the preliminary credential). Once these requirements are met, the individual may then apply for the **Clear Credential**.

Requirements for foreign-trained individuals differ from requirements for those prepared in the United States. Visit the Commission's website for details.

Direct application is allowed if the teacher preparation program was completed out-of-state, an out-of-state certificate was issued, and the candidate has met the basic skills requirement.

If the teacher preparation program was completed in California, the applicant must be formally recommended for the credential by the college or university where the program was completed. California-trained applicants will receive a five-year preliminary credential. Within five years, the individual must complete a Commission-approved professional teacher induction program in order to receive the Clear Credential. See notes [1], [2] and [3] below.

SCHOOL COUNSELOR
SCHOOL PSYCHOLOGIST
(Valid 5 years)

The **Clear School Counselor Credential** requires:
- (a) Bachelor's degree;
- (b) A one year postgraduate professional approved program in school counseling, including a practicum;
- (c) Recommendation of a California college or university with a Commission-approved school counseling program[4]; and
- (d) Basic Skills requirement.

NOTE: Individuals prepared outside of California may satisfy requirements (b) and (c) above by verifying completion of a professional preparation program consisting of at least 48 semester units of post baccalaureate study and a minimum of 600 clock hours of supervised field experience in a public school at two of three school levels (elementary, middle and high school). Up to 150 of the 600 clock hours need to be devoted to issues of diversity. A letter verifying practicum must be on original, official letterhead from the college or university's education department and must accompany the application packet. The applicant must also verify eligibility for the equivalent credential authorization in the state where the program was completed. If the out-of-state preparation does not fit this pattern, the applicant must contact a California college or university with a Commission-accredited school counseling program for evaluation.

The **Clear School Psychology Credential** requires:
- (a) Bachelor's degree;
- (b) A two year postgraduate professional approved program in school psychology, including a practicum with children; and
- (c) Recommendation of a California college or university with a Commission-approved Basic Pupil Personnel Services Program[4].
- (d) Basic Skills requirement.

NOTE: Individuals prepared outside of California may satisfy requirements (b) and (c) above by verifying completion of a professional preparation program consisting of at least 60 semester units of post baccalaureate study and a minimum of 450 clock hours of practicum, of which 300 clock hours must be in a preschool to grade 12, and 150 hours must be through on-campus or community agencies, and 1200 clock hours of supervised field experience. A letter verifying practicum must be on original, official letterhead from the college or university's education department and must accompany the application packet. The applicant must also verify eligibility for the equivalent credential authorization in the state where the program was completed. If the out-of-state preparation does not fit this pattern, the applicant must contact a California college or university with a Commission-accredited school psychology program for evaluation.

18

SCHOOL ADMINISTRATOR
(Valid 5 years)

The **Preliminary Administrative Credential** requires:
  (a)   Bachelor's degree;
  (b)   Hold a valid California credential. Note: Out-of-state trained administrators are not required to hold a valid California Elementary, Secondary, or Special Education teaching credential.
  (c)   Three years of successful teaching or counseling experience;
  (d)   Recommendation of California college or university with a Commission-approved Administrative Service Program[4];
  (e)   Special Education training (including "mainstreaming")[4];
  (f)   The basic skills requirement; and
  (g)   A one year postgraduate professional approved program in school administration including a practicum, *OR* pass SLLA exam.

The holder of an Administrative Services Credential is required to complete a second tier of course work, including two years of successful full-time experience while in an administrative position over a five year period. They would then qualify for a five year **Clear Administrative Credential**.

[1] "Single Subject" Subject Matter Competence: verification of subject matter competency is met by one of two methods: (1) completing a commission-approved subject matter program or its equivalent and obtaining a statement from the authorized person in the education department of California college or university with an approved program (California colleges and universities may have recency requirements that have to be met before a waiver may be granted) **OR** (2) achieving a passing score on the appropriate California Subject Examinations for Teachers (CSET), administered by NES. Information about the appropriate subject assessment(s), including passing scores and registration may be requested. The statutory subjects available for Single Subject Teaching Credentials are Agriculture, Art, Business, English, Foreign Language (non-English), Health Science, Home Economics, Industrial and Technology Education, Foundational Mathematics, Mathematics, Music, Physical Education, Physics, Physics (Specialized), Biological Sciences, Biological Sciences (Specialized), Chemistry, Chemistry (Specialized), Geoscience, Geosciences (Specialized) and Social Science. Contact the Commission for complete information.

"Single Subject" Competence (*out-of-state applicants*): The out-of-state credential authorization must correspond to a California subject area in order for the Commission to issue a credential. If the credential is in a subject area that does not correspond with an area that may be listed on a California credential, the candidate must have completed 32 semester units of course work in the California subject area. If the subject matter course work has not be completed, a preliminary credential will be issued but the applicant will be required to meet California subject-matter requirements before the Clear Credential may be issued. More information may be found in leaflet CL674S, *Verifying Subject Matter Competence for Single Subject Teaching Credentials.*

[2] "Multiple Subject" Subject Matter Competence: Verification of subject matter competency is met by one of two methods: (1) completing a Commission-approved liberal arts subject matter program or its equivalent and obtaining a subject matter from the authorized approved program (California colleges and universities may have recency requirements that have to be met before a waiver can be granted–availability may also be limited as colleges and universities continue to phase out programs) **OR** (2) achieving a passing score on the appropriate CSET examination. Information about the appropriate subject assessment, including passing scores and registration may be requested. Contact the Commission for more information.

"Multiple Subject" Competence (*out-of-state applicants*): The out-of-state credential authorization must correspond to a California subject area in order for the Commission to issue a credential. If the subjects listed on the out-of-state credential are other than "elemetary teaching" or "self-contained", a preliminary credential will be issued but the applicant will be required to meet California subject-matter requirements before the Clear Credential may be issued. More information may be found in leaflet CL674M, *Verifying Subject Matter Competence for Multiple Subject Teaching Credentials.*

[3] Teaching of Reading: a course in the teaching of reading is required for both the Multiple Subject and Single Subject Teaching Credential for those trained in California and outside of the U.S. The Reading Instruction Competence Assessment (RICA) is required for Multiple Subject applicants who are trained in California.

[4] Not Required of out-of-state applicants.

STATE OF COLORADO

Colorado Department of Education
Educator Licensing Unit
201 East Colfax Avenue
Denver, Colorado 80203-1799
Phone: 303-866-6628 / Fax: 303-866-6866
Web Site: **http://www.cde.state.co.us/index_license.htm**

INITIAL REQUIREMENTS AT A GLANCE:

Also needed will be items: A, B, C, E, G, J (one original copy), K and O - See page 2. The fee is $60.00 for initial and renewal evaluations and $39.50 for the fingerprinting/background check for all initial applicants. A state-administered Content Test, PLACE, is required for most certificates though in 2003-2004, Colorado has authorized the use of five PRAXIS content knowledge exams as alternatives (see below). Colorado DOES belong to the NASDTEC Interstate Contract (Teachers, Support Professionals, and Administrators). Courses in Special Education are NOT required. Colorado now employs performance-based standards for all initial instructional certificates. For complete information on these standards, visit http://www.cde.state.co.us/cdeprof/download/pdf/li_perfbasedstandards.pdf. For complete information, contact the Department.

Renewal Requirements: A valid professional license may be renewed every five years with six semester hours of college/ university credit or 90 contact hours of Professional Development (inservices, workshops, being on a committee, etc.) earned during the validity (from the issuance date to the expiration date) of your professional license.

GENERAL LICENSE REQUIREMENTS

A.   **Initial License:** Valid 3 years, renewable.
This is Colorado's entry level license. Issued upon completion of an approved preparation program or an alternative teacher program. It entitles the holder to teach in any public school offering an approved induction program. The holder must complete an approved induction program, fulfill on-going professional development activities, and successfully complete a performance evaluation.

Authorization: Interim, valid 1 year, renewable once for out-of-state applicants who haven't completely fulfilled Colorado's licensing requirements. Authorization may be issued to an applicant who:
1.   holds, or is eligible for a valid educator certificate or license, as a teacher, principal, or administrator, in another state;
2.   has not successfully passed the Colorado State Board of Education-approved assessment(s) and does not have three years of full-time successful teaching experience; and
3.   meets the requirements for an Initial educator license.

The employing school district may provide an induction program for holders of a Interim authorization. Induction programs completed while holding such authorizations may apply toward fulfilling the requirements of a Colorado Initial or Professional educator license.

C. **Alternative Teacher License:** Valid 1 year, non-renewable.
Issued to an applicant who has earned a bachelor's degree from an accredited institution and possesses subject matter knowledge appropriate for teaching in public schools; who agrees to participate in an on-the-job, 1 year, alternative teacher preparation program; and who has received a contract as an alternative teacher from an authorized school or district for one full academic year.

D. **Initial Special Service License:** Valid 3 years, renewable.
1. See A above
2. Issued to an applicant who has completed an approved Special Services program and holds appropriate professional registration, certificate or license.

E. **Initial Principal License:** Valid 3 years, renewable.
1. See A above
2. Issued to an applicant who has completed an approved graduate program for principals.

F. **Initial Administrator License:** Valid 3 years, renewable.
Issued to an applicant who has completed requirements for superintendents.

G. **Professional License:** Valid 5 years, renewable.
Available for all endorsements. Renewal must include completion of on-going professional development activities.

Master Certificate (voluntary): Valid 7 years, renewable. This certificate is held in conjunction with a professional license and is **not** a stand-alone certificate.
Available for all endorsements. Issued to holders of the Professional License who demonstrate advanced competencies by attaining National Board for Professional Teaching Certification.

ENDORSEMENTS AND LEVELS

Early Childhood Education .... Ages 0-8	Physical Education K-12
Elementary Education K-6	Science 7-12
Agriculture 7-12	Social Studies 7-12
Art K-12	Speech 7-12
Business Education 7-12	Technical Education (Industrial Arts) 7-12
Marketing Education 7-12	Instructional Technology Teacher K-12
Drama K-12	Audiologist 0-21
Bilingual & ESL K-6, K-12, 7-12	Occupational Therapist 0-21
Mathematics 7-12	Orientation & Mobility (Peripatology) 0-21
Music K-12	Physical Therapist 0-21
Foreign Language K-12	School Nurse 0-21
French, German, Italian, Japanese,	School Psychologist 0-21
Latin, Russian, and Spanish	School Social Worker 0-21
Special Education Endorsements:	Speech/Language Pathologist 0-21
Special Education Specialists:	Principal K-12
Visually Impaired	Administrator K-12
Deaf/Hard of Hearing	Counselor 0-21
Early Childhood Education Specialist	Director of Special Education K-12
Special Education Generalist	Reading Teacher K-12
Early Childhood Special Education	Reading Specialist K-12
Gifted and Talented Specialist	School Library Media K-12

STATE OF CONNECTICUT

State Department of Education
Bureau of Educator Standards and Certification
P.O. Box 150471
Hartford, Connecticut 06115-0471
Phone: 860-713-6969 / Fax: 860-713-7017
Web Site: **http://www.ct.gov/sde**
E-Mail: teacher.cert@ct.gov

INITIAL REQUIREMENTS AT A GLANCE:

Also needed will be items A, B, C, E, G, K, N, O, and Q - See page 2. Connecticut fees: Application review and processing is $50.00; Initial Educator certificate: $100.00; Provisional Educator certificate: $200.00; Professional Educator certificate: $300.00 (NO personal checks accepted.) Individuals seeking certification must demonstrate one or both of the following competencies: 1) essential skills in reading, writing and mathematics which are fulfilled by taking and meeting Connecticut's standards on the Praxis I Pre-Professional Skills Tests (PPST) or meeting the approved waiver standards; and 2) subject knowledge in the candidate's intended teaching areas(s) which must be fulfilled by taking and meeting Connecticut's standards on the Praxis II subject knowledge tests. All early childhood, elementary, middle grades, and secondary education candidates must also pass the Praxis II specialized assessments. (See "A Guide to Educator Assessments in Connecticut.")

Applicants from out-of-state programs or with out-of-state successful experience may obtain deferrals of the assessments for a period of one year with an interim certificate. A third competency exists: professional knowledge through the Beginning Educator Support and Training (BEST) program. This program, which includes components of both support and assessment, is applicable only to beginning teachers who are employed under an Initial Educator Certificate. A course in Special Education IS required for all certificates, and a survey course in United States History (3 sem. hrs.) IS required for all teaching certificates. Connecticut DOES belong to the NASDTEC Interstate Contract (Teachers, Support Professionals, and Vocational Educators). Connecticut DOES belong to the Interstate New Teacher Assessment and Support Consortium (INTASC). Major revisions are expected in 2010.

Renewal Requirements: For the holder of a Professional Educator Certificate, a completed application form, and a minimum of six (6) credit hrs., or nine (9) CEUs, or a combination of three (3) credit hrs. and 4.5 CEUs every five (5) years. Renewal Fees: Initial - $100; Provisional - $200; and Professional - $0

The **Initial Educator Certificate** will usually be issued before beginning employment. Valid three years. The **Provisional Educator Certificate** is valid for eight years. The **Professional Educator Certificate** is renewable every five years. The **Interim Educator Certificate** may be issued at the initial or provisional level and is valid for one calendar year. There are two types of interim educator certificates:

1. **The Nonrenewable Interim Educator Certificate** is issued with Connecticut test deferrals and/or specific course deficiencies as provided by certification regulations.
2. **The Interim Educator Certificate** is issued with specific course deficiencies as provided by certification regulations.

EARLY CHILDHOOD CERTIFICATES
(Birth - K and Nursery - 3)

This certificate, or another appropriate grade level certificate, shall be required for anyone serving as a teacher of infants, toddlers, nursery school, kindergarten and grades one through three in the employ of a board of education. The endorsement for birth through kindergarten authorizes the holder to teach students in both special and regular education settings in the appropriate grades; and the endorsement for nursery through grade three authorizes the holder to teach nursery through kindergarten students in both special and regular education settings and to teach grade one through grade three students in regular education.

I.   **Initial Educator Certificate (Birth - K and N - 3):** To receive an initial educator certificate for early childhood teaching with an endorsement in birth through kindergarten and nursery through grade three, an applicant shall present evidence of meeting the following requirements in addition to meeting the assessment requirements, as appropriate:

    A.   Holds a bachelor's degree from an approved institution;

    B.   Has completed a minimum of 15 semester hours of credit in human growth and development, including: typical and atypical development, psychology of learning and family studies. This may be completed as part of a subject-area major or general academic courses;

    C.   Has a minimum of 39 semester hours of credit in general academic courses in five of the six following areas: natural sciences; social studies; fine arts; English; mathematics; and foreign language. A survey course in United States history of at least 3 sem. hrs. shall be included;

    D.   Has completed a subject area major consisting of one of the following:

        1.   A major awarded by an approved institution in any one subject area, except that a major in professional education may not be accepted in fulfillment of this requirement; or

        2.   A 39 sem. hr. credit interdisciplinary major consisting of a concentration of at least 18 sem. hrs. in human growth and development, including: typical and atypical development, psychology of learning and family studies, with the remainder distributed among no more than three additional subjects related to human growth and development, except that a major or course work in professional education may not be accepted in fulfillment of this requirement; and

    E.   Has a minimum of 36 sem. hrs. of credit in professional education in a planned program of study and experience in early childhood education to be distributed among each of the following:

        1.   Foundation of education. This group includes areas such as: philosophy of education; history of education; and comparative education;

        2.   Curriculum and methods of teaching including course work in:

            (a)   For birth-K and N-3 this group shall include course work in:

                i.   Curriculum and methods for typical and special-needs children, taught in a manner that would facilitate the understanding of children with special-needs in a least-restrictive environment, and shall consist of course work in integrated curriculum and strategies for developmentally appropriate nursery-kindergarten programs, to include study in each of the following areas, with at least 6 credits in the area (*) of which at least 3 credits shall be in methods of teaching language arts;
(*) Learning and teaching of language arts, children's literature, mathematics, science, social studies, expressive arts, health/safety through an integrated curriculum; or developmentally appropriate curriculum for early childhood; or integrated early childhood curriculum;

                ii.   Observation and assessment of development in young children and planning individualized programs;

                iii.   Classroom organization and facilitating play; or effective teaching and organizational skills in an environment with play; or role of play and the learning environment;

                iv.   Early childhood program models, and issues including family and professional collaboration and diversity;

                v.   Program adaptations for children with special needs; or teaching strategies and related services for children with special needs; or program planning for children with special needs; and

            (b)   For birth-K, this group shall consist of course work in facilitating development and programming for normal and special-needs infants and toddlers with study in at least 3 of the following 4 areas:

                i.   Infant/toddler development and assessment; or assessment of behavior and development in infants and toddlers;

    ii. Curriculum development for infants and toddlers; or appropriate environment and the role of play;

    iii. Infant/toddler program models, issues and collaborations; or programs for infants and toddlers with parent and professional support;

    iv. Adaptations for infants and toddlers with special needs; or adapting the infant/toddler environment for children with special needs; and

(c) For N - 3, this group shall consist of course work in:

    i. Curriculum and strategies for developmentally appropriate practices in the primary grades including study in:

    ii. Learning and teaching of language arts, children's literature, mathematics, science, social studies, the arts, health/safety, physical education; or curriculum for the primary grades; and 2 of the following: (1) Assessment of learning in the primary grades; or evaluation of primary-grade children for program planning; (2) Classroom organization and management using media technology, or effective teaching and classroom organization with media technology; (3) Elementary school models, programs, issues, collaborative efforts; or primary-grade program models and partnerships; (4) Strategies for integrating children with special needs; or adapting curriculum and strategies for primary-grade children with special needs; and

3. Field experiences should include observation and limited participation teaching prior to full-time student teaching and practicum. All students will complete (a) and (b) below totaling at least 6 but not more than 12 sem. hrs. of credit: (a) Supervised student teaching or practicum in Pre-Kindergarten or Kindergarten, including children with special needs; and (b) One of the following: **for Birth-K,** supervised student teaching in a program serving infants and toddlers, including children with special needs; or **for Nursery-3** supervised student teaching in grades one, two or three.

II. **Provisional Educator Certificate:** To receive a Provisional Educator certificate to teach early childhood education, an applicant shall present evidence of meeting the assessment requirements, as appropriate, and the preparation and eligibility requirements for an initial educator certificate, **AND** the following:

    A. Successfully completed the BEST assessment with at least 10 school months of successful teaching under an initial educator certificate, interim initial educator certificate, or durational shortage area permit. Persons who obtained the initial educator certificate upon completion of successful service under the temporary 90-day certificate shall be required to complete 15 school months of successful teaching under the initial educator certificate; **OR**

    B. Has completed, within ten years prior to application, at least 30 school months of successful teaching in a subject area or field appropriate to the subject area or field for which the provisional educator certificate is sought, in a public, approved nonpublic school or nonpublic school approved by the appropriate governing body in another state; **OR**

    C. Has served a board of education successfully under a provisional teaching certificate for the school year immediately preceding application. The subject area or field taught during the preceding year shall be the same for which provisional educator certification is sought.

III. **Professional Educator Certificate:** An applicant shall present evidence of having met the assessment requirements, as appropriate, in addition to meeting the following requirements:

    A. Has completed 30 school months of successful teaching under the provisional educator certificate, interim educator certificate or provisional teaching certificate; and

    B. Has met one of the following requirements for course work at an approved institution or institutions:

        1. *Prior to July 1, 2003,* an applicant who holds or held a provisional educator certificate shall have completed not less than 30 semester hours of credit beyond

the bachelor's degree. Such course work need not necessarily lead to a master's degree and may include graduate or undergraduate courses. It shall consist of:

    a.   A planned program at an approved institution related directly to the subject areas or grade levels of the endorsement, or in an area or areas related to the teacher's ability to provide instruction effectively or to meet locally determined goals and objectives; or

    b.   An individual program which is mutually determined or approved by the teacher and the employing agent of the board of education and which is designed to increase the ability of the teacher to improve student learning.

2.   *Prior to July 1, 2003,* an applicant who holds or held a 10 year provisional teaching certificate shall have completed 30 semester hours of credit beyond the bachelor's degree. Such course work need not necessarily lead to a master's degree and may include graduate or undergraduate courses. It shall consist of:

    a.   A planned program at an approved institution; or

    b.   An individual program which is mutually determined or approved by the teacher and the employing agent of the board of education and which is designed to increase the ability of the teacher to improve student learning. Such an individual program may include course work taken at one or more approved institutions of higher education and may include registered in-service programs sponsored by local or regional boards of education or approved nonpublic schools upon the approval of the joint subcommittee of the Board of Governors of Higher Education and the Board established pursuant to Section 10-155b of the Connecticut general statutes, revision of 1958, revised to January 1, 1983.

3.   *Prior to July 1, 2003,* an applicant who holds or held a five-year provisional teaching certificate shall have completed either a master's degree or not less than 30 semester hours of credit beyond the bachelor's degree. Such course work need not necessarily lead to a master's degree and may include graduate or undergraduate courses. Except as otherwise provided, it shall consist of:

    a.   A master's degree at an institution; or

    b.   An individually planned program consisting of at least 30 semester hours of credit beyond the bachelor's degree, which includes at least 15 semester hours of credit in general academic courses in addition to the credits offered to fulfill the requirements for the provisional educator certificate. Exceptions to the requirement of 15 semester hours of credit in general academic courses may be granted when an approved institution or the Department determines that the applicant has, in the combined program of undergraduate and post-baccalaureate preparation, met this requirement.

4.   *On and after July 1, 2003,* any applicant who holds or held a provisional teaching or provisional educator certificate shall have completed, at an approved institution, either a master's degree or at least 30 semester hours of graduate credit.

ELEMENTARY CERTIFICATE
(Grades K - 6)

This certificate shall authorize the teaching of all elementary academic subjects and special subject or fields as taught within the self-contained classroom in the grade levels of the endorsement, except that it shall not authorize the teacher to be the sole provider for teaching of art, health, music, or physical education. Elementary certificates shall be endorsed for the grade levels in accordance with the recommendation of the preparing institution.

I.   **Initial Educator Certificate:** To receive an initial educator certificate for elementary teaching, an applicant shall present evidence of meeting the following requirements in addition to meeting the assessment requirements, as appropriate:

    A.   Holds a bachelor's degree from an approved institution;

    B.   Has completed a minimum of six semester hours of credit in child and or human growth and development;

    C.   See Section IC in Early Childhood Certification.

D. Has completed a subject-area major consisting of one of the following:
    1. A major awarded by an approved institution in any one subject area, except that a major in professional education may not be accepted in fulfillment of this requirement; or
    2. A 39 sem. hr. credit interdisciplinary major consisting of a concentration of at least 18 sem. hrs. of credit in any one subject area with the remainder distributed among no more than 3 additional subjects related to the area of concentration, except that a major or course work in professional education may not be accepted in fulfillment of any portion of this requirement.
E. Has a minimum of 30 semester hours of credit in professional education in a planned program of study and experience in elementary education to be distributed among each of the following: (1) Foundations of education; (2) Educational psychology; (3) Curriculum and methods of teaching, including 6 sem. hrs. of credit in language arts; (4) Supervised observation, participation, and full time responsible student teaching in an elementary school, totaling at least six but not more than 12 semester hours of credit; and (5) A course of study in special education comprised of not fewer than 36 clock hours which shall include study in understanding the growth and development of exceptional children, including handicapped and gifted and talented children and children who may require special education and methods for identifying, planning for and working effectively with special-needs children in the regular classroom.

II. **Provisional Educator Certificate:** (See Section II in Early Childhood Certification.)

III. **Professional Educator Certificate:** (See Section III in Early Childhood Certification.)

MIDDLE GRADES CERTIFICATE
(Grades 4 - 8)

This certificate, or another certificate appropriate to the grade level of the students to be taught, shall authorize the teaching of grades 4 through 8 in the endorsed subjects.

I. **Initial Educator Certificate:** To receive an initial educator certificate for teaching at the middle grades, an applicant shall present evidence of meeting the following requirements in addition to meeting the assessment requirements, as appropriate:
    A. Holds a bachelor's degree from an approved institution;
    B. See Section IC in Early Childhood Certification;
    C. Has completed study in two areas of concentration. The **primary area of study** is to consist of a minimum of 24 semester hours of credit in one of the following subjects: English, history and social science, mathematics, biology, chemistry, physics, earth science, political science, economics, geography, anthropology or sociology; and a **secondary area of study** consisting of a minimum of 15 semester hours in an academic subject (English, history and social science, mathematics, biology, chemistry, physics, earth science, political science, economics, geography, anthropology or sociology) which may result in endorsements in the two subject areas, or in an all level endorsement subject such as special education or related subjects which will not qualify for a second middle level endorsement. (NOTE: for complete information on required courses for middle level areas, contact the Department); and
    D. See Section IE in Elementary Certification, although focused for middle grades.

II. **Provisional Educator Certificate:** (See Section II in Early Childhood Certification.)

III. **Professional Educator Certificate:** (See Section III in Early Childhood Certification.)

SECONDARY ACADEMIC CERTIFICATE
(Grades 7 - 12)

This certificate, or another certificate appropriate to the subject and grade level taught, shall be required or anyone employed by a board of education as a secondary education teacher in grades seven through twelve. This certificate shall be valid for endorsed subjects, unless otherwise specified. When departmentalized instruction is offered in grades below the seventh, this certificate may be considered valid for such instruction in grades 5 and 6 in endorsed subjects only.

I. **Initial Educator Certificate:** To receive an initial educator certificate for secondary academic subjects, an applicant shall present evidence of meeting the following requirements in addition to meeting assessment requirements:
- A. Holds a bachelor's degree from an approved institution;
- B. See Section IC in Early Childhood Certification
- C. Has completed a subject area major consisting of ONE of the following:
  1. A major awarded by an approved institution in the subject area for which certification is sought except that a major in professional education may *not* be accepted in fulfillment of this requirement except that physical education and technology education are acceptable majors for physical education and technology education; *OR*
  2. A minimum of 30 semester hours of credit in the subject for which endorsement is sought and a minimum of nine semester hours of credit in a subject or subjects directly related to the subject for which endorsement is sought, except that a major or course work in professional education may not be accepted in fulfillment of the requirement, except that physical education and technology education are acceptable majors for physical education and technology education; and except that:
     - a. For the general science endorsement, a major consisting of minimum of 39 semester hours of credit in science including study in biology, chemistry, physics and earth science. Professional education course work shall not be accepted;
     - b. For the history and social studies endorsement, a major awarded by an approved institution in history, including at least 18 semester hours of credit in social studies; *or* a major in political science; economics; geography; anthropology or sociology including at least 18 semester hours of credit in history, **or** an interdisciplinary major consisting of 39 semester hours of credit in subjects covered by the endorsement, each of which shall include 18 semester hours of credit in history including i) United States history, ii) western civilization or European history and iii) non-western history, and shall include a minimum of one course in each of the following areas: political science; economics; geography; sociology, anthropology or psychology. Professional education course work may not be accepted;
     - c. For the business endorsement, a major awarded by an approved institution in business or in any one of the subjects covered by the endorsement or an interdisciplinary major consisting of 39 semester hours of credit in subjects covered by the endorsement. Professional education course work may not be accepted;
     - d. For a foreign language endorsement, 24 semester hours of credit in the foreign language in which endorsement is sought, except that this course work shall be in addition to the basic course of six semester hours of credit or the equivalent in that foreign language, and a minimum of 9 semester hours of credit in a subject or subjects directly related to the subject for which endorsement is being sought. Professional education course work shall not be accepted; and
- D. Has a minimum of 18 semester hours in professional education in a planned program of study and experience to be distributed among each of the following: foundations of education; educational psychology; curriculum and methods of teaching; supervised observation, participation and full time responsible student teaching totaling at least 6, but not more than twelve semester hours; and a course of study in special education comprised of not less than 36 clock hours.

II. **Provisional Educator Certificate:** (See Section II in Early Childhood Certification.)

III. **Professional Educator Certificate:** (See Section III in Early Childhood Certification.)

SPECIAL SUBJECTS
(Grades K-12)

This certificate shall authorize the teaching of the endorsed special subjects at the elementary and secondary levels in agriculture, art, health, home economics, technology education, music and physical education.

I.   **Initial Educator Certificate:** (See Section I in Secondary Academic Certification)

II.   **Provisional Educator Certificate:** (See Section II in Early Childhood Certification)

III. **Professional Educator Certificate:** (See Section III in Early Childhood Certification)

SCHOOL COUNSELOR

I.   **Initial Educator Certificate:** To receive an initial educator certificate to serve as a school counselor, the applicant shall meet the following requirements in addition to meeting the assessment requirements:
    A.   Holds a professional educator certificate, or holds or is eligible for an initial educator certificate and has had either 30 school months of successful teaching experience, or has completed a full-time supervised school internship of 10 school months in a (PK - 12) school setting. This internship is in addition to that required in a practicum, as described in subsection (E) below;
    B.   Holds a master's degree;
    C.   Has completed, as part of, or in addition to the master's degree, a minimum of 30 semester hours of graduate credit in a planned program for school counseling services as attested to by an institution approved for the preparation of school counselors;
    D.   Presents the recommendation of the preparing institution, which shall be based on evidence of knowledge, skills, and understanding gained from study or experience in the following areas: principles and philosophy of developmental guidance and counseling; psychological and sociological theory as related to children, youth and families; career development theory and practice; individual and group counseling procedures; organizational patterns and relationships of pupil personnel services to total school program and community; pupil appraisal and evaluation techniques; and school-based consultation theory and practice;
    E.   Presents evidence from the preparing institution of a progression of supervised experiences in counseling and guidance through laboratory and practicum; and
    F.   A course of study in special education comprised of not fewer than 36 clock hours, as described under the elementary certificate requirements.

II.   **Provisional Educator Certificate:** (See Section II in Early Childhood Education Certification)

III. **Professional Educator Certificate:** To receive a professional educator certificate for school counselor, an applicant shall present evidence of having met the following: completion of 30 school months of successful service under the provisional educator certificate, interim provisional educator or provisional teacher certificates; and completion of 45 semester hours of graduate credit at an approved institution or institutions in counseling and related areas including those required for the initial educator certificate and course work in related areas such as psychology, sociology and special education. (Pertains to Connecticut provisional certificate holders.)

SCHOOL PSYCHOLOGIST

I.   **Initial Educator Certificate:** To serve as a school psychologist, the applicant shall meet the following requirements in addition to meeting the assessment requirements:
    A.   Holds a master's degree;
    B.   Has completed, as part of or in addition to the master's degree, a minimum of 45 semester hours of graduate credit in a planned program for school psychological services as attested to by an institution approved for the preparation of school psychologists;
    C.   Presents the recommendation of the preparing institution, which shall be based upon evidence of knowledge, skills and understanding gained from study in each of the following: evaluation techniques, including observation, clinical appraisal and testing, and integration and interpretation of data; a supervised practicum or field work experience with school-age children; characteristics of and programs for exceptional

children; human growth and personality development and the implications of individual differences among normal and exceptional children for the planning of educational programs; individual and group counseling skills, modification of behavior techniques and interviewing skills; and learning theories as applied to the teaching process;

D. Has completed, in addition to the supervised practicum or field work experience, an internship consisting of 10 school months or its equivalent in a period not to exceed 20 school months, of supervised experience in a school setting under the supervision of a certified school psychologist, the local school system and the preparing institution; and

E. Has completed a course of study in special education comprised of not fewer than 36 clock hours.

NOTE: If all other requirements are met except the internship, an initial educator certificate may be issued and re-issued once conditionally. For further information, contact the Department.

II. **Provisional Educator Certificate:** (See Section II in Early Childhood Certification)

III. **Professional Educator Certificate:** To receive a professional educator certificate for school psychologist, an applicant shall present evidence of having met the general conditions, in addition to meeting the following requirements: has completed 30 school months of successful service under the provisional educator certificate, interim educator certificate or provisional teaching certificate; and has completed 60 semester hours of graduate credit in psychology and related areas at an approved institution, including those required for the initial educator certificate.

INTERMEDIATE ADMINISTRATOR OR SUPERVISOR CERTIFICATE

This certificate or another appropriate certificate shall be required for anyone serving in the employ of a board of education who is designated by the employing agent or board of education as: deputy superintendent, assistant superintendent, principal, assistant principal, curriculum coordinator, supervisor of instruction or any person who has the primary responsibility for directing or coordinating or managing certified staff and resources, or any person responsible for summative evaluation of certified staff. This certificate may authorize service as a department chairperson or school business administrator.

Persons hired on or after September 1, 1980, to serve in supervisory positions in special education and related services shall be required to hold the intermediate administrator or supervisor certificate and shall be appropriately certified according to the following: (1) Whenever a board of education is required to employ a full-time supervisor of special education instruction, the supervisor shall be required to hold both the intermediate administrator or supervisor certificate and special education certification; (2) whenever a board of education is required to employ a full-time supervisor of pupil personnel services, the supervisor shall be required to hold both the intermediate administrator or supervisor certificate and certification in any of the service categories to be supervised; (3) after 7/1/91, whenever a board of education is required to employ a full-time supervisor of special education personnel, including instructional and pupil personnel services personnel, the supervisor shall be required to hold both intermediate administrator or supervisor certificate and certification in special education or in a service category of pupil personnel services.

I. **Initial Educator Certificate:** In addition to meeting the assessment requirements, an applicant shall present evidence of meeting the following requirements:

A. Holds a master's degree from an approved institution;

B. Has completed 18 semester hours of graduate credit in addition to the master's degree;

C. Has completed 50 school months of successful teaching or service, which shall have been in public schools or nonpublic schools approved by the appropriate governing body in another state in a position or positions requiring certification in the state where employed, or in a position or positions which would have required certification had the service been in Connecticut public schools, or in a state education agency as a professional or managerial staff member. Consideration may be given toward fulfillment of the requirements of this subsection to applicants who have completed, as part of a planned program of preparation, a one-year period of internship in areas of school administration and supervision under the supervision of the recommending institution;

D. Presents the recommendation of an approved institution where the applicant has completed a planned program of preparation for administrative and supervisory personnel. The recommendation shall state that the applicant is personally and professionally qualified to serve as a public school administrator or supervisor, and has completed an approved program at the institution specifically for school administration and supervision. The program on which the institutional recommendation has been based shall aggregate not less than 15 semester hours of graduate credit taken at the recommending institution.

    E.   Has completed graduate study in each of the following areas: Psychological and pedagogical foundations of learning; curriculum development and program monitoring; school administration; personnel evaluation and supervision; and contemporary educational problems and solutions from a policy-making perspective, which may include the use of research; and

    F.   Has completed a course of study in special education comprised of not fewer than 36 clock hours as described in the requirements for the elementary certificate.

II.   **Provisional Educator Certificate:** (See Section II in Early Childhood Certification)

III.   **Professional Educator Certificate:** To receive a professional educator certificate for Intermediate Administrator or Supervisor, an applicant shall meet the following requirements: has completed 30 school months of successful service under the provisional educator certificate, interim provisional certificate or provisional teaching certificate; and has completed not less than 30 semester hours of graduate credit at an approved institution in addition to the master's degree. (Pertains to Connecticut provisional certificate holders.)

SUPERINTENDENT OF SCHOOLS
(For Superintendent, Deputy Superintendent, Assistant Superintendent or Executive Director of a Regional Educational Service Center)

I.   **Initial Educator Certificate:** In addition to meeting the general conditions, an applicant shall present evidence of meeting the following requirements will have:

    A.   A master's degree from an approved institution;

    B.   Completed 30 semester hours of graduate credit beyond the master's degree;

    C.   Completed a minimum of 80 school months of successful teaching or service, at least 50 school months of which shall have been in public schools, approved nonpublic schools or nonpublic schools approved by the appropriate governing body in another state, in a position or positions which would have required certification had the service been in Connecticut public schools, or as a professional or managerial staff member in a state education agency. This total may include the 30 school months of administrative experience required in accordance with subsection (D) of this section;

    D.   Completed a minimum of 30 school months of full-time administrative or supervisory experience in public schools, approved nonpublic schools or nonpublic schools approved by the appropriate governing body in another state, in a position or positions which would have required certification had the service been in Connecticut public schools, or as a managerial staff member in a state education agency, in a position or positions which if in Connecticut public schools would have required intermediate administrator or supervisor certification. On specific recommendation of the preparing institution, consideration may be given toward fulfillment of the requirements of this subsection to applicants who have completed, as part of a planned program of preparation for the superintendency, a one-year period of internship in general school administration under the supervision of the institution recommending the applicant for certification;

    E.   Presents the recommendation of an accredited college or university approved for the preparation of superintendents of schools. The recommendation shall state that the applicant is personally and professionally qualified to serve as a superintendent of schools, and has completed an approved program at the institution specifically in preparation for the position of superintendent of schools. The program on which the institutional recommendation has been based shall aggregate not less than 30 semester hours of graduate credit in addition to the master's degree. Not less than 15 semester hours of this requirements shall have been completed at the recommending institution, and additional course work aggregating not less than 15 semester hours of credit shall have been completed either at the recommending institution or at another approved institution by arrangement with, or with the approval of, the recommending institution;

F. Completed in a graduate program, study in each of the following areas: Psychological and pedagogical foundations of learning; curriculum development and program monitoring; school administration; personnel evaluation and supervision; contemporary educational problems and solutions from a policy making perspective; and

G. Completed a course of study in special education comprised of not fewer than 36 clock hours, as described in the requirements for the elementary certificate.

II. **Provisional Educator Certificate:** (See Section II in Early Childhood Education Certification)

III. **Professional Educator Certificate:** To receive a professional educator certificate for superintendent of schools, an applicant shall present evidence of having served successfully under the provisional educator, interim provisional educator or provisional teaching certificates for a period of at least 30 school months. (Pertains to Connecticut provisional certificate holders.)

STATE OF DELAWARE

Department of Education
Licensure/Certification Office
401 Federal Street, Suite 2
Dover, DE 19901
Phone: (302) 735-4120 / toll-free (888) 759-9133
Web Site: **https://deeds.doe.k12.de.us/default.aspx**

INITIAL REQUIREMENTS AT A GLANCE:

Also needed will be items: B, C, D, E, N (Official Grade slip with scores on the PRAXIS Pre-professional skills Tests of Reading (175), Writing (173), and Mathematics (174)) and a Social Security Card copy and O - See page 2. They also require a photocopy of applicant's social security card. The fee is $10.00. A state administered certification test is NOT required. Delaware DOES belong to the Interstate Certification Agreement and has teacher contract agreements with Maryland, District of Columbia, Virginia, Pennsylvania, and New Jersey. Delaware DOES belong to the NASDTEC Interstate Contract (Teachers only). *Reciprocity:* Educators who hold a full and current license/certificate in another U.S. state (including District of Colombia, Guam, and Puerto Rico) will receive a comparable license/certificate upon applying for licensure/certification in Delaware. Courses in Special Education ARE required for all certificates.

Renewal Requirements: Continuing license - Valid for an additional five years, 90-clock hours of professional development. At least one-half of the required hours (45 hours every five 5 years) for educators must be in activities that relate to the educator's work with students or staff. The 90-clock hours of professional development must have taken place during the term of the continuing license. No Fees.

DELAWARE LICENSURE TIERS

Tier One: Initial Licensure Requirements:
Issued to educators with less than 3 years full time (non-substitute) teaching experience. Valid three years (up to six years for trade and industry teachers): Bachelor's degree from an accredited 4-year institution; Completed a student teaching program or the Alternative Routes to Licensure and Certification program; and passing scores on an examination of general knowledge such as the Praxis I.

Tier Two: Continuing Licensure Requirements:
Valid five years: Applicant has completed requirements for an Initial License and has received no more than one unsatisfactory annual evaluation; 90 clock hrs. of professional development; and passing a Criminal History background check.

Tier Three: Advanced Licensure Requirements:
Valid ten years: For applicants who have received National Board for Professional Teaching

Standards certification or an equivalent program and passing a Criminal History background check.

CERTIFICATE TYPES
(All Levels)

A.   **Standard Certificate** - Valid five years. Issued to a candidate who has met all the requirements for initial certification. Renewable with three years service in Delaware schools or six semester hours of course work.

B.   **Emergency Certificate** - Valid for up to three years (or up to six years in the case of skilled and Technical Sciences). Issued to an educator eligible for, or holding, a Delaware license but who has not met the requirements for Standard Certification in a specific content area but has met the requirements for an Initial or Continuing License.
NOTE: An emergency certificate is issued only at the request of the hiring authority.

EARLY CHILDHOOD CERTIFICATE
(Birth - Grade 2)

A Standard Early Childhood Teacher Certificate will be issued to an applicant who holds a valid Delaware Initial, Continuing, or Advanced License; or Standard or Professional Status Certificate issued by the Department prior to August 31, 2003, and who meets ONE of the following five requirements:

A.   A bachelor's degree from an NCATE specialty organization recognized educator preparation program offered by a regionally accredited college or university, with a major in Early Childhood Education; **OR**

B.   A bachelor's degree from a state approved educator preparation program offered by a regionally accredited college or university, with a major in Early Childhood Education, where the state approval body employed the appropriate NCATE specialty organization standards for early childhood teacher education; **OR**

C.   Passage of the appropriate PRAXIS II test approved by the Standards Board and the State Board; **OR**

D.   A bachelor's degree from an NCATE or state approved program, where the state approval body employed the appropriate NASDTEC standards or NCATE specialty organization standards, offered by a regionally accredited college or university, with a major in Primary or Elementary Education; **AND** at least eighteen (18) semester hours of course work, specific to the birth to age five (5) child, taken either as part of the degree program or in addition to it, as follows:
   (1) Children's Growth, Development and Learning (birth - age five (5)) (3 credits);
   (2) Early Childhood Curriculum Development, Assessment, Content, and Implementation (6 credits);
   (3) Language Development and Early Literacy in Young Children (3 credits);
   (4) Family Development and Service Systems for Children and Families (3 credits); and
   (5) Development and Programming for Young Children with Special Needs (3 credits);
   (OR)

E.   A bachelor's degree from a regionally accredited college or university in any field, **AND** a minimum of forty-five (45) semester hours of general content course work, taken either as part of the degree program or in addition to it; **AND** a minimum of thirty-nine (39) semester hours of course work, taken either as part of the degree program or in addition to it, as follows:
   (1) Children's Growth, Development, and Learning (Birth - age 8) (6 sem hours);
   (2) Identifying and Teaching Children with Exceptional Needs (6 sem hours);
   (3) Early Childhood Curriculum Development, Assessment, Content, and Implementation, including a practicum of no less than 50 hours (Birth - age 8) (9 sem hours);
   (4) Professional Issues in Early Childhood Education (3 sem hours);
   (5) Language Development, Early Literacy and Reading in Young Children (9 sem hours);
   (6) Parent, Family Community Interactions (3 sem hours); and
   (7) Family Development and Service Systems for Children and Families (3 sem hours).

ELEMENTARY CERTIFICATE
(K - 6)

The Department shall issue a Standard Certificate as an Elementary Teacher to an educator who holds a valid Delaware Initial, Continuing, or Advanced License; or a Limited Standard, Standard or Professional Status Certificate issued by the Department prior to August 31, 2003 who has met the following requirements:

A.   Acquired the prescribed knowledge, skill or education to practice in a particular area, to teach a particular subject or to instruct a particular category of students by:

     1.   Obtaining National Board for Professional Teaching Standards certification in the area, subject, or category for which a Standard Certificate is requested; **OR**

     2.   Graduating from an NCATE specialty organization recognized educator preparation program or from a state approved educator preparation program, where the state approval body employed the appropriate NASDTEC or NCATE specialty organization standards, offered by a regionally accredited college or university, with a major or its equivalent in Elementary Education; **OR**

     3.   Satisfactorily completing the Alternative Routes for Licensure and Certification Program, the Special Institute for Licensure and Certification, or such other alternative educator preparation programs as the Secretary may approve; **OR**

     4.   Holding a bachelor's degree from a regionally accredited college or university in any content area and for applicants applying after June 30, 2006 for their first Standard Certificate, satisfactory completion of fifteen (15) credits or their equivalent in professional development related to their area of certification, of which at least six (6) credits or their equivalent must focus on pedagogy, selected by the applicant with the approval of the employing school district or charter school which is submitted to the Department; **AND**

B.   For applicants applying after December 31, 2005, where a PraxisT II examination in the area of the Standard Certificate requested is applicable and available, achieving a passing score as established by the Standards Board, in consultation with the Department and with the concurrence of the State Board, on the examination; **OR**

C.   Meeting the requirements for licensure and holding a valid and current license or certificate from another state in Elementary Education; The Department shall not act on an application for certification if the applicant is under official investigation by any state or local authority with the power to issue educator licenses or certifications, where the alleged conduct involves allegations of immorality, misconduct in office, incompetence, willful neglect of duty, disloyalty or falsification of credentials, until the applicant provides evidence of the investigation's resolution; **OR**

D.   Meeting the requirements for a Meritorious New Teacher Candidate Designation

MIDDLE LEVEL CERTIFICATE
(Grades 6 - 8)

A.   Bachelor's degree from a regionally accredited college or university with a major or its equivalent in the content area to be taught; **AND**

B.   Appropriate pedagogical content courses consistent with the NASDTEC or NCATE specialty organization standards for middle school or the content specialization to be taught; **OR**

C.   Bachelor's degree from a regionally accredited college or university in an NCATE specialty organization or state approved program, where the state employed the appropriate NASDTEC or NCATE specialty organization standards in Elementary or Middle School Education.

SECONDARY SCHOOL CERTIFICATE

A.   Bachelor's degree from an accredited institution; **AND**

B.   Completion of teacher education in the area of endorsement, **OR**

C.   Pedagogy and major or equivalent, **OR**

D.   Passing scores on the appropriate Praxis II Specialty Area test.

ELEMENTARY AND SECONDARY SCHOOL COUNSELOR

A. Master's degree in school counseling at the appropriate school level;
B. Completion of a graduate degree in school counseling at the appropriate level;
C. Three years of professional experience in the school, or Delaware Department-approved experiences or internship.
    (OR)
    Graduate degree from and accredited institution; and 30 graduate semester hours.

LIBRARIAN AND MEDIA SPECIALIST

A Standard Library/Media Specialist Certificate will be issued to an applicant who holds a valid Delaware Initial, Continuing, or Advanced License; or Standard or Professional Status Certificate issued by the Department prior to August 31, 2003, and who meets the following requirements:
A. Bachelor's degree in any content area from a regionally accredited college/university; **AND**,
B. Completion of a Master's degree from a regionally accredited college/university in an American Library Association (ALA) approved program in School Library/Media; **OR**,
C. Master's degree from a regionally accredited college/university in any other content area, including a general Media Library Specialist (MLS) degree, and completion of a program in School Library/Media approved by the Department.

ELEMENTARY & SECONDARY PRINCIPAL
SUPERINTENDENT

A. Three years of classroom teaching experience at level appropriate to certification;
B. Master's degree; and
C. Recommendation of preparing institution.
    OR
D. Specific coursework (21 hrs.) and a master's degree.
E. **Superintendent**: Master's degree plus 30 graduate credits, or 60 graduate credit hours including a master's degree, or a doctor's degree from an accredited institution. Three years of teaching experience or two years of teaching and one year of supervised internship in a 60 sem. hour program for school administration.

DISTRICT OF COLUMBIA

Office of Academic Credentials and Standards
51 N Street NE, 3rd Floor
Washington, D.C. 20002
Phone: 202-727-6436 / Fax: 202-727-2019
Web Site: **http://www.k12.dc.us/dcsea/certification**

INITIAL REQUIREMENTS AT A GLANCE:

Also needed will be items A, B, C, E, G, N and O - See page 2. There is a $30.00 evaluation fee. Passing scores on the Praxis I Pre-Professional Examination in Reading, Writing and Mathematics are required for initial licensure. Additionally, passing scores on the Praxis II Subject Area test must be achieved within the 3 year Provisional Certification period. A course in Special Education IS required. District of Columbia does NOT belong to the Interstate Certification Compact and the NASDTEC Interstate Contract (Teachers and Administrators). District of Columbia DOES belong to the Interstate New Teacher Assessment and Support Consortium (INTASC). Additional coursework in Special Education is NOT required for all certificates. Revisions are effective as of January, 2005.

Renewal Requirements: Every five years: six (6) semester hours of college work, or 90 seat hours of in-service training (professional growth).

TEACHING CERTIFICATES
Early Childhood (Grades Pre-K - 3); Special Education (K - 12);
Elementary (Grades 1 - 6); Middle School (Grades 4 - 8); and Secondary (Grades 7 - 12)

Licenses:

Provisional License - valid 3 years, non-renewable. Issued to candidates while working to complete requirements for the Standard License.

Standard License - valid 5 years, renewable. Issued upon completion of bachelor-level, state approved teacher education program, and with passing scores on the Praxis I and Praxis II (subject area) tests.

Professional License - valid 5 years, renewable. Issued to candidates who have met the Standard License requirements and who have two years of satisfactory teaching experience and permanent tenure.

Out-of-State Applicants - the issuance of a DC teaching license based on reciprocity applies only to individuals who have been issued a full license from another (other than DC) participating member jurisdiction under the National Association of State Directors of Teacher Education and Certification (NASDTEC) Interstate Agreement.

General Requirements (all certificates):
A.   Bachelor's Degree from an accredited institution.
B.   Teacher preparation course work at the level of endorsement, including specific course work for each level.
C.   A minimum of 48 semester hours of general or liberal education courses in the Humanities, Social and Natural Sciences, Mathematics, and Health and Physical Education.
D.   Thirty (30) semester credits in the secondary subject area to be taught.
E.   At least 6 semester hours with not less than 200 clock hours of student teaching at the level of endorsement, OR, a minimum of one year of satisfactory teaching experience at the level of endorsement.

SCHOOL COUNSELOR

A.   Master's Degree from an accredited institution in guidance and counseling;
B.   Preparation course work in counseling in specific areas; and
C.   Practicum in a guidance setting and two years of successful academic counseling. One year may be met with satisfactory counseling or pupil personnel work in business or industry.

MEDIA SPECIALIST / SCHOOL LIBRARIAN (K-12)

A.   Master's Degree from an accredited institution;
B.   Course work in library science;
C.   Preparation course work at the level sought including directed field experiences in a school library **or** two years of successful teaching **or** one year of library work experience; and
D.   Completion of the School Leaders Licensure Assessment (SLLA - Administered by ETS).

ADMINISTRATIVE SERVICES CREDENTIAL (Valid 5 Years)
Principal, Assistant Principal, Director, and other school-site Administrators

Licenses:

Provisional License - **valid 2 years, non-renewable.**

   Applicants who have completed a state-approved administrative services preparation program from an accredited educational institution outside of the District of Columbia, hold a valid administrative services license from another state, and have not taken the School Leaders Licensure Assessment (SLLA), shall be eligible for a two year, non-renewable Provisional Administrative Services credential, provided they satisfy the requirements of sub-sections (A), (B), and (C) below.

Standard Professional License - **valid 5 years.**
Minimum Requirements: *Applies only to applicants employed since January 1, 2000.*
   A.   Valid teaching credential (requiring at least a bachelor's degree); Professional preparation program (including student teaching); or School Psychologist, School Librarian, School Social Worker, Speech and Language Pathologist, or Pupil Personnel Worker; and
   B.   Completion of a minimum of three years of successful, full time classroom teaching

35

experience in public or private schools of equivalent status, or three years of experience in the fields of pupil personnel, health, clinical or rehabilitative services.

C.   Completion of a program of specialized and professional preparation in Administrative Services approved by the Superintendent, including a master's degree program of a minimum of thirty semester hours from an accredited institution of higher education; or a one year Superintendent approved Administrative Services Internship consisting of supervised inservice training taken through an accredited District of Columbia college or university, to include a master's degree.

D.   Completion of the School Leaders Licensure Assessment (SSLA - *administered by ETS*).

Superintendent - eligibility determined by a special panel.

STATE OF FLORIDA

Florida Department of Education
Bureau of Educator Certification
325 West Gaines Street, Suite 201
Tallahassee, Florida 32399-0400
Phone: 800-445-6739 or 850-245-5049 (outside U.S.) / Fax: 850-245-0602
Web Site: **http://www.fldoe.org/edcert/**

INITIAL REQUIREMENTS AT A GLANCE:

Also needed will be items A, B, E, H, I (or Green Card), and K (See page 2). The fee is $75.00 for each subject area or endorsement. A state administered certification test (General Knowledge Test, Florida Professional Education Test or Florida Subject Area Examination) is required in lieu of recent NTE and Praxis test scores. Contact the Bureau for complete testing information. Florida DOES belong to the Interstate Certification Compact, but there are contingencies. Florida DOES belong to the NASDTEC Interstate Contract (Teachers, Administrators, and Support Professionals). Florida is NOT a member of the Interstate New Teacher Assessment and Support Consortium (INTASC). Coursework in Special Education is NOT required.

Renewal Requirements: Every 5 years: six (6) semester hours of college work, **or** 120 Florida master inservice program points, **or** other training and coursework approved by Florida statutes. Fee: $75.00

GENERAL CERTIFICATE REQUIREMENTS

Note: An applicant for certification in Florida will first be issued a **Statement of Status of Eligibility**. This document summarizes additional requirements (if any) needed to qualify for a **Temporary Certificate** which is valid three years and non-renewable. With a Temporary Certificate, an applicant may seek employment from a school district, where requirements for the **Professional Certificate** are expected to be completed.

Temporary Academic or Vocational Certificate: (Valid three years, non-renewable)

Bachelor's or higher degree. Several optional certification routes may be considered such as: Florida graduates of approved programs; Florida education majors who haven't completed their programs; out-of-state graduates of approved teacher education programs; and education majors from countries other than the United States.

Completed application process requirements;

A.   Obtain employment in a Florida school which has an approved Professional Education Competence Program;

B.   Demonstrate Mastery of Subject Area Knowledge or meet Subject Specialization with a 2.5 GPA for a requested subject; and

C.   Fingerprint clearance by both the Florida Department of Law Enforcement and the FBI.

Professional Academic or Vocational Certificate (Valid 5 years, renewable):

A.   Meet all requirements for the three year non-renewable Temporary Certificate;
B.   Demonstrate Mastery of Subject Area Knowledge for a requested subject;
C.   Demonstrate Mastery of General Knowledge;
D.   Demonstrate Mastery of Professional Preparation and Education Competence; and
E.   Completion of the Florida Professional Education Competence Program.

SUBJECT COVERAGES AND ENDORSEMENTS

Elementary Level: **Grade Levels**

   Elementary Education . . . . K - 6

   Prekindergarten/Primary Education . . . . age 3 through grade 3

   Preschool Education . . . . birth through age 4

Middle Level (Grades 5 - 9):

   English; General Science; Integrated Curriculum; Mathematics; and Social Science.

Secondary Level (Grades 6 - 12):

   Agriculture, Business Education, Drama, English, Family and Consumer Science, Technology Education, Journalism, Marketing, Mathematics, Science (Biology, Chemistry, Physics, or Earth-Space), Social Science, and Speech.

Elementary and Secondary Level (Grades K - 12):

   Art, Computer Science, Exceptional Student Education, Hearing Impaired, Speech-Language Impaired, Visually Impaired, Health, Physical Education, Humanities, Music, Reading; and *Foreign Languages*: including Chinese; French; German; Greek; Hebrew; Italian; Japanese; Latin; Portuguese; Russian; Arabic; Haitian Creole; Farsi; and Spanish.

Level PK - 12:

   Guidance and Counseling; Education Media Specialist; School Social Worker; and School Psychologist.

Vocational Endorsements:

   Teacher Coordinator of Cooperative Education; and Teacher Coordinator of Work Experience Programs.

Other Academic Endorsements:

   Athletic Coaching; Autism; Driver Education; English to Speakers of Other Languages (ESOL); Gifted; Orientation and Mobility; Prekindergarten Disabilities; Reading; American Sign Language; and Severe or Profound Disabilities

Administrative Coverages:

   Administration of Adult Education (adult); Educational Leadership; School Principal; and Local Director of Vocational Education (vocational).

EDUCATIONAL MEDIA SPECIALIST (PK - 12)

Bachelor's or higher degree majoring in educational media **or** 30 semester hours in educational media including: management of library media programs, collection development, library media resources, reference sources and services, organization of collections, and design and production of educational media.

GUIDANCE AND COUNSELING CERTIFICATE (PK - 12)

A.   Master's or higher degree in guidance and counseling including 3 semester hours of supervised counseling practicum completed in an elementary or secondary school; **OR**
B.   Thirty semester hours of graduate credit with at least 3 hours in each of the following: administration of guidance services, administration and interpretation of standardized tests, career development information, learning and personality theory, counseling theories and individual counseling techniques, group counseling and guidance techniques, group consultation

skills, legal issues in school counseling, specialized counseling techniques for use with elementary and secondary special populations, **and** 3 semester hours in a supervised counseling practicum in an elementary or secondary school.

SCHOOL PSYCHOLOGIST (PK - 12)

Plan One: A specialist's or higher degree with a major in school psychology at the specialist's or higher degree level which includes six (6) semester hours of graduate credit in a year-long supervised school psychology internship in an elementary or secondary school, or

Plan Two: A master's or higher degree and completion of a graduate program in school psychology which includes sixty (60) semester hours of graduate credit in school psychology to include the areas of:

Psychological foundations; Educational foundations; Psychoeducational assessment; Interventions and specialized techniques; Statistics, measurement, and research design; and Professional school psychology; **and**

Three (3) semester hours in a supervised practicum in school psychology in addition to an internship; and Six (6) semester hours in a year-long supervised school psychology internship in an elementary or secondary school. No more than twelve (12) semester hours of credit in the internship shall be accepted; **or**

Three additional plans are available. For further information, contact the department.

SCHOOL SOCIAL WORKER (PK - 12)

A bachelor's or higher degree with an undergraduate major in social work. The program shall be accredited by the National Council on Social Work Education or the institution shall be accredited or approved in accordance with the provisions of Florida statutes.

ADMINISTRATIVE / SUPERVISORY CERTIFICATION

Florida classifies administrative certification on two levels. Level I, Educational Leadership, certification holders may serve as intern assistant principals, assistant principals, or interim principals or principals. Additional requirements apply to Level II School Principals. For further details, contact the Department.

Requirements:
Florida is currently in the process of making revisions to, and pilot testing revisions to their Florida Educational Leadership Examination (FELE) which are presently scheduled to take effect in July, 2008. The revised examination will contain subtests covering the following three areas:

A. Instructional Leadership with standards in (1) Instructional Leadership, (2) Managing the Learning Environment, and (3) Learning, Accountability and Assessment;

B. Operational Leadership with standards in (1) Human Resource, (2) Decision Making Strategies, (3) Ethical Leadership, and (4) Technology; and

C. School Leadership with standards in (1) Community and Stakeholder Partnerships, (2) Diversity, and (3) Vision.

STATE OF GEORGIA

Georgia Professional Standards Commission
Certification Section
Two Peachtree Street, Suite 6000
Atlanta, Georgia 30303
Phone: 404-232-2500 or 800-869-7775 (Outside Metro Atlanta) / Fax: 404-232-2560
Web Site: http://www.gapsc.com/TeacherCertification.asp

INITIAL REQUIREMENTS AT A GLANCE:

Also needed are items A, B, C, E, G, and O - See page 2. There is a fee of $20.00 unless employed in a Georgia public school. Minimum scores on the CBT or Praxis I PPST exams ARE required (see chart and Praxis II requirements below). The original certificate is valid for from one to five years. Courses in Special Education ARE required. Georgia DOES belong to the Interstate Certification Compact (Teachers, Support Personnel, Administrators, and Vocational). For 2004-2005, Georgia is reviewing major changes to their certification, preparation and ethics standards. Georgia has established a special requirement (to be met at the date for certificate renewal) for educators to demonstrate satisfactory proficiency on a test of computer skill competency. Successful completion of the *InTech* model training at a state educational technology center or PSC approved courses or test-out option will satisfy the requirement. All Georgia educators holding the Clear Renewable Certification must satisfy this requirement by 6/30/06.

Renewal Requirements: 6 semester hours of college course work or 10 credits of Georgia Professional Learning Units (PLUs) or 10 credits of Continuing Education Units, and a criminal record check. *Types and Timing of Renewal Credit* - Credit may be in any combination of the following: (1) College course work reflected on official transcripts with a grade of "c" or better; 3 semester hours is equivalent to 5 quarter hours and developmental studies courses and course work that is audited and/or exempted without credit shall not be accepted; (2) Professional Learning Units (PLUs) reflected on official transcripts from school systems, colleges or other state agencies approved by the Georgia Department of Education; **or** (3) Continuing Education Units (CEUs) issued by a provider authorized by the International Association for Continuing Education and Training (IACET).

Renewal credit for certificates that are currently valid must have been completed during the validity period established on the certificate. Renewal credit for inactive certificates must have been completed within the 5-year period preceding the date of renewal application.

Beginning in 2003, the Professional Standards Commission (PSC) revised certification requirements and procedures to improve "the interstate mobility of out-of-state certified educators".

The Special Georgia Requirements for content assessment (PRAXIS II), Recency of Study/Experience, Standards of Conduct, Computer Competency and coursework in Special Education and the Teaching of Reading will continue to exist and be a part of all Georgia state-approved preparation programs. *However, specific experience gained by veteran and out-of-state educators moving to Georgia may now be used to exempt all Special Georgia Requirements except computer competency and the standards of conduct.* To be acceptable, the out-of-state experience must be directly related to the type (teaching, service, leadership) and field (subject area) of the Georgia certificate being requested. For further information, contact the Commission.

New Praxis I Series Requirements (*Effective 6/7/2001*)
Either Individual or Composite Scores must be met

Praxis I	Reading	Writing	Mathematics	Composite Score
PPST	176	174	176	526
CBT	322	321	321	964

REQUIREMENTS FOR TEACHING CERTIFICATES

The following teaching certification fields are available:
Teaching fields are divided into several classifications including Early Childhood (Preschool-5); Middle Grades (4-8); Secondary (7-12) with fields such as English, Math, Science, History, Business, and Home Economics; and Preschool-12 fields such as Art, Music, Health and Physical Education, Foreign Language, and Special Education. Additional teaching fields include:

Agriculture Education	Interrelated Special Education	Trade and Industrial Education
Art Education	Interrelated Special Education /	Visually Impaired
Behavior Disorders	Early Childhood	Vocational Fields

Biology	Italian	Teaching Endorsements
Chemistry	Japanese	Career Exploration (PECE)
Chinese	Latin	Coordinator of Cooperative
Dance	Learning Disabilities	Education (CVAE)
Drama	Marketing Education	Diversified Cooperative
Earth/Space Science Economics	Mental Retardation	Training (DCT)
French	Music	English to Speakers of Other
Geography	Orthopedically Impaired	Languages (ESOL)
German	Physics	Gifted In-Field
Greek	Political Science	Preschool Special Education
Health Education	Reading	Related Vocational Instruction
Health Occupations, Health and	Russian	(RVI)
Physical Education	Social Science	Safety and Driver Education
Hearing Impaired	Spanish	Reading Endorsement
Hebrew	Speech	Middle Grades Endorsement
Family and Consumer Science	Technology Education	Early Childhood Mathematics
		Early Childhood Science

An applicant may be certified in Georgia who has completed one of the following: (a) **Approved Programs** - Candidate has completed a teacher preparation program during the time, in the field, and at the level for which it was approved either by the state authority in a state approved teacher education program, or (b) **Reciprocity** - Candidate holds or has held professional certification in another state, or (c) **Alternate Provisional** - Candidates who may have completed college degrees in disciplines other than education and programs such as Troops to Teachers or others may be used.

CERTIFICATION CLASSIFICATIONS

All certificates are classified in the following manner: Type, Title, Level, Field (see above), and Category (effective 10/1/01) Types of certification recognize three school personnel functions defined as Teaching, Leadership and Service. All fields shall be grouped under one of these functions.

Certificate Types:
Teaching certificates are issued in fields that prepare an individual to teach the subject matter offered as a part of the school curriculum.
Leadership certificates are issued in fields that prepare an individual to administer or supervise a school system, school or school program. Leadership Fields include Education Leadership, Director of Media Centers, Director of Pupil Personnel Services, Director of Special Education, and Instructional Supervision.
Service certificates are issued in fields that prepare an individual to provide support services to students, school personnel and school operations. Service Fields include Audiologist, Media Specialist, School Counselor, School Nutrition Director, School Psychologist, School Social Worker, and Speech and Language Pathologist.

Certificate Titles[*]:
Provisional certificates are issued to individuals who have satisfied the minimum job-entry level requirements for a specific field.
Professional renewable certificates are issued to individuals employed in all school personnel functions who completed applicable requirements
Probationary certificates are issued to professionally certified individuals who are completing requirements to add a new field of certification while they are employed in the field being added. Initial probationary certificates are not issued in certain fields.
Emergency certificates are issued to teachers who lack renewal credit, recent study, and/or the appropriate assessment(s) under certain conditions. Such certificates are issued in teaching or service fields only.

[*]   For a complete list of Georgia Certificate Titles, contact the Commission or visit their web site.

Certificate Levels:
   There are seven certification levels, some containing sub-levels. The following are generally considered minimums: (a) *Level I* - Vocational Education Fields - H.S. diploma or GED; (b) *Level II* -

Vocational Education - A.S. Degree; (c) *Level IV* - Bachelor's degree; *Level V* - Master's degree; (d) *Level VI* - Ed. Specialist's degree; and (e) *Level VII* (minimum of Ph. D or Ed. D).

Certificate Categories:

A.   *Clear Renewable Certificate* - Valid 5 years - All professional requirements for certification in the field have been met. Clear renewable status applies to Teaching, Service, and Leadership fields.

B.   *Conditional Certificate* - Variable Validity - Issued at the request of a Georgia employer when one or more conditions have to be met in order to be issued the Clear Renewable Certificate. Conditional certificates fall under the following titles: Provisional, Probationary, Emergency, or Non-renewable Professional.

C.   *Life Certificate* - Discontinued in 1974; however, Georgia educators issued life certification before 1974 may continue to use these certificates.

SPECIAL GEORGIA REQUIREMENTS

Through either State law or Professional Standards Commission policy there are special requirements for certification in Georgia. These requirements must be met regardless of whether an applicant is seeking certification through the approved program approach or through certification by reciprocity from another state, D.C., DODDS, NBPTS or U.S. Territory. An initial certificate at the request of an employing superintendent may be issued for one year to allow the applicant to meet special course work and test requirements. Special requirements address course work, performance and experience as described by the following provisions.

A.   Course Work:
    1.   Exceptional Children and Youth - Any person certified as a teacher, principal, superintendent, guidance counselor, or media specialist must complete or have completed acceptable college credit or its equivalent through a Georgia-approved, local staff development program in the identification and education of children with special needs.
    2.   The Teaching of Reading - Any teacher certified in Elementary Grades (P - 8), Early Childhood (P - 5), Middle Grades (4 - 8), English and certain special education fields, including mental retardation, learning disabilities, behavior disorders, and interrelated teacher of special education, must complete acceptable college credit or its equivalent through a Georgia-approved, local staff development program in the teaching of reading.

B.   Certification Test - All applicants, seeking certification in Georgia must pass the appropriate subject matter assessments applicable to the field of certification (PRAXIS II.)

C.   Experience is a prerequisite requirement for certification in certain fields. Three categories of experience have been defined: teaching, school, and occupational.
    1.   School Experience - Three years of acceptable school experience are required for educational leadership certificates;
    2.   Occupational Experience
        a.   A minimum of two years of full-time employment in business or industry in the field of certification is required as a prerequisite to certification in vocational-technical teaching fields at level below the Bachelor's Degree; and
        b.   One year of full-time employment is required as a minimum of applicants as a prerequisite for certification in vocational-technical teaching fields at the Bachelor's Degree level or higher; and

D.   Recency-of-study must be established by having earned a minimum of 10 quarter hours or 6 semester hours within the last five years or by having one year of approved teaching or school experience within the last five years.

TEACHING CERTIFICATES
Clear Renewable
Valid five years; Renewable

Requirements are:

A.   Bachelor's or higher Degree from a regionally accredited institution;

B.   Approved professional preparation program, including either student teaching or internship; AND recommendation of the institution; OR holding or having held professional certification out-

41

of-state; and

C.   Special Georgia requirements including the appropriate assessment, credit in the identification and education of exceptional children and credit in teaching reading for select fields.

SCHOOL COUNSELOR
School Service Field

Requirements are:

A.   Master's or higher degree from a regionally accredited institution;

B.   Approved professional preparation program and recommendation of the institution; OR holding or having held professional certification out-of-state;

C.   Special Georgia requirements including the appropriate assessment, and credit in the identification and education of exceptional children; and

D.   A Conditional Certificate may be issued to applicants with a master's degree or higher in a counseling area other than school counseling who have passed the appropriate assessment and are employed.

ADMINISTRATION
Educational Leadership Fields

Superintendent, Associate/Assistant Superintendent
Principal, and Assistant Principal

Requirements:

A.   Master's or higher degree from a regionally accredited institution;

B.   Approved professional program and recommendation of the institution, OR holding or having held professional certification out-of-state;

C.   Three years of acceptable school experience; and

D.   Special Georgia requirements including the appropriate assessment, and credit in the identification and education of exceptional children.

STATE OF HAWAII

Hawaii Teacher Standards Board
650 Iwilei Road, #201
Honolulu, Hawaii 96817
Phone: 808-586-2600 / Fax: 808-586-2606
Web Site: **http://www.htsb.org/**

INITIAL REQUIREMENTS AT A GLANCE:

Also needed are items A, C, D, E, F, G, N and O - See page 2. Fee is $240.00 for the five year license. Passing scores on the PPST, CBT, and PRAXIS II are required. Standards for passing scores are changing. Hawaii DOES belong to the Interstate Certification Compact and the NASDTEC Interstate Contract (Teachers only) and is a member of the Mid-Atlantic agreement. Hawaii DOES belong to the Interstate New Teacher Assessment and Support Consortium (INTASC). Coursework in Special Education is NOT required. *The Hawaii Teacher Standards Board (HTSB) has revised their certification requirements for Teachers, Librarians, and Counselors.* Certification is now standards/performance-based. Contact the Board for complete information. Revisions are ongoing.

Renewal Requirements: License renewal is still under evaluation during a formal "Pilot" test. Renewal will become a 5 years process. Requirements may include the following:
1. Year 1: Submission of a Professional Development Growth Plan (PDGP);
2. Years 2 - 4: Document linkage between their Plan and their subject matter field and their pedagogy. Demonstrate and document, using multiple criteria, its potential for positively affecting student learning;

4. Year 5: Teachers will complete and submit the Reflection Report at least 6 months prior to expiration of their license.

Teaching Fields for Licensure:

Agricultural Arts
Art
Business Education
Computer Education
Drama / Theatre Arts
Early Childhood Education
Elementary Education
Marketing/Distributive Education*
English
ESL
Family Consumer Science
Guidance

Hawaiian Language
Hawaiian Studies
Hawaiian Language Immersion
Health
Health and Physical Education
Industrial Arts
Industrial Technical*
Languages
Mathematics
Middle School Teaching
Music
Physical Education

Reading
School Librarian
Science
School Counselor
Social Studies
Special Education
Speech
Vocational Office Education*
Vocational Family Consumer Science*
Vocational Agriculture*

*Trade experience requirements apply. Contact the Board for further information.

REQUIREMENTS FOR TEACHING LICENSE, CREDENTIAL, AND CERTIFICATES

Teaching licenses are issued in the following areas: Early Childhood PK-3, Elementary K-6; Secondary Subject Fields 7-12; Special Education areas of Mild/Moderate, Severe/Profound, Middle Level 5-9, Orthopedically Disabled, Blind/Visually Impaired, Deaf/Hard of Hearing and Orientation/Mobility; and K-12 in Art, Hawaiian Language Immersion, Music, P.E., and Reading.

License: (Valid five years) Renewal is based upon standards established by the HTSB. Requirements: completion of undergraduate, advanced, or graduate level state approved teacher education program including K-12 student teaching or validation of teaching competencies based upon HTSB performance standards or submittal of passing scores on the PPST, PLT, and Praxis Content Area Test(s).

Out-of-State Teachers: *Effective June 6, 2007* to qualify, a teacher must provide documentation of all of the following:
A.   A valid, un-revoked professional (not provisional or temporary) license from another state; and
B.   Completion of a State-Approved Teacher Education Program; and
C.   Passed all licensing tests required by the State which issued the valid license; and
Passed tests for content knowledge, basic skills, and pedagogy. Note: For any tests not required and taken for the out-of-state license, the teacher must pass the required Hawaii Praxis tests and will be issued a license based on the date when these required tests are passed and application and required documentation submitted.

STANDARDS FOR TEACHING LICENSES

Standard 1: Focuses on the Learner
Standard 2: Creates and maintains a safe and positive learning environment
Standard 3: Adapts to Learner Diversity
Standard 4: Fosters effective communication in the learning environment
Standard 5: Demonstrates knowledge of content
Standard 6: Designs and provides meaningful learning experiences
Standard 7: Uses active learning strategies
Standard 8: Uses assessment strategies
Standard 9: Demonstrates professionalism
Standard 10: Fosters parent and school community relationships

STANDARDS FOR LIBRARY LICENSES

Standard 1: Focuses on the Learner
Standard 2: Creates and maintains a safe and positive learning environment
Standard 3: Adapts to learner diversity
Standard 4: Fosters effective communication in the learning environment
Standard 5: Demonstrates knowledge of content
Standard 6: Designs and provides meaningful learning experiences
Standard 7: Uses active learning strategies
Standard 8: Uses assessment strategies
Standard 9: Demonstrates professionalism
Standard 10: Fosters parent and school community relationships
Standard 11: Designs and provides quality library media programs and services

STANDARDS FOR COUNSELORS LICENSES

Standard 1: Focuses on the Learner
Standard 2: Creates and maintains a safe and positive learning environment
Standard 3: Adapts to learner diversity
Standard 4: Fosters effective communication in the learning environment
Standard 5: Demonstrates knowledge of content
Standard 6: Designs and provides meaningful learning experiences
Standard 7: Uses active learning strategies
Standard 8: Uses assessment strategies
Standard 9: Demonstrates professionalism
Standard 10: Fosters parent and school community relationships

STATE OF IDAHO

State Department of Education
Office of Certification and Professional Standards
650 W. State St., P.O. Box 83720
Boise, Idaho 83720-0027
Phone: 800-432-4601 or, Local 208-332- 6881 / Fax: 208-334-2228
Web Site: **http://www.sde.idaho.gov/site/teacher_certification/**

INITIAL REQUIREMENTS AT A GLANCE:

Also needed will be items A, B, C, E, G, J (one copy), K and O (See page 2). The fee is $75.00 and $100.00 for the Alternate Route approval. Background check and fingerprint card fee $40.00. Scores on the Praxis II Content, Pedagogy, or Performance test ARE required. All certificates are valid for five (5) years. Idaho DOES belong to the NASDTEC Interstate Contract (Teachers and Support Professionals). Idaho IS a member of the Interstate New Teacher Assessment and Support Consortium (INTASC). Coursework in Special Education is NOT required. There is a requirement for completing a 3 sem. hr. course: Idaho Comprehensive Literacy Course (ICLC). New Alternate Routes to Certification were effective 7/1/2006. Please contact the Bureau or visit their web site for complete details.

Renewal Requirements: Six sem. credit hours must be completed within past five years, **or** 3.5 sem. credit hours and 45 clock hours of professional development. All teachers must show successful completion of the Idaho State Board approved Technology Assessment. Elementary, Special Ed., ESL and Bilingual employed in Idaho must successfully complete a three (3) semester credit hour course: Idaho Comprehensive Literacy Course, or pass the Idaho Comprehensive Literacy Assessment.

EARLY CHILDHOOD / EARLY CHILDHOOD
SPECIAL EDUCATION BLENDED CERTIFICATE
(Birth to Grade 3)

1. Minimum of thirty (30) semester hours in the philosophical, psychological, methodological foundations in instructional technology and in the professional subject matter of Early Childhood and Early Childhood Special Education. The Professional subject matter of Early Childhood and Early Childhood Special Education must include course work specific to the young child from birth through grade 3 in the areas of: (a) child development and learning; (b) curriculum development and implementation; (c) family and community relationships; (d) assessment and evaluation; (e) professionalism; and (f) application of technologies.
2. Proficiency in these areas is measured by semester credit hours and/or achievement of content competency as determined by assessment developed by institutions of higher education and approved by the State Board of Education.
3. An institutional recommendation from an accredited college or university.

A Blended Early Childhood Certificate is valid in grades K-3 in an elementary school. It is valid, also, in inclusive preschools and other programs designed to serve typically and atypically developing young children from birth through age eight.

K-12 endorsements may be added to the Blended Birth through Grade Three Certificate through completion of currently adopted requirements.

STANDARD ELEMENTARY CERTIFICATE

A. Bachelor's Degree;
B. 24 semester hours of Professional Education including philosophical, psychological and methodological foundations;
C. Six semester hours of student teaching or three years of successful experience in an elementary school;
D. Six semester hours in developmental reading; and
E. Requires Praxis II Elementary Content test and the PLT.

STANDARD EXCEPTIONAL CHILD CERTIFICATE

A. Bachelor's degree;
B. 30 semester hours in the area of endorsement approved either by the Idaho State Board or the state education agency from the state of origin. Endorsements include: Generalist (Educationally Disabled) and Hearing Impaired; Visually Impaired; Physically Disabled; Multiply Disabled; Severe Retardation; and Seriously Emotionally Disturbed / Severe Behavior Disorders.
C. Requires an Institutional Recommendation
D. Requires completion of Praxis Skills test (Special Ed.) and Specialty test for endorsement area.

STANDARD SECONDARY CERTIFICATE

A. Bachelor's Degree;
B. 20 semester hours of Professional Education including philosophical, psychological, and methodological foundation of education;
C. Six semester hours of secondary student teaching;
D. Three semester hours of reading in the content area; and
E. Preparation in two fields of secondary teaching with a major of 30 semester hours and a minor of 20 semester hours or in a single area of 45 semester hours.
F. Requires completion of Praxis II Specialty Area tests for all endorsements.

SCHOOL COUNSELOR
Pupil Personnel Services, Standard Counselor Endorsement

Requirements are:
A. Master's Degree;
B. Approved program of graduate study in school guidance and counseling including a supervised practicum;
C. Successful completion of 700 hours of supervised field experience, one half of which must be in a K-12 school setting; and
D. Recommendation of the institution.

SCHOOL PRINCIPAL (PRE-K - 12)

Requirements are:

A.   Master's Degree;

B.   Four years of full time certified experience working with Pre-K - 12 students while under contract in a school setting;

C.   Completed an administrative internship or have 1 year experience as an administrator; and

D.   Verification of completion of an approved program of graduate study with at least thirty semester credit hours (45 quarter hours) of graduate study in school administration for the preparation of school principals. This program shall include the following competencies:

(1) leadership, ethics, and management of change;

(2) all forms of communication, including technology, advocacy, and mediation;

(3) customer involvement and public relations;

(4) staff development and supervision of instruction;

(5) school law and finance (including special education), and grant writing;

(6) curriculum development, integration of technology, delivery, and assessment; and

(7) Education of all populations, including special education; and student behavior management/positive behavior supports/effective discipline.

An institutional recommendation is required for a School Principal, Pre-K - 12.

SUPERINTENDENT

Requirements are:

A.   Hold the Educational Specialist or Doctorate degree or a comparable post-master's sixth year program at an accredited college or university;

B.   Four years of full time experience working with K - 12 students while under contract in a school setting;

C.   Have completed and administrative internship for the superintendent endorsement or have 1 year of out-of-state experience as an assistant superintendent or superintendent in grades Pre-K - 12 while holding that state's administrative certificate;

D.   Verification of completion of a state approved program of at least thirty semester credit hours (45 quarter hours) of post masters degree graduate studies for the preparation of school superintendents at an accredited institution. This program in school administration and interdisciplinary supporting areas shall include the following competencies in addition to those required for the Principal Pre-K - 12 endorsement:

(1) Advanced school finance, grant writing, and generation of additional sources of revenue;

(2) policy development and school board operations/relations;

(3) District-wide support services;

(4) Employment practices and negotiations;

(5) educational product marketing and community relations; and

(6) Special services and federal programs.

An institutional recommendation is required for a school superintendent.

STATE OF ILLINOIS

State Board of Education
Educator Certification
100 North 1st Street
Springfield, Illinois 62777
Phone: 217-557-6763 / Fax: 217-524-1289
Web Site: **http://www.isbe.net/certification/**

INITIAL REQUIREMENTS AT A GLANCE:

Also needed will be items A, B, C, E, G, and M - See page 2. The fee is $30.00. The Illinois Certification Testing System (ICTS) Basic Skills test and the appropriate ICTS content area test ARE required. Teaching certificates require the successful completion of the Assessment of Professional Teaching (APT) test. Out-of-state applicants may be issued a Provisional Illinois

Certificate and then must pass the required state administered certification tests within nine months from the issue date or it will be canceled. An applicant with less than 4 years of teaching experience will be issued an Initial Teaching Certificate. At the completion of 4 years teaching, the applicant is eligible for a 5 year, renewable Standard teaching certificate. Illinois DOES belong to the Interstate Certification Agreement Contract, the NASDTEC Interstate Contract (Teachers and Administrators), and Interstate New Teacher Assessment and Support Consortium (INTASC). Illinois has additional reciprocity with Iowa, Kansas, Michigan, Missouri, Nebraska, Oklahoma, South Dakota and Wisconsin. Courses or competencies in Special Education ARE required. Please contact the Division for complete details.

NOTE: The Illinois State Board of Education has adopted new standards that will guide the preparation of all certified educators. Beginning fall 2001, Illinois colleges and universities must meet the National Council for Accreditation of Teacher Education (*NCATE*) 2000 standards (http://www.ncate.org/standard/m_stds.htm).

Renewal Requirements: Every 5 years. If you plan to maintain your certificate as valid and active, you must develop and submit to your Local Professional Development Committee (LPDC) a Certificate Renewal Plan that includes your personal improvement goals, proposed activities or types of activities, and projected time lines. Registration fees: $25 for a Standard Certificate, $50 for a Master Certificate, $25.00 for Administrator, and $25.00 for School Service Personnel renewal.

Illinois Standards-Based Certification

As of July 1, 2003, all college and university professional preparation programs for teachers and administrators were redesigned to address the content area standards for regular education teachers and administrators. These include the content area standards that define the knowledge and performance standards necessary for the preparation of teachers in specific fields, such as elementary education, mathematics, or foreign language, and for administrators preparing for roles as principals, superintendents, and chief school business officials.

As of July 1, 2004, all college and university preparation programs for school service personnel were redesigned to address the content area standards for the specific professional roles. These include programs preparing school counselors, school nurses, school psychologists, school social workers, and speech language pathologists.

The special education expectations for general education teachers are an integral part of the Illinois Professional Teaching Standards, and are presented as knowledge and performance indicators related to the specific standards. These became effective July 1, 2003.

Although some endorsements will be maintained under the new system, the State Board has expressed a commitment to eliminate many of the current categories.

Standards-Based Assessment Implementation Schedule

Date	Test to be Implemented	Explanation
January 2003	**Learning Behavior Specialist I (LBS I)**	For current special education teachers seeking to remove an LBS I limitation on their certificate. The LBS I test will be required of all new candidates seeking an LBS I endorsement on a certificate as of July 2003.
July 2003	**Special Education Content-Area Tests**	All other special education tests implemented
October 2003	**Assessment of Professional Teaching (APT)** *Four Versions:* Early Childhood; Elementary; Secondary; and Special (K-12)	This is a new test that will assess candidates' knowledge of the Illinois Professional Teaching Standards, Core Technology Standards, and Core Language Arts Standards.
July 2004	**Content-Area Test: All Teaching and**	New content tests, replacing existing content tests required of individuals

	Administrative Certificates	seeking a teaching or administrative certificate, will be administered.
July 2005	Content-Area Test: School Service Personnel	New content tests, replacing existing content tests required of individuals seeking certification for school counselor, school nurse, school psychologist, school social worker, or speech language pathologist will be administered.

LEVELS AND TYPES OF TEACHER CERTIFICATION

I. **Initial Certificate** - Valid 4 years, non-renewable. For candidates with less than 4 years teaching experience. Available for Early Childhood, Elementary, Secondary, Special K-12, and Pre-K to Age 21.

II. **Standard Certificate** - Valid 5 years, renewable upon completion of continual professional development. Candidate must have a minimum of 4 years teaching experience. Available as in (I.) above.

III. **Master Certificate** - Valid 10 years, renewable upon completion of continual professional development. Available for candidates awarded certification by the National Board for Professional Teaching Standards. Available as in (I.) above and school counselor.

Teaching Certificates	School Service Personnel Certificates	Administrative Certificates
Early Childhood Elementary High School Special Special K-12 Special Pre-K to Age 21	School Social Worker Endorsement School Psychologist Endorsement Guidance Endorsement School Nurse Endorsement Speech Language Pathologist	General Administrative Endorsement Chief School Business Official Endorsement Director of Special Education Superintendent Endorsement

ILLINOIS CERTIFICATIONS & STANDARDS
Language Arts and *Technology Core Standards* (Illinois Professional Teaching Standards) apply to ALL certifications

EARLY CHILDHOOD - (Birth - Grade 3)

  The Initial Early Childhood certificate is valid for 4 years of teaching and is registered 4 years at a time. During the validity period, the holder must obtain four years of teaching experience. When the holder has completed four years of teaching experience, the Initial certificate becomes invalid and the holder must obtain a Standard certificate.

A. A bachelor's degree from a regionally accredited university;

B. Less than four years of teaching experience on an Illinois certificate;

C. Proof of completion of an approved program in Illinois or of an approved program in another state comparable to the certificate sought or possession of a comparable certificate from another state;

D. Identification and teaching methods for exceptional children, explicitly including the learning disabled child;

E. Pre-student teaching clinical experiences with infants/toddlers, preschool/kindergarten children, and primary school students;

F. Student teaching at the Birth - Grade 3 level credit in a student teaching course at any grade level, and evidence of three months of successful teaching experience; and

G. Passing score on the basic skills, early childhood examination, and assessment of professional teaching from the Illinois Certification Testing System.

SPECIAL EDUCATION

Special Education Certifications:

Learning Behavior Specialist I (LBS I)	LBS II/Technology Specialist
Blind or Visually Impaired	LBS II/Bilingual Education Specialist
Deaf or Hard of Hearing	LBS II/Deaf-Blind Specialist
Speech Language Pathologist	LBS II/Behavior Intervention Specialist
Early Childhood Special Education	LBS II/Curriculum Adaptation Specialist
Learning Behavior Specialist II (LBS II)	LBS II/Multiple Disabilities Specialist
LBS II/Transition Specialist	

For complete information on Special Education certification, contact the Division.

ELEMENTARY - (K - 9)

The **Initial Elementary Certificate** is valid for 4 years of teaching and is registered 4 years at a time. During the validity period, the holder must obtain four years of teaching experience. When the holder has completed four years of teaching experience, the Initial certificate becomes invalid and the holder must obtain a Standard certificate. The holder of an elementary certificate may obtain endorsements at the middle grades level (grades 5-8 for the elementary certificate) by having 18 semester hours in the subject, by also meeting the middle grades course requirements and, where required, meeting other course distribution requirements. Limited Primary level (K - 4) endorsements may be granted on the Elementary certificate. For complete information, contact the Division.

Requirements:
A.   A bachelor's degree from a regionally accredited university;
B.   Less than four years of teaching experience on an Initial certificate;
C.   Proof of completion of an approved program in Illinois or completion of an approved program in another state for a comparable certificate or a comparable certificate from another state;
D.   Identification and teaching methods for exceptional children, explicitly including the learning disabled child;
E.   Pre-student teaching clinical experiences at the K-9 level or proof of teaching experience at the K-9 level;
F.   Student teaching at the K-9 level, credit in a student teaching course at any grade level and evidence of three months of successful teaching experience; and
G.   A passing score on the basic skills, elementary examinations, and assessment of professional teaching for elementary teachers from the Illinois Certification Testing System.

MIDDLE GRADES - (5 - 8)

See description for **Initial Elementary and Secondary Certificates**.

SECONDARY - (6 - 12)

The **Initial Secondary Certificate** is valid for 4 years of teaching with 4 year registration periods. During the registration period, the holder must obtain four years of teaching experience. When the holder has completed four years of teaching experience, the Initial certificate becomes invalid and the holder must obtain a Standard certificate. The holder of a Secondary certificate may obtain endorsements at the middle grades level (grades 6-8 for the Secondary certificate) by having 18 semester hours in the subject. For complete information, contact the Division or visit their web site. Most Senior High endorsements (grades 9 - 12 for the secondary certificate) are obtained by having 24 semester hours in the subject and passing the content area test - OR - having 32 semester hours in the subject. There are some exceptions.

Requirements:
A.   A bachelor's degree from a regionally accredited university.
B.   Less than four years of teaching experience;
C.   Proof of completion of an approved program in Illinois or of completion of an approved program in another state for a comparable certificate or proof of possession of a comparable certificate from another state;
D.   Identification and teaching methods for the exceptional children explicitly including the learning disabled child;
E.   Pre-student teaching clinical experiences at the 6-12 level or proof of teaching experience at the 6-12 level;

F.   Student teaching at the 6-12 level, credit in a student teaching course at any grade level and evidence of three months of successful teaching experience;

G.   A major area of specialization (or 32 semester hours); and

H.   A passing score on the basic skills and secondary certificate subject matter knowledge, and the secondary APT examination of the Illinois Certification Testing System.

SCHOOL SERVICE PERSONNEL

School Counselor:
All persons requesting a School Counselor endorsement on the School Service Personnel certificate must meet the following requirements and must successfully complete the required certification examinations.

A.   School Counselors must hold or be qualified for a standard teaching certificate.

B.   School Counselors must hold a master's degree from a recognized teacher education institution.

C.   School Counselors must complete an approved program in guidance from a recognized college or university, consisting of 39 semester hours of coursework at the graduate level.

D.   Successful completion of the required certification examinations.

School Psychologist: All persons seeking endorsement as a School Psychologist on the School Service Personnel certificate must have completed an approved program for the endorsement, either in Illinois or in another state. Educational requirements:

A.   Candidates must have graduated with a master's degree or higher degree in psychology or educational psychology with specialization in school psychology and have completed, in a school setting, a field experience and internship at the graduate level. All applicants must successfully complete the required certification examinations. The field experience must be at least 250 hours and the internship at least a full year, under the direction of an intern supervisor.

ADMINISTRATIVE CERTIFICATES

Administrative certificates are required for persons serving in administrative roles. These certificates are valid for five-year periods and may be renewed. The certificate is available by transcript evaluation only to persons who have completed an approved school administrator program in another state or country or who hold another state's comparable certificate.

Provisional Administrative Certificates: Should applicants from other states who hold valid comparable certificates from their states not meet all of Illinois' requirements, they can be issued a provisional Illinois certificate. The first year of the two year certificate expires on June 30 following the date of issue. When a provisional certificate has been issued and the holder has not passed the required Illinois examinations within nine months after the issue date, the certificate will be canceled.

General Administrative Endorsement: This endorsement is required for principals, assistant principals, assistant or associate superintendents, and staff filling other similar or related positions.

1. Candidates for the general administrative endorsement shall hold a master's degree awarded by a regionally accredited institution of higher education that encompasses the coursework in educational administration and supervision.

2. Candidates shall have completed an Illinois program approved for the preparation of administrators or a comparable approved program in another state or country or hold a comparable certificate issued by another state or country.

3. Candidates shall have two years' full-time teaching or school service personnel experience in public schools, schools under the supervision of the Department of Corrections, schools under the administration of the Department of Human Services, or nonpublic schools recognized by the State Board of Education or meeting comparable out-of-state recognition standards.

4. Candidates shall be required to pass the applicable content-area test, as well as the test of basic skills if its passage would be required for receipt of a standard certificate.

Chief School Business Official:

1. Candidates for the chief school business official's endorsement shall hold a master's degree awarded by a regionally accredited institution of higher education.

2. Candidates, whose master's degrees were earned in business administration, finance, or accounting, shall be required to pass the basic skills and content area tests.

3. All other candidates shall:

a. have completed an Illinois program approved for the preparation of school business officials or a comparable approved program in another state or country or hold a comparable certificate issued by another state or country; and

b. have two years' administrative experience in school business management.

4. Each candidate shall be required to pass the applicable content-area test, as well as the test of basic skills if its passage would be required for receipt of a standard certificate.

Superintendent (2004):

This endorsement is required of school district superintendents.

1. Candidates for the superintendent's endorsement shall hold a master's degree awarded by a regionally accredited institution of higher education.

2. Candidates shall have completed an Illinois program approved for the preparation of superintendents or a comparable approved program in another state or country or hold a comparable certificate issued by another state or country.

3. Candidates shall have at least two years' administrative or supervisory experience in schools, on at least a half-time basis, on a general supervisory, general administrative, or all-grade supervisory endorsement on an administrative certificate, or a comparable out-of-state credential; the superintendent's endorsement shall not be issued as an individual's first endorsement on the administrative certificate unless issued on the basis of a comparable out-of-state credential.

4. Candidates shall be required to pass the applicable content-area test, as well as the test of basic skills if its passage would be required for receipt of a standard certificate.

Director of Special Education: This endorsement is required for directors and assistant directors of special education, effective July 1, 2005. All candidates are subject to the requirements of subsections (1) through (4).

1. Candidates for the director of special education endorsement shall hold a master's degree awarded by a regionally accredited institution of higher education; and

2. Candidates shall have completed an Illinois program approved for the preparation of directors of special education (complete entitlement application process)

(OR)

1. Hold a comparable certificate issued by another state or country (complete application for administrative certificate process); OR

2. Submit evidence of having completed 30 semester hours of coursework, distributed among all the following areas (complete application for endorsement process), **OR**

    1. Survey of exceptional children
    2. Special methods courses covering at least three areas of disability
    3. Educational and psychological diagnosis and remedial techniques
    4. Supervision/administration of special education programs and personnel
    5. Guidance and counseling

3. Candidates shall have two years' full-time teaching experience or school service personnel experience in a field other than school nursing in public schools, schools under the supervision of the Department of Corrections, schools under the administration of the Department of Human Services, or nonpublic schools recognized by the State Board of Education or meeting comparable out-of-state recognition standards.

4. Candidates shall be required to pass the Director of Special Education test (#180), as well as the test of basic skills if its passage would be required for the receipt of a standard certificate.

STATE OF INDIANA

Indiana Department of Education
Division of Professional Standards
101 West Ohio Street, Suite 300
Indianapolis, Indiana 46204
Phone: 317-232-9010 / Toll-free: 866-542-3672 / Fax: 317-232-9023
Web Site: **www.doe.state.in.us/dps**

INITIAL REQUIREMENTS AT A GLANCE:

Also needed will be items A, B, D, E, G, K, N, O and Q - See page 2. The fee is $35.00. Applicants must submit a Limited Criminal History Check ($7.00 fee.) Indiana DOES belong to the Interstate Certification Compact and the Interstate New Teacher Assessment and Support Consortium (INTASC). Indiana belongs to the NASDTEC Interstate Contract (Teachers, Support Professionals, and Administrators). Indiana recognizes NCATE accreditation. Passing scores on the PRAXIS I: PPST ARE almost universally required. Praxis II Specialty Area tests ARE required for most content areas. Course work in Special Education IS required for all teaching certificates. Effective 7/1/2007, all applicants for licensure must have a valid certification from either the American Red Cross or the American Heart Association in CPR and the Heimlich Maneuver.

NOTES: All *Rules 2002* licenses issued are renewable only upon satisfactory completion of a Professional Growth Plan (PGP). All licenses may be renewed under previous rules provided that all necessary courses or Continuing Renewal Units (CRUs) are completed. For a more complete summary of changes and performance requirements, contact the DPS directly or visit their web site.

Renewal Requirements: Fee: $35.00. Under prior rules, recertification requires six semester hours or 90 Certification Renewal Units (CRUs), or a combination equal to 90 CRUs. 1 Credit equals 15 CRUs. Under the new *Rules 2002*, licenses must be renewed with a Professional Growth Plan (PGP) every 5 years.

TEACHER LICENSE FRAMEWORK

Initial Practitioner License - Valid two years.
A.   Bachelor's or higher degree;
B.   met INTASC standards; and
C.   met Indiana DEVELOPMENTAL standards* including (1) Early Childhood; (2) Middle Childhood; (3) Early Adolescence; and/or (4) Adolescence/Young Adulthood;
D.   met Indiana CONTENT standards* in at least one of the following license areas:

Vocational Education (Career/Technical)	Gifted and Talented Education
English as a New language	Journalism
Exceptional Needs	Reading
Fine Arts	Reading Specialist
World Language	Technology Education
Generalist: Early Childhood	Workplace Specialist
Generalist: Early and Middle Childhood	**District Administrators:**
Generalist: Early Adolescence	Superintendent
Health/Physical Education	Exceptional Needs Director
Language Arts	Career/Technical Education Director
Library Media	Curriculum and Instruction Director
Mathematics	**Building Level Administrator**
Science	**School Services:**
Social Studies	School Psychology
Adaptive Physical Education	School Nurse
Business	School Counselor
Communication Disorders	School Social Worker
Computer Education	

*   See School Settings table below

Initial Practitioner License - Valid two years. Complete Indiana Mentoring and Assessment Program (IMAP).

Proficient Practitioner License - Valid five years, renewable.

Accomplished Practitioner License - Valid ten years initially. Renewable every five years thereafter.

SCHOOL SETTINGS FOR TEACHING LICENSES

School Setting on license	Developmental Level Standards Required	Content Standards Applicable to School Setting
PRESCHOOL *	Early Childhood	Generalist Standards for Early Childhood ** or Specific Content (Which will appear on the license as Preschool Generalist or as a specific content area)
ELEMENTARY/ PRIMARY *	Early Childhood	Generalist Standards for Early and Middle Childhood, or Specific Content (Which will appear on the license as either Elementary/ Primary Generalist or as a specific content area)
ELEMENTARY/ INTERMEDIATE	Middle Childhood	Generalist Standards for Early and Middle Childhood, or Specific Content (Which will appear on the license as either Elementary: Intermediate Generalist, or as a specific content area)
MIDDLE SCHOOL/ JUNIOR HIGH	Early Adolescence	Early Adolescence Generalist plus two core content areas, or Specific Content (Which will appear on the license as Early Adolescence Generalist with two content areas noted).
HIGH SCHOOL	Adolescence / Young Adulthood	Specific Content (Which will appear on the license as a specific content area)

* Preschool is Pre-Kindergarten, and that Elementary/Primary begins with Kindergarten.

For a complete summary of the new performance-based requirements within each license and area, contact the Division directly or visit their web site.

STATE OF IOWA

Iowa State Board of Educational Examiners
Grimes State Office Building
400 East 14th Street
Des Moines, Iowa 50319
Phone: 515-281-3245 / Fax 515-281-7669
Web Site: **http://www.boee.iowa.gov**

INITIAL REQUIREMENTS AT A GLANCE:

Also needed will be items A, B, C, I, J (1 copy), and K - See page 2. The fee is $85.00 for the Initial License and $85.00 for subsequent Licenses and renewals. There is a $60.00 evaluation fee for examining out-of-state candidates' credentials. A state administered certification test is NOT required for out-of-state applicants. Scores on the National Teacher's Examination test IS required for beginning teachers. Iowa IS a member of the Interstate New Teacher Assessment and Support Consortium (INTASC). Iowa does NOT belong to the NASDTEC Interstate Contract, however they currently maintain exchange agreements with Illinois, Michigan, Kansas, Missouri, Nebraska, Oklahoma, South Dakota and Wisconsin. Courses in Human Relations and ARE required to meet Iowa requirements. A course in Special Education IS required.

TYPES OF LICENSES

A.   **Initial License** (valid two years; renewable for a second two years)
1.   Baccalaureate degree from an approved institution.
2.   Completion of an approved teacher education program.
3.   Completion of an approved human relations component.
4.   Completion of requirements for one of the teaching endorsements.

B.   **Standard License** (valid five years; renewable)
1.   See A, 1-4.
2.   Two years of successful teaching experience (based on a local evaluation process.)

C.   **Master Educator's License** (valid five years; renewable)
1.   Holder of or eligible for an Standard License.
2.   Five years of teaching experience.
3.   Master's degree in an area of one of the teaching endorsements.

D.   **Professional Administrator's License** (valid five years; renewable)
1.   See C, 1-2.
2.   Completion of requirements for one of the administrative endorsements.

E.   **Class A License** (valid one year; non-renewable). May be issued if the candidate:
1.   Has not completed all required components in the professional education core.
2.   Has not completed an approved human relations component.
3.   Recency -- meets requirements for a valid license but has less than 160 days of teaching during last 5 - year period.
4.   Degree not granted until next regular commencement.

TEACHING ENDORSEMENTS[*]

[*] for a complete listing of Iowa endorsements, please visit http://www.state.ia.us/boee/addition.html

A.   **Subject area (K - 6 and 7 - 12)**
1.   See Initial License (A, 1-3).
2.   Professional Education Core: Completed or evidence of competency in (a) Student Learning; (b) Diverse Learners; (c) Instructional Planning; (d) Instructional Strategies; (e) Learning Environment/Classroom Management; (f) Communication; (g) Assessment; (h) Foundations, Reflection, and Professional Development; and (i) Collaboration, Ethics, and Relationships.
Computer technology related to instruction;
Completion of pre-student teaching field-based experiences;
Methods of teaching with an emphasis on the subject and grade level endorsement desired.
Content/subject matter specialization. The practitioner understands the central concepts, tools of inquiry, and structure of the discipline(s) the practitioner teaches and creates learning experiences that make these aspects of subject matter meaningful for students. This is evidenced by completion of a 30 semester hour teaching major which must minimally include the requirements for at least one of the basic endorsement areas or special education teaching endorsements.
A minimum of 12 weeks of student teaching in the subject area and at the grade level in which the endorsement is desired.

B.   **Elementary (K - 6)**
1.   See Initial License (A, 1-3).
2.   See Subject Area (A, 2).
3.   Curriculum Content:
a.   Methods and materials of teaching a variety of elementary subjects.
b.   Pre-student teaching experience in at least two different grades.
c.   Specialization in a single discipline or a formal interdisciplinary program of at least 12 semester hours.

C. **Prekindergarten/Kindergarten**
   1. See Initial License (A, 1-3).
   2. See Subject Area (A, 2).
   3. Curriculum to include courses related to young children.

D. **Middle School (5 - 8)**
   The new endorsement is available to all teachers who hold a current Iowa teaching license with a K-6 elementary classroom endorsement or a secondary teaching endorsement. This endorsement will allow the holder to teach all subjects in grades five through eight (except art, music, industrial arts, physical education, reading and special education). The new endorsement is available to all teachers who hold a current Iowa teaching license with a K-6 elementary classroom endorsement or a secondary teaching endorsement. Other requirements are as follows:
   1. three semester hours of course work in the growth and development of the middle school age child. This course work shall specifically address the emotional, physical and mental characteristics and needs of middle school age children. (This course work must be in addition to related studies completed as part of the professional education core);
   2. three semester hours of course work in middle school curriculum design and instruction; including, but not limited to, instruction in interdisciplinary teaming, pedagogy, and methods. (This course work must be in addition to related studies completed as part of the professional education core);
   3. The applicant must have completed six semester hours of course work in the social studies to include course work in American history, world history, and geography;
   4. six semester hours in mathematics to include course work in algebra;
   5. The applicant must have completed six semester hours in science to include course work in life science and physical science; and
   6. The applicant must have completed six semester hours in language arts to include course work in grammar, composition, and speech.

   It is important to note that the work completed to fulfill items number one and number two in the above requirements must be in addition to work completed in the core of the applicant's teacher education program. Note also that the course work in areas three though six carries no similar restriction; course work completed as a part of fulfilling the college's general education requirements may be used to add this endorsement; however, methods (of teaching) courses may not be used.

E. **English as a Second Language**
   1. See Initial License (A, 1-3).
   2. See Subject Area (A, 2).
   3. Completion of 18 semester hours of course work in ESOL.

F. **Elementary Counselor (K - 6)**
   1. Master's Degree
   2. Completion of counseling competencies focusing on guidance and counseling on the elementary level, including a practicum in elementary school counseling.

G. **Secondary Counselor (7 - 12)**. Same as for Elementary Counselor except that competencies and practicum focus on secondary level.

H. **Other Teaching Endorsements**: Reading Specialist; Elementary School Medial Specialist (K - 6); Secondary School Medial Specialist (7 - 12); School Medial Specialist (K - 12 - A master's degree program.)

ADMINISTRATIVE ENDORSEMENTS

A. **Principal (PK - 12)**
   1. Master's Degree
   2. Meet course work and competencies in elementary and secondary administration, supervision, and curriculum.
   3. Three years of teaching experience on the PK - 12 level.

B. **Superintendent (PK - 12)**
   1. Master's degree, plus at least 30 semester hours of planned graduate study in administration beyond the master's degree. Overall, at least 45 semester hours of course

work must be in school administration and related subjects.

2. Three years' experience as a building principal or other PK - 12 district wide or education agency administrative experience.

3. Three years of teaching experience on the K - 12 level.

Note: Graduates from institutions in other states who are seeking initial Iowa certification and an administrative endorsement must also meet the requirements for the standard license.

STATE OF KANSAS

Kansas State Department of Education
Teacher Education and Licensure
120 SE 10th Avenue
Topeka, KS 66612-1182
Phone: 785-296-2288 / Fax: 785-296-4318
Web Site: **http://www.ksde.org/Default.aspx?tabid=84**

INITIAL REQUIREMENTS AT A GLANCE:

Also needed will be items A, B, C (approved by the state where program was completed), E, G (Kansas Form), J, K ($44.00 fee), O and Q - See page 2. The fee is $39.00. A state administered certification test is NOT required for out of state applicants. Passing scores on the Praxis II - Principles of Learning and Teaching AND the Praxis II - Specialty Area tests ARE required. Other tests of pedagogy and content may be acceptable. An Initial Conditional License is valid two years and renewable one time. A performance assessment must be completed during the conditional licensing period to move to a five-year Professional License. Out of state applicants may be eligible for the Professional or Accomplished License as their initial Kansas license dependent upon their qualifications and experience. Kansas DOES belong to the NASDTEC Interstate Contract (Teachers Support Professionals and Administrators) and the Interstate New Teacher Assessment and Support Consortium (INTASC). They also participate in the Central States Exchange Agreement with South Dakota, Nebraska, North Dakota, Oklahoma, Missouri, Minnesota, Ohio, and Wisconsin. Coursework in Special Education IS required for all teaching certificates.

Renewal Requirements - All Renewals: Professional development must be completed to maintain the **Professional License**. Eight (8) post-graduate credit hours every 5 years, **or** 120 - 160 Professional Development Points PDPs (depending on the degree level), **or** four (4) post-graduate credit hours **and** 80 PDPs (at the bachelor's degree level). All credit hours and PDPs for renewal must be approved by a local Kansas Professional Development Council. Educators become eligible for a ten-year **Accomplished Teaching License** if the achieve National Board Certification from NBPTS.

TEACHING ENDORSEMENTS

Teaching endorsements shall be based upon completion of the approved teacher education program in the field of specialization. Verification of completion of the approved program will be required from the university where the program was completed. License Levels include: (a) early childhood, birth-grade 3; (b) early childhood through late childhood, kindergarten - grade 6; (c) late childhood through early adolescence, 5 - 8; (d) early adolescence through late adolescence and adulthood, 6 - 12; and (e) early childhood through late adolescence and adulthood, Pre-K - 12.

ELEMENTARY AND/OR SECONDARY

Conditional License: Valid two years. Baccalaureate degree; completion of state-approved teacher education program in the subject and field of endorsement; recent college credit or recent accredited experience; and completion of pedagogy and content assessments as described above. Recent college credit means credit hours earned within the six years immediately preceding application (8 semester hours). Recent accredited experience means one year of experience under contract, half-time or more, in an accredited school within the six years prior to application while holding a certificate valid for the assignment.

Professional License: Completion of a teaching performance assessment from a state-accredited school; verification of at least one year of recent accredited experience or at least eight semester hours of recent credit; and an application and license fee. **NOTE:** Experienced out-of-state candidates may be able to acquire this license. Contact the Department for complete information.

Accomplished Teaching License: Verification of achieving National Board Certification issued by the National Board for Professional Teaching Standards (NBPTS); verification of a currently valid Professional level teaching license; and an application and license fee.

SCHOOL SPECIALIST
Including: SCHOOL COUNSELOR, READING SPECIALIST, LIBRARY MEDIA

Conditional License: Valid two years. Hold or be eligible for a Professional Teaching License; a graduate degree; completion of state-approved graduate level school counselor program; minimum cumulative GPA of 3.25 in graduate coursework; recent college credit or accredited teaching experience; successful completion of school specialist assessment. A performance assessment that consists of a one full school year or two full semesters of supervised internship beyond the approved graduate-level program must be completed during the conditional license period to move to the professional school specialist license. Out of state applicants may be eligible for a professional school specialist license for school counselor if they meet conditional license requirements and meet specific experience requirements as a school counselor.

Professional License: Verification of successful completion of the school specialist performance assessment prescribed by the state board; verification of at least one year of recent accredited experience or at least eight semester hours of recent credit; and an application and license fee.

SCHOOL LEADERSHIP - ALL LEVEL BUILDING LEADERSHIP

Conditional License: Valid two years. Hold or be eligible to hold a Professional Teaching License; a graduate degree; completion of a graduate level program for building leadership; minimum 3.25 cumulative GPA in graduate coursework; recent college credit or accredited experience; successful completion of school building leadership assessment; minimum of three years of experience in an accredited school system while holding a professional level license. A performance assessment that consists of a one full school year or two full semesters of supervised internship beyond the approved graduate-level program must be completed during the conditional license period to move to the professional school leadership license for building leadership. Out of state applicants may be eligible for a professional level building leadership license if they meet conditional license requirements and meet specific experience requirements as a building administrator (principal).

Professional License: Verification of successful completion in a state-accredited school of the school leadership performance assessment prescribed by the state board; verification of at least one year of recent accredited experience or at least eight semester hours of recent credit; and an application and license fee.

SCHOOL LEADERSHIP - DISTRICT LEADERSHIP

Conditional License: Valid two years. A graduate degree; completion of a graduate level program for district leadership; minimum 3.25 cumulative GPA in graduate coursework; recent college credit or accredited experience; successful completion of school district leadership assessment; minimum of three years of experience in an accredited school system while holding a professional level license. A performance assessment that consists of a one full year or two full semesters of supervised internship beyond the approved graduate-level program must be completed during the conditional license period to move to the Professional School Leadership License for District Leadership. Out of state applicants may be eligible for a Professional Level District Leadership License if they meet conditional license requirements and meet specific experience requirements as a district administrator (superintendent).

Professional License: See School Leadership - All Level Building Leadership

COMMONWEALTH OF KENTUCKY

Education Professional Standards Board
Division of Certification
100 Airport Road, 3rd Floor
Frankfort, Kentucky 40601
Phone: 502-564-4606 / Toll Free: 888-598-7667 / Fax: 502-564-7092
Web Site: **http://www.kyepsb.net/**

INITIAL REQUIREMENTS AT A GLANCE:

Also needed are items A, B, C, E, G, (signed by Superintendent), O and Q - See page 2. *Note:* J, K & L are done at the school district level. There is a $50 fee for initial issuance and renewal. National and/or state-created certification assessments ARE required for Early Childhood and Administrative certificates. Scores on the Praxis II tests ARE required in the specialty areas and the Principles of Learning and Teaching (PLT) at the appropriate level(s). Kentucky DOES belong to the Interstate Certification Compact (with contingencies) and the NASDTEC Interstate Contract (Teacher--with qualifications) and the Interstate New Teacher Assessment and Support Consortium (INTASC). A course in Special Education IS required for new instructors.

Renewal Requirements: A renewal of the Initial Professional Certificate requires the completion of at least 15 graduate semester hours applicable to a master's degree or fifth year program for the first renewal and the completion of a master's degree, or a 5th year graduate program consisting of at least 32 graduate hours, prior to the second renewal (within 10 years). All subsequent five year renewals require either three years of successful teaching experience or six additional semester hours of graduate credit. Contact the Division of Certification for complete certification options. Fee: $50.00

Note: Kentucky is now a standards-based state and as such does not dictate a specific set of courses for any certificate. However, they do approve the programs which align with their standards.

Initial Provisional Certificates: Valid for one year and may be extended four years upon successful completion of an internship (as judged by a beginning teacher committee,) to a Professional Certificate. There is a one year beginning teacher internship for new teachers and those from out-of-state with less than two years experience.

Approved Programs: Interdisciplinary Early Childhood Education (Birth to Primary); Elementary School (Primary - Grade 5); Middle School (5 - 9); Secondary School (8 - 12); Middle/Secondary School (5 - 12); Elementary/Middle/Secondary (Primary - 12); Exceptional Children (Primary - 12); Endorsements to Certificates (Primary - 12); and Professional Certificate for Instructional Leadership (all grades).

Alternative Routes to Certification: Option I - Exceptional Work Experience (8 -12); Option II - Local District Training Program Certification (Birth-12); Option III - College Faculty Certification (8 -12); Option IV - Adjunct Instructor Certification (Birth-12); Option V - Veterans of Armed Services (Birth-12); Option VI - University Based Alternative Certification (Birth-12); and Related Programs. For more information, contact the Division or visit their web site.

STATEMENT OF ELIGIBILITY

The completion of an approved program of preparation in the appropriate program area; Passing scores on the PRAXIS II Subject Assessment in the appropriate program area and the PLT at the appropriate level.

Upon successful completion of an approved preparation program and required tests, the Education Professional Standards Board shall issue an eligibility statement for employment that shall be valid for a five year period. Renewable for five years with at least six semester hours of graduate credit or by retaking the Praxis II exams.

PROVISIONAL CERTIFICATE: GUIDANCE COUNSELOR
K - 12 (Valid 5 years)

58

Eligibility for *appropriate* teaching certificate (all levels); one year of full-time teaching experience; and master's degree. Renewable with the completion of nine semester hours of additional graduate credit, selected from the program leading to the Standard Guidance Certificate.

STANDARD CERTIFICATE: GUIDANCE COUNSELOR
K - 12 (Valid 5 years)

One year experience as a full time guidance counselor; Master's degree including approved instructional areas (see Provisional Certificate requirements: a - l); additional course work to increase skills and knowledge of school guidance counseling. Renewable with 60 clock hours of training at the appropriate level or 6 semester hours of graduate credit related to the position.

PROVISIONAL CERTIFICATE: SCHOOL PSYCHOLOGIST
(Valid 1 year, Non-renewable)

Applicant must have completed 48 semester hours of a 60 hour program for the Standard Certificate (see below.)
Applicant must be Eligible for the Standard Certificate.

STANDARD CERTIFICATE: SCHOOL PSYCHOLOGIST
(Valid 5 years, Renewable for 5 year)

Master's degree of not less than 60 semester hours with professional education. Renewable within 5 years with two years experience as a school psychologist and 42 clock hours of professional development.

PROFESSIONAL CERTIFICATE: PRINCIPAL
(All Grades)

The prerequisites for the Level I initial Professional Certificate for Instructional Leadership, in accordance with the pertinent Kentucky statutes and State Board of Education regulations, an applicant shall: (1) have been admitted to the preparation program; (2) have completed 3 years of full time teaching; (3) hold at least a Master's degree; and (4) qualify for a Kentucky teaching certificate.

The initial Professional Certificate for Instructional Leadership shall be issued for one year upon completion of the Level I preparation, above. There is a one year principal internship for new principals and those from out-of-state with less than two years experience as a principal or assistant principal. Upon successful completion of the prescribed testing and internship program, the certificate shall be extended four years.

The certificate shall be renewed subsequently for 5 year periods. The first renewal shall require the completion of the Level II program in the curriculum standards. Each subsequent five year renewal shall require the completion of two years of principal experience or three additional hours of related graduate credit, or 42 clock hours of approved training.

PROFESSIONAL CERTIFICATE: SCHOOL SUPERINTENDENT

The Professional Certificate for Instructional Leadership--School Superintendent shall be valid for the position of school superintendent or assistant superintendent.

The prerequisites for the program of preparation for the Professional Certificate for Instructional Leadership--School Superintendent, the candidate shall: (1) Have been admitted to the preparation program on the basis of criteria developed by the teacher education institution; (2) Have completed at least 3 years of full-time teaching experience, including at least 140 days per year, and also at least 2 years of additional experience, including at least 140 days per year, in a position(s) of elementary, middle, or secondary principal, or supervisor of instruction, guidance counselor, director of pupil personnel, director of special education, school business administrator, local district coordinator of vocational education, or coordinator/ administrator/supervisor of district-wide services; (3) Have completed the master's degree; and (4) Have completed both Level I and Level II preparation and certification for any one of the positions of elementary, middle, or secondary school principal or supervisor of instruction.

The initial **Professional Certificate**--School Superintendent shall be issued for a duration period of 5 years and shall be renewed subsequently for 5 year periods. Each 5 year renewal shall require the completion of 2 years of experience as a school superintendent, or 3 semester hours of additional graduate credit related to the position of school superintendent, or 42 hours of approved training selected from programs approved for the Kentucky Effective Instructional Leadership Training Program.

STATE OF LOUISIANA

Louisiana Department of Education
Division of Certification and Preparation
Claiborne Building, 1201 North Third Street
P.O. Box 94064
Baton Rouge, Louisiana 70804-9064
Phone: 1-877-453-2721 or 225-342-3490 / Fax: 225-342-3499
Web Site: **http://www.doe.state.la.us/lde/tsac/home.html**

INITIAL REQUIREMENTS AT A GLANCE:

Also needed will be items A, B, C, E, G, K (by district, upon employment), M, N, O and Q - See page 2. A professional conduct form is also required. A personal conduct form is also required of candidates. The fee is $25.00 ($50.00 for out-of-state applicants). Scores from the PRAXIS/National Teachers Examination ARE required for all teaching certificates except the 3-year certificate. A three year non-renewable certificate is available for out-of-state applicants who have not taken the Praxis/NTE. Experienced teachers from other states who enter Louisiana schools for the first time and provide appropriate evaluation results from their immediate previous teaching assignment, and have taught for 2 years or more within the last five years, may be excluded from participation in the State Assessment Program. Louisiana DOES belong to the NASDTEC Interstate Contract (Teachers) and the Interstate New Teacher Assessment and Support Consortium (INTASC). A course or competencies in Special Education IS required.

Renewal Requirements: Every five years Level 2 or Level 3 certificate holders must complete 150 clock hours of professional development in order to be recertified. Fee is $25.00.

CERTIFICATION CHANGES
Effective July, 2002

For all new certificates issued after July 1, 2002, universities must now recommend students to the Department for Level 1 Professional Certification. This certifies that they have prepared their students to meet Louisiana state certification requirements. The universities will now also be held responsible for the success of the teachers they recommend. For further information, contact the Department.

The **Louisiana Alternative Certification Program** provides opportunities for individuals with non-education degrees to become certified public school teachers. There are three alternative certification paths: (1) *Practitioner Teacher Program*; (2) *Masters Degree Program*; and (3) *Non-Masters/Certification-Only Program.*
Candidates for admission to any one of the programs must possess a baccalaureate degree from a regionally accredited university and must pass the Pre-Professional Skills Test, PRAXIS I and a content-specific PRAXIS examination. Individuals seeking certification under the Practitioner Teacher Program must submit an official transcript for evaluation to a Louisiana college or university with an approved teacher education program or to a state-approved private practitioner program provider. Individuals seeking certification under the Masters Degree Program or the Non-Masters/Certification-Only Program must submit an official transcript for evaluation to a Louisiana college or university with

an approved teacher education program.

Revised Certification Titles and General Requirements:

A. **Level 1 Professional Certificate** - 3 yrs., then renewable once, for three (3) years
    1. Graduate from a state-approved teacher preparation program;
    2. Passing scores on Praxis; and
    3. Be recommended by a university to receive the certification.
        (OR)
    4. Complete an approved Practitioner Teacher Program;
    5. Passing scores on Praxis; and
    6. Be recommended by the Practitioner Teacher Program to receive certification.
        (OR)
    7. Meet the requirements of an out-of-state certified teacher.

B. **Level 2 Professional Certificate** - 5 years, Renewable
    1. Possess a Level 1 Professional Certificate;
    2. Pass the Louisiana Assistance and Assessment Program; and
    3. Have three years of teaching experience in area(s) of certification.

C. **Level 3 Professional Certificate** - 5 years, Renewable
    1. Possess a Level 1 or Level 2 Professional Certificate;
    2. Complete a Master's Degree;
    3. Have five years of teaching experience in area(s) of certification; and
    4. Pass the Louisiana Assistance and Assessment Program.

D. **Out-of-State Certificate** - 3 years, Non-renewable
    1. Take and pass the appropriate PRAXIS examinations;
        (OR)
    2. Provide evidence of at least 4 years of successful teaching experience in another state, completes one year of employment as a teacher in Louisiana's public school systems, and secures recommendation of the local superintendent of the employing school system for continued employment.

Previous Certifications (issued prior to 7/1/2002):
A. **TYPE C** - Will no longer be issued.
B. **TYPE B** - Candidates will retain these certificates that are valid for life for continuous service.
C. **TYPE A** - Candidates will retain these certificates that are valid for life for continuous service.

EARLY CHILDHOOD
(Pre-K - 3)

Education Program Requirements: 124 semester hour minimum
A. General Education .... 39 hrs
    Including: English (12); Mathematics (9); Sciences (9); Social Studies (6); and Arts (3)
B. Focus Area Requirements: Early Childhood, Reading/Language Arts, and Mathematics .. 33 hrs
C. Knowledge of the Learner and Learner Environment: .... 15 hrs
D. Methodology and Teaching: .... 15 hrs
E. Flexible hours (university's discretion) .... 22 hrs
F. 270 Clock hours of student teaching with 180 of those in actual teaching with a substantial portion being on an all day basis.

ELEMENTARY TEACHERS
(Grades 1 - 5)

Education Program Requirements: 124 semester hour minimum
A. General Education .... 54 hrs
    Including: English (12); Mathematics (12); Sciences (15); Social Studies (12); and Arts (3)
B. Focus Area Requirements: Reading/Language Arts, and Mathematics .... 21 hrs
C. Knowledge of the Learner and Learner Environment: .... 15 hrs

| D. | Methodology and Teaching: . . . . | 15 hrs |
| E. | Flexible hours (university's discretion) . . . . | 19 hrs |

F. 270 Clock hours of student teaching with 180 of those in actual teaching with a substantial portion being on an all day basis.

MIDDLE GRADES TEACHERS
(Grades 4 - 8)

Education Program Requirements: 124 semester hour minimum

A.   General Education . . . . 54 hrs
        Including: English (12); Mathematics (12); Sciences (15); Social Studies (12); and Arts (3)

B1.   Generic: for additional content knowledge . . . . 12 hrs
        Including: English (3); Mathematics (3); Sciences (3); Social Studies (3)
        (OR)

B2.   Generic - Two teaching areas: *In-depth Teaching Area 1* . . . . 19 hrs
        Must Include: English, Social Studies, Mathematics (7+ hrs) or Science (4+ hrs)
        (OR)

B3.   Generic - Two teaching areas: *In-depth Teaching Area 2* 19hrs
        Must Include: English, Social Studies, Mathematics (7+ hrs) or Science (4+ hrs)

C.   Focus Area Requirements: Early Childhood, Reading/Language Arts, and Mathematics . . 33 hrs

D.   Knowledge of the Learner and Learner Environment: . . . . 15 hrs

E.   Methodology and Teaching: . . . . 24 hrs

F.   Flexible hours (university's discretion) . . . . 19 hrs

G. 270 Clock hours of student teaching with 180 of those in actual teaching with a substantial portion being on an all day basis.

SECONDARY TEACHERS
(Grades 6 - 12)

Education Program Requirements: 124 semester hour minimum

A.   General Education . . . . 39 hrs
        Including: English (6); Mathematics (6); Sciences (9); Social Studies (6); and Arts (3)

B1.   Primary Teaching Area - Science . . . . 22 hrs
        (OR)

B2.   Primary Teaching Area English, Social Studies or Mathematics . . . . 25 hrs
        (OR)

B3.   Primary Teaching Area - Other . . . . 31 hrs

C1.   Secondary Teaching Area English, Social Studies or Mathematics (minimum) . . . . 13 hrs
        (OR)

C2.   Secondary Teaching Area Science (minimum) . . . . 10 hrs
        (OR)

C3.   Secondary Teaching Area - Other (minimum) . . . . 19 hrs

D.   Knowledge of the Learner and Learner Environment: . . . . 15 hrs

E.   Methodology and Teaching: . . . . 24 hrs

F.   Flexible hours (university's discretion) . . . . 17 - 26 hrs

G. 270 Clock hours of student teaching with 180 of those in actual teaching with a substantial portion being on an all day basis.

SCHOOL LIBRARIAN

Elementary or Secondary teaching certificate; and
Library science coursework . . . . 21 semester hours

SCHOOL COUNSELOR
(K - 12)

A..   **Counselor** in the School Setting:
        An applicant who holds a valid Louisiana teaching certificate and meets the following requirements may be issued an endorsement for Counselor in a school setting. The applicant must hold a master's degree in school counseling from a regionally accredited institution or a

master's degree with the equivalent hours and courses required for a master's degree in school counseling. The graduate training must include a total of 24 semester hours of professional courses distributed so that at least one course will be taken in each of the following basic areas: (a)Principles and Administration of School Counseling Programs; (b) Career and Lifestyle Development; (c) Individual Appraisal; (d) Counseling Theory and Practice; (e) Group Processes; (f) Human Growth and Development; (g) Social and Cultural Foundations in Counseling; and (i) Supervised Practicum in a School Setting

B. **Professional Counselor** in the School Setting
A professional endorsement may be issued to an applicant who has met the requirements for counseling in the school setting and holds current licensure as a Licensed Professional Counselor in Louisiana (LPC) in accordance with Act 892 L.S. 1987 et.seq.

NOTE: An applicant who does not hold a Louisiana teaching certificate but meets all other requirements will be issued an Ancillary Counselor K-12 or Professional Counselor K - 12 certificate.

SCHOOL PSYCHOLOGIST

A. **Provisional Psychologist Certificate:** Valid for one (1) year, renewable once, unless lapsed. Additional Requirements: Academic preparation in school psychology that meets the Standards of Training Programs in School Psychology, except for the internship. The certificate may be renewed once in order to complete the internship.

B. **Level B Standard Certificate:** Valid five years, renewable.
Additional Requirements: Meet the requirements for Standard Certificate and applicant must hold a master's or specialist degree, including internship from a school psychology training program at.

C. **Level A Certificate:** Valid five years, renewable.
Additional Requirements: Meet the requirements for Standard Certificate and applicant must hold a degree in psychology from a regionally accredited institution.

EDUCATIONAL LEADER CERTIFICATES
(Effective 7/1/2006)

A. **Level 1** - Asst. Principal, Principal, Supervisor of Instruction, etc. - Valid 5 years. Renewable. Note: for complete information, contact the Division.
1. **Master's Degree Path**
   a. Hold or be eligible to hold a valid Louisiana Type B or Level 2 teaching certificate or have a comparable level out-of-state teaching certificate and three years of teaching experience in the area of certification requested

   b. Complete a competency-based graduate degree preparation program in the area of educational leadership from a regionally accredited institution; and
   c. Passing score on the School Leaders Licensure Assessment (SLLA).
2. **Alternate Path 1** - for applicants holding a master's degree and seeking to add Educational Leader certification to a valid teaching certificate:
   a. Hold or be eligible to hold a valid Louisiana Type B or Level 2 teaching certificate or have a comparable level out-of-state teaching certificate and three years of teaching experience in the area of certification requested;
   b. Completed a graduate degree program from a regionally accredited institution;
   c. Meet competency-based requirements by completion of and individualized program of educational leadership; and
   d. Passing score on the SLLA.
3. **Alternate Path 2** - for applicants holding a master's degree in education and are seeking to add Educational Leader certification to a valid teaching certificate:
   a. Hold or be eligible to hold a valid Louisiana Type B or Level 2 teaching certificate or have a comparable level out-of-state teaching certificate and three years of teaching experience in the area of certification requested;

  b. Completed a graduate degree program in education from a regionally accredited institution;

  c. Provide documented evidence of leadership experiences (240 clock hours or more) at the school and/or district level; and

  d. Passing score on the SLLA.

 4. **Alternate Path 3** - for applicants already holding a bachelor's degree from a regionally accredited institution and seeking to add Educational Leader certification to a valid teaching certificate through a competency-based educational leader practitioner (residency) program:

  a. Hold or be eligible to hold a valid Louisiana Type B or Level 2 teaching certificate or have a comparable level out-of-state teaching certificate and three years of teaching experience in the area of certification requested;

  b. Demonstrate a strong knowledge of instruction through a rigorous screening process by and approved program provider;

  c. Complete a competency-based educational leader practitioner/residency preparation program in the area of educational leadership from a state-approved private provider or a regionally accredited institution; and

  d. Passing score on the SLLA.

B. **Level 2** - Valid 5 years. Renewable based upon successful completion and verification of required continuing learning units.

 1. To receive the Level 2 Educational Leader certificate, the candidate must:

  a. Hold a valid Level 1 certificate, Louisiana provisional principal certification, or comparable level out-of-state educational leader certificate;

  b. Have three years of teaching experience in their area(s) of certification;

  c. Have completed the Educational Leader Induction Program under the administration of the Louisiana Department of Education:

   i. The induction period begins upon the candidate's first full-time administrative appointment (permanent or acting) as an assistant principal, principal, parish or city supervisor of instruction, supervisor of child welfare and attendance, or comparable school/district leader position;

   ii. The Educational Leader Induction Program must be completed within a three year period;

  d. Have three years of educational leadership experience at the level of assistant principal or above.

C. **Level 3 (Superintendent)** - This endorsement is required to serve as a school system superintendent or assistant superintendent. Valid 5 years and renewable every 5 years.

 1. Eligibility requirements:

  a. Valid Level 2 Educational Leader certificate or one of the Louisiana administrative/supervisory certifications that preceded the 2006 Educational Leadership Certification structure;

  b. Five years of teaching experience in their area of certification;

  c. Five years of successful administrative or management experience in education at the level of assistant principal or above. The assistant principal experience would be limited to a maximum of two years of experience in that position; and

  d. Passing score on the SLLA.

STATE OF MAINE

Department of Education
Certification Office
23 State House Station
Augusta, Maine 04333-0023
Phone: 207-624-6603 / Fax: 207-624-6604
Web Site: **http://www.maine.gov/education/cert/index.html**

INITIAL REQUIREMENTS AT A GLANCE:

Also needed will be items A, B, C (if applicable), E, J, K, M and O are required - See page 2. The fees are $100.00 (Instructional and Educational Specialist) and $200.00 (Administrative). A criminal history record check is $55.00. Passing scores on the Pre-Professional Skills Test (PPST) or the Praxis I Computer-Based Tests. Maine DOES belong to the Interstate Certification Compact, the NASDTEC Interstate Contract (Teachers and Support Professionals), and the Northeast Regional Credential Program established between Connecticut, Massachusetts, New Hampshire, New York, Rhode Island, and Vermont. Maine DOES belong to the Interstate New Teacher Assessment and Support Consortium (INTASC). A course in Special Education IS required for all teaching certificates.

Renewal Requirements: Renewable every five years with six Renewal Credits, or six semester hours, or 90 clock hours of professional development; The completion of all professional activities and observations as described in an approved Action Plan. An applicant will develop an Action Plan following the guidelines of their district certification process. For further information, contact the Department or visit their web site.

CERTIFICATION LEVELS

I.   **Conditional** - Valid 1 year; renewable two times. Offered for candidates who have not met all professional requirements. Bachelor's degree from a regionally accredited college, completion of all content area courses, and affidavit of employment from local school district.
II.   **Provisional** - Valid 2 years; renewable. Bachelor's degree from an approved institution; Completion of an approved preparation program including a formal recommendation from that institution; Qualifying scores on the NTE Core Battery; and fulfillment of all requirements for one or more endorsements or education specialist certificates.
III. **Professional** - Valid 5 years; renewable. Applicant must hold a provisional certificate; and must have the recommendation for a professional certificate.
IV.   **Master** - Valid 5 years; renewable. Applicant must hold a professional certificate; demonstrate exemplary professional skills; possess knowledge of current theories of effective instruction; made outstanding contributions to the teaching profession in curriculum design, staff development, clinical supervision or student teachers or peer observation of teachers, or educational leadership; and must have the recommendation for a master certificate.
V.   **Conditional** - Valid 1 year; renewal only with approval. Intended for applicants who have not met all professional requirements. Applicants should complete professional requirements during the term of this certificate.

Northeast Regional Credential: Valid one year (in Maine), non-renewable; The Northeast Regional Credential permits a like-for-like certification exchange between member states. The applicant must still complete all requirements for the Provisional, Professional, or Conditional certifications.

ELEMENTARY TEACHER
(K-8)

I.   Authorization: Teaches students kindergarten through grade eight.
II.   Academic Requirements: Eligibility for this endorsement shall be established by:
      A.   Graduation from an accredited baccalaureate program approved for the education of elementary teachers which is comprised of at least 50 percent liberal arts and a distribution of 6 semester hours in each of four content areas (math, English, science, social sciences) together with the formal recommendation of the preparing institution **(OR)**
      B.   Preparation which includes:
            A bachelor's degree from an accredited institution with 60 semester hours in liberal arts distribution and at least 6 semester hours in each of four content areas (math, English, science, social sciences)
III. Professional Requirements: A minimum of 33 semester hours in the following: (A) Knowledge of the learner and learning process; (B) Computer literacy and computer applications; (C) Teaching exceptional students in the regular classroom; (D) Content area methods in reading, math, science, social studies and language arts; (E) Curriculum design and methods of program evaluation; (F) Early and on-going experience or practicum; and (G) Student Teaching: One academic semester or 15 weeks of full-time student teaching experience.

MIDDLE LEVEL
(5 - 8)

I.   Teaches English/language arts, mathematics, science and social studies.

II.   Eligibility for this endorsement shall be established by:
- A.   Possession of a valid provisional or professional Maine teaching certificate (K-8, 7-12 or K-12);
- B.   7 - 12 endorsement area of authorization, semester hours 24
- C.   Praxis II.

SECONDARY
(7 - 12)

I.   Teaches English/language arts, mathematics, life science, physical science and social studies.

II.   Eligibility for this endorsement shall be established by:
- A.   Graduation from an accredited baccalaureate program approved for the education of secondary English language arts teachers which includes a major in English language arts together with the formal recommendation of the preparing institution.
  (OR)
- B.   Preparation which includes:
  1.   A bachelor's degree from an accredited institution; and
  2.   A minimum of 24 semester hours in the following: English/language arts, mathematics, social studies and science.

III.   Professional education - 15 semester hours including:(1) teaching exceptional children in the regular classroom; (2) content area methods; and one academic semester or 15 weeks of full time student teaching experience.

LIBRARY-MEDIA SPECIALIST

I.   Valid for two years.

II.   Possession of a provisional or professional teaching certificate in a subject area; and completion of a graduate approved program for the preparation of Library-Media Specialists.

SCHOOL GUIDANCE COUNSELORS

I.   Authorization: Serves as a school guidance counselor to provide guidance services from Kindergarten through grade 12.

II.   Academic Requirements: Eligibility for this certification shall be established by:
- A.   A master's degree from an accredited institution and an approved program to prepare school guidance counselors together with formal recommendation of the preparing institution; and
- B.   A minimum of 33 graduate semester hours in the following areas: (1) Understanding of the profession of school guidance; (2) Understanding of educational philosophies and school operations; (3) Consultation skills; (4) Individual counseling skills; (5) Group counseling, including classroom group work; (6) Understanding of human development and behavior; (7) Knowledge of career development and career education; (8) Knowledge of assessment and testing; (9) Research skills related to the field of guidance; and (10) Participation in a K-12 internship relating to the duties of a school guidance counselor in a school setting.

III.   Professional Requirements:
Prior to application the candidate must document the equivalent of two full years of work experience.

BUILDING ADMINISTRATOR[1]

I. This certificate allows the holder to serve as *Principal, Career and Technical Education Administrator, Assistant Principal, Assistant Career Technical Education Administrator*, or *Teaching Principal*.

II. Maine provides multiple *pathways* for certificate eligibility. Applicants not meeting requirements for the standard pathways described below, may be eligible for a conditional certificate (see E below).

    A. General Certificate Eligibility for all Pathways - requirements:

        1. Bachelor's degree from an accredited college or university;

        2. Master's degree, in any field, from an accredited college or university; and

        3. Evidence of a minimum of three years of satisfactory public or private school teaching experience, or three years of equivalent teaching experience in an instructional setting (e.g., military, business, post-secondary institution, industry schools);

        4. Completed through approved courses the following two knowledge areas:

            a. Teaching exceptional students in the regular classroom; and

            b. Federal and Maine civil rights law and education laws;

        5. Meets, through one of the following pathways below, the standards of the Interstate School Leaders Consortium (ISLLC), as follows:

            a. Facilitating the development, articulation, and stewardship of a vision of learning that is shared by the school community;

            b. Advocating, nurturing, and sustaining a school culture and instructional program conducive to student learning and staff professional growth;

            c. Ensuring management of the organization, operations, and resources for a safe and effective learning environment;

            d. Collaborating with families and community members, responding to diverse community interests and needs, and mobilizing community resources;

            e. Acting with integrity, fairness, and in an ethical manner; and

            f. Understanding, responding to, and influencing the larger political, social, economic, legal, and cultural context.

        6. Satisfactory completion of an approved internship or practicum based on the ISLLC Licensure standards and relating to the duties of a principal or career and technical education administrator, which shall take place in a school setting and shall be met by one of the following:

            a. Completion of a graduate level state-approved administrator internship or practicum program with a minimum term of 15 weeks;

            b. Completion of a minimum of one full year of employment as an assistant principal, assistant career and technical education administrator, principal out-of-state, or career and technical education administrator out-of-state; or

            c. Completion of a mentorship plan reviewed and approved by the Commissioner, with the duration of the plan being for one academic year.

B. Pathway I Certificate Eligibility

    Meets the ISLLC standards through completion of a Maine approved program for principals.

C. Pathway II Certificate Eligibility

    Meets the ISLLC standards through coursework or equivalent training experiences. Specifically, applicants shall provide evidence of a basic knowledge, training, or experience in all of the following knowledge areas:

        (1) school finance and budget; (2) supervision and evaluation of personnel; (3) organizational theory and planning; (4) community relations; (5) educational leadership; (6) instructional leadership; (7) curriculum development; (8) cultural difference; and (9) ethical decision making.

D. Pathway III Certificate Eligibility

    Meets ISLLC standards through successful completion of the School Leader Licensure Assessment, in accordance the Maine DOE.

E. Conditional Certificate

    1. Meets the requirements of General Certificate Eligibility, in Sections A(1) and A(3) above;

    2. Meets the knowledge area requirement specified in Section C(2), above;

    3. Meets the majority of the remaining knowledge area requirements specified in Section C, above; and

    4. Meets the internship requirement for this certificate specified in Section A(6), above, or has a supervised internship plan approved by the Department prior to the issuance of the conditional certificate.

III. Renewal Requirements

    A. For those employed in Maine under this certificate, completed an approved administrator action plan; and

B. For those not employed in Maine under this certificate, completed a minimum of six credits of approved study.

[1] For complete requirements, please contact the Department.

ADMINISTRATOR CERTIFICATE [2]

I. This certificate allows the holder to serve as superintendent, assistant superintendent, principal, assistant principal, career and technical education administrator, assistant career and technical education administrator, teaching principal, or curriculum coordinator.

II. Maine provides multiple *pathways* for certificate eligibility. Applicants not meeting requirements for the standard pathways described below, may be eligible for a conditional certificate (see E below).

A. General Certificate Eligibility for all Pathways - requirements:

1. Bachelor's degree from an accredited college or university;
2. Master's degree, in any field, from an accredited college or university; and
3. Evidence of a minimum of three years of satisfactory public or private school teaching experience, or a minimum of three years of equivalent teaching experience in an instructional setting (e.g., military, business, post-secondary institution, industry schools);
4. Evidence of a minimum of three years of previous administrative experience in schools or an institutional setting (e.g., military, business, industry, public or private agency);
5. See A(4a-4b) for Building Administrator above;
6. See B(5a-5f) for Building Administrator above;
7. Satisfactory completion of an approved internship or practicum based on the ISLLC Licensure standards and relating to the duties of a superintendent in a school setting by one of the following:
   a. Completion of a graduate level state-approved administrator internship or practicum program with a minimum term of 15 weeks;
   b. Completion of a minimum of one full year of employment as an assistant superintendent or superintendent out-of-state; or
   c. Completion of a mentorship plan reviewed and approved by the Commissioner, with the duration of the plan being for a minimum of one academic year.

B. Pathway I Certificate Eligibility

Meets the ISLLC standards through completion of a Maine approved program for superintendents.

C. Pathway II Certificate Eligibility

Meets the ISLLC standards through coursework or equivalent training experiences. Specifically, applicants shall provide evidence of knowledge in all of the following areas:
   (1) school finance and budget; (2) supervision and evaluation of personnel; (3) organizational theory and planning; (4) community relations; (5) educational leadership; (6) instructional leadership; (7) curriculum development; (8) cultural difference; and (9) ethical decision making.

D. Pathway III Certificate Eligibility

Meets ISLLC standards through successful completion of the School Superintendent Assessment, in accordance the Maine DOE.

E. Conditional Certificate

1. Meets the requirements of General Certificate Eligibility, in Sections A(1) through A(4) above;
2. Meets the knowledge area requirement specified in Section C(1) and C(2), above;
3. Meets a majority of the remaining knowledge area requirements specified in Section C, above; and
4. Meets the internship requirement for this certificate specified in Section A(7), above, or submits a plan for a supervised internship plan to be approved by the Department prior to the issuance of the conditional certificate.

III. Renewal Requirements

First Renewal:

A. For those employed in Maine under this certificate, completed an approved administrative action plan; and
B. For those not employed in Maine under this certificate, completed a minimum of six credits of approved study.

Second Renewal:
> Documentation of a minimum of 30 additional credits of approved study or equivalent professional development beyond the master's degree required for the initial professional certificate.

[2] For complete requirements, please contact the Department.

STATE OF MARYLAND

Maryland State Department of Education
Division of Certification and Accreditation
200 West Baltimore Street
Baltimore, Maryland 21201
Phone: 410-767-0412 / Fax: 410-333-8963
Web Site: **http://www.mdcert.org**

INITIAL REQUIREMENTS AT A GLANCE:

Also needed will be items A, B, C, E, G (principals also), J & K (upon employment), N, O and Q - See page 2. The fee is $10.00. A state administered certification test is NOT required. Official scores on the National Teacher's Examination test ARE required. Maryland DOES belong to the Interstate Certification Compact, the NASDTEC Interstate Contract (all areas), and the Interstate New Teacher Assessment and Support Consortium (INTASC). A course in special education is required only for Specialist Area certificates. Maryland is revising their requirements effective in 2008.

Renewal Requirements: Fee: $10.00. **Professional Eligibility Certificate**: 6 semester hours of acceptable credit every 5 years which may include reading, if needed. **Standard Professional Certificate I:** Six semester hours of acceptable credit. Renewable only once, with conditions, by request of a local superintendent. **Standard Professional Certificate II:** Non-renewable. **Advanced Professional Certificate** (including Administrator I): 6 semester hours of acceptable credit that may include reading, if needed; and verification of 3 years of satisfactory professional school-related experience completed during the validity period of the certificate; and a professional development plan. **Administrator II:** The local school system and each Administrator II shall develop an Individualized Professional Development Plan (IPDP) for each renewal period by the end of the third year of service as a principal. Upon successful completion of the plan and before the date of certificate renewal, the local superintendent of schools shall recommend to the State Superintendent of Schools that the applicant be certified as Administrator II for another 5 years.

REQUIREMENTS FOR TEACHING CERTIFICATE

CONDITIONAL CERTIFICATE - Valid for two years, this certificate is issued to an employed applicant at the request of the local school system if they are unable to fill a position with a qualified person who holds a Professional Certificate.

PROFESSIONAL ELIGIBILITY CERTIFICATE - Valid for five years, renewable with six credits. This is the initial certificate issued to an applicant meeting certification requirements but is not employed.
Requirements: Bachelor's degree; completes a Maryland-approved teacher education program, including teaching in the area of endorsement or completion of course and experience requirements; and qualifying scores on ACT, SAT, or GRE, and Praxis I (PPST) and appropriate Subject Assessment(s).

STANDARD PROFESSIONAL CERTIFICATE I - Valid for five years. Renewable once.
Requirements: Applicant must meet all requirements for the Professional Eligibility Certificate and is employed in a Maryland School.

STANDARD PROFESSIONAL CERTIFICATE II - Valid 5 years, non-renewable.
Requirements: Meets the requirements for a Standard Professional Certificate I; 3 years of satisfactory

professional experience; 6 semester hours of credit; and submits a professional development plan for the Advanced Professional Certificate.

ADVANCED PROFESSIONAL CERTIFICATE - Valid for five years.

Requirements: Satisfy requirements for the Standard Professional Certificate, 6 semester hours of acceptable credit; presents verification of 3 years of satisfactory school-related experience; and meets one of the following standards:

(1)   Earned a Master's or higher degree from an Institution of Higher Eduction (IHE) in a certification area directly related to public school education with 6 sem. hrs. related to the teacher's specific discipline or the specialist's specific assignment; **or**

(2)   Earned at least 36 sem. hrs. of approved content or professional education course work directly related to public school education earned after a bachelor's degree, including at least 21 graduate credits, of which at least 6 shall be related to the the teacher's specific discipline or the specialist's specific assignment; **or**

(3)   Obtained National Board Certification and earned a minimum of 12 sem. hrs. of approved graduate course work earned after a bachelor's or higher degree, and related to the the teacher's specific discipline or the specialist's specific assignment.

An applicant for the Advanced Professional Certificate in a vocational education area who does not possess a bachelor's or higher degree shall complete the requirements for a Standard Professional Certificate, a planned program of 36 sem. hrs. taken at an IHE. A maximum of 12 CPDs for the trade-related reading course work may be applied to the total of 36 sem. hrs.

TEACHING ENDORSEMENTS:

Early Childhood: (PreK - 3);
Elementary: (Grades 1-6, and middle school);
Secondary: (7-12 depending on the subject area);
Special Education: Birth - Grade 3; Grades 1 - 8; Grades 6 - 12; Hearing Impaired, Visually Impaired, Severely and Profoundly Handicapped.
Specialty Areas: (PreK - 12): Art; English for Speakers of Other Languages; Health; Music; and Physical Education.

EARLY CHILDHOOD EDUCATION

Complete either (A) or (B) below:
Bachelor's or higher degree from an accredited institution with a major in interdisciplinary studies, or a major in an academic field taught in Early Childhood Education including a minimum of 12 semester hours of course work in both mathematics and science and 9 semester hours of course work in both English and social studies; **OR**

B.   Bachelor's or higher degree from an accredited institution and complete not less than 48 semester hours of content coursework including a minimum of 12 semester hours of coursework in both mathematics and science and 9 semester hours of course work in both English and social studies;

AND

C.   Complete 27 semester hours of professional education course work taken at an accredited college or university, including a course in each of the following at the appropriate age or grade level:
        (1) Child development; (2) Human learning; (3) Teaching methodology; (4) Inclusion of special needs student populations; (5) Assessment of students; (6) Processes and acquisition of reading skills; (7) Best practices in reading instruction that include the cuing systems of graphophonics, semantics, and syntactics; (8) Use of reading assessment data to improve instruction; and (9) Materials for teaching reading to gain literary experience, to perform a task, and to read for information; **AND**

D.   Complete a teaching experience in one of the following two ways:
        1. A supervised experience in a public or accredited nonpublic school setting at the Pre-K or kindergarten and primary age/grade level; **OR**
        2. One year of successful full-time teaching experience in a public or accredited nonpublic school setting at the Pre-K or kindergarten or primary age/grade level.

E.   The required coursework in (C)(6), above, may also be taken through Continuing Professional Development (CPD) credits; and

F.   A minimum of 50 percent of the required coursework in either (A) or (B), **and** (C), above, must be

70

taken at the same institution.

ELEMENTARY EDUCATION

Same as for Early Childhood Education except preparation must be at the appropriate Elementary grade level(s).

SECONDARY EDUCATION

To receive certification in the areas of agriculture (agribusiness and renewable natural resources), biology, business education, chemistry, computer science, earth/space science, English, foreign language-classical, foreign language -modern, geography, history, mathematics, physical science, physics, speech communication, and theater, the applicant shall:

Complete one of the following options:
A. Earn a bachelor's or higher degree from an accredited institution with a major in the certification area; **OR**
B. Complete 36 semester hours or more of content course work taken at an accredited institution in the certification area. **Note:** A minimum of 50 percent of this content course work shall be taken at the same institution and, a minimum of 12 semester hours of the required content course work shall be upper division course work; **AND**
C. Complete 21 semester hours of professional education course work taken at an accredited institution at the appropriate age or grade level including:
> 1. At least one 3 semester hour course in each of the following: (a) Adolescent development; (b) Human learning; (c) Teaching methodology; (d) Inclusion of special needs student populations; and (e) Assessment of students; **and**
> 2. Six semester hours covering the following which may also be taken through CPDs:
>> (a) Types of reading; (b) Use of reading assessment data to improve instruction; (c) Skills in reading including cognitive strategies in reading; (d) Reading instruction including reading aloud strategies and methods for diagnosing reading difficulties and making instructional modifications and accommodations for the student; (e) Strategies for intrinsic and extrinsic motivation for reading; (f) Teaching students to learn from text by applying theories, strategies, and practices in daily classroom use including additional content in types of reading using authentic texts; (g) Skills in reading including processing of multimedia information and strategies to connect reading with study skills; and (h) Reading instruction that integrates content area goals with reading goals including strategies for students to communicate effectively orally and in writing about what they have read in content area texts; **AND**
D. Complete a teaching experience in one of the following two ways:
> 1. A supervised experience in a public or accredited nonpublic school setting at the appropriate age or grade level and in the subject area for which the applicant is seeking certification; **or**
> 2. One year of satisfactory full-time teaching experience in a public or accredited nonpublic school setting at the appropriate age or grade level and in the subject area for which the applicant is seeking certification; **AND**
F. A minimum of 50 percent of the professional education course work required in (C), above, must be taken at the same institution.

LIBRARY MEDIA SPECIALIST[1]

An applicant for certification as library media specialist shall meet the requirements of one of the following two certification options:

Option I: The applicant shall have a master's degree from a program at an institution of higher education (IHE) that would lead to State certification as a library media specialist or a comparable position as determined by the State Department of Education.

Option II: Bachelor's or higher degree from an IHE; satisfactory experience; and satisfactorily completed a program of 36 semester hours of post-baccalaureate or graduate credits with 15 semester hours completed at one institution. A minimum of 24 semester hours of the post-baccalaureate credits shall be met by graduate credits in the content course work. The professional education course work may be met by course credits earned in addition to, or as part of, the undergraduate degree program.

A.   Professional education course work for certification as a library media specialist;
B.   Content course work for certification as a library media specialist;
C.   The total number of post-baccalaureate credits needed for certification will not be reduced for course requirements that are met in the applicant's bachelor's degree program. Additional post-baccalaureate or graduate courses may be substituted if some of the course work has been acquired as a part of the undergraduate degree program; and
D.   An applicant shall satisfactorily complete a school library media practicum, 1 year of full-time teaching experience, or 1 year of full-time school library media-related experience.

[1] For complete requirements, contact the Department

GUIDANCE COUNSELOR

The requirements for certification as a guidance counselor are:
A.   **Option I:**
     1. A master's degree in school guidance and counseling from an accredited institution;
     2. A National Board of Certified Counselors (NBCC) certificate; **and**
     3. Two years of satisfactory performance as a teacher or counselor in a school setting.
B.   **Option II:**
     1. A master's degree in school guidance and counseling in a program approved using State-approved standards; **and**
     2. Two years of satisfactory performance as a teacher or counselor, or 500 clock hours in a supervised practicum in school guidance and counseling.
C.   **Option III:** A master's degree in school guidance and counseling from a program approved by the Council for Accreditation of Counseling and Related Educational Programs (CACREP).
D.   **Option IV:**
     1. A master's degree in school guidance and counseling from an approved program under the Interstate Contract agreement for support services; **and**
     2. 2 years of satisfactory performance as a teacher or counselor.

SCHOOL PSYCHOLOGIST

B. The requirements for certification as a school psychologist are:
A.   **Option I:**
     1. Have an advanced graduate specialist's, or doctoral degree in school psychology from a National Association of School Psychologists, NCATE, American Psychological Association, or Department approved program; **and**
     2. Meet qualifying scores on the State-approved test for school psychologist;
B.   **Option II:**
     1. Have a master's, advanced graduate specialist's, or doctoral degree in either psychology, education, or human development from an approved ; and
     2. Have completed 60 semester hours of graduate courses at an accredited institution, 30 of which must be from one institution. For a complete list of coursework areas, contact the Department.
     3. Meet qualifying scores on the State-approved test for school psychologist; **OR**
C.   **Option III:** Have a valid Nationally Certified School Psychologist certificate issued by the National School Psychology Certification Board; **AND**
D.   **Experience Requirements:** For a complete summary of the experience requirements, contact the Department.

PRINCIPALS AND SUPERVISORS

This regulation applies for obtaining certification as an Administrator I or Administrator II. NOTE: A principal transferring from a regular school to a special education school must have special education certification. However, a principal transferring from a special education school to a regular school will require no additional certification.

A.   **Administrator I:** This certificate qualifies an individual to be assigned as a supervisor in instruction or an assistant principal. The applicant shall have:
1. A master's degree from an IHE;
2. 27 months of satisfactory teaching performance or satisfactory performance on a professional certificate or as a certified specialist; and
3. Completed one of the following:
    (a) A Department approved program leading to certification as a supervisor of instruction, assistant principal, or principal including outcomes in the Maryland instructional leadership framework;
    (b) An approved program leading to certification as a supervisor of instruction, assistant principal, or principal in accordance with the interstate agreement; *or*
    (d) 18 semester hours of graduate course work taken at an IHE at the post-baccalaureate level to include a balance of content in the following categories: (i) curriculum, instruction, and assessment; (ii)Development, observation, and evaluation of staff; (iii) Legal issues and ethical decision-making; (iv) School leadership, management and administration; and (v) Practicum, internship or a collaboratively designed and supervised experience by the local school system and IHE to include Department approved instructional leadership outcomes with verification of this experience from the applicant.

B.   **Administrator II:**
1. This certificate qualifies an individual to be assigned as a school principal.
2. The applicant, before initial appointment as principal, shall complete the requirements for Administrator I and present evidence of a qualifying score as established by the State Board on a Department-approved principal certification assessment.
3. A principal who enters Maryland from another state may obtain an Administrator II certificate if they held a valid professional state certficate and verification of at least 27 months of satisfactory performance as a principal during the past 7 years where the application is for a like or comparable Maryland certificate.
4. Special Provisions:
    (a) An applicant who successfully completes the requirements for resident principal certificate may obtain an Administrator II certificate.
    (b) A Standard Professional certificate or Advanced Professional Certificate shall be considered valid for service as principal of an elementary school of not more than six teachers if the principal teaches at least 50 percent of the school day.
    (c) A person who holds the position of assistant principal on the date this regulation becomes effective shall meet the requirements of this regulation not later than the end of the first full validity period after the renewal of the currently held certificate.

SUPERINTENDENT

The requirements for a certificate as superintendent or deputy, associate and assistant superintendent or equivalent position shall be:
A.   Eligibility for a professional certificate.
B.   A Master's Degree from an accredited institution.
C.   Three years of successful teaching experience and two-years of administrative and/or supervisory experience.
D.   Successful completion of a two year program with graduate courses in administration and supervision in an institution or institutions approved by an accrediting agency recognized by the State Superintendent of Schools; graduate work under the second requirement (Master's Degree) may be applied toward the requirements of this particular requirement, provided that a minimum of 60 semester hours of graduate work is presented.

STATE OF MASSACHUSETTS

Department of Elementary and Secondary Education
Office of Educator Licensure
350 Main St., PO Box 9140
Malden, Massachusetts 02148
Phone: 781-338-3000
Web Site: **http://www.doe.mass.edu/educators/**

INITIAL REQUIREMENTS AT A GLANCE:

Also needed will be items A, B, C, D (when applicable), E, G, K, and M - See page 2. The fee for an initial or renewal license is $100.00 with any additional credentials costing $25.00 each. A two-part, state-administered certification test, the Massachusetts Tests for Educator's Licensure (MTEL) in Communications and Literacy, as well as content areas IS required for all certificates. Massachusetts DOES belong to the Interstate Certification Compact and the NASDTEC Interstate Contract (Teachers, Support Professionals, and Administrators). Competencies in special education ARE required for the Initial and Professional certificate. Major revisions are planned for 2008.

Renewal Requirements: Based upon the successful completion of the requisite number of Professional Development Points (PDPs) within a five year validity period. In addition to collecting PDPs, an Individual Professional Development Plan (IPDP) must be approved if employed under the license. If not employed under the license, an IPDP is not necessary. IPDPs must include at least 150 PDPs. At least 80% of those PDPs must be in areas of the content and professional skills of the certificate. The remaining 20% of those points may be in areas of other educational issues and topics that improve student learning. A minimum of 10 PDPs must be earned in a particular topic for the PDPs to count toward recertification. Professional Development Plans must include an additional 30 PDPs in the content and skills of any additional certificate to be renewed. For complete information, contact the Department.

ROUTES TO INITIAL TEACHER LICENSE[2]

A. **Route One** is for in-state teacher candidates who receive their preparation in approved undergraduate programs. Route One cannot be used to prepare for a license as a library teacher.

B. **Route Two** is for in-state teacher candidates who receive their preparation in approved post-baccalaureate programs, including approved alternative programs.

C. **Route Three** is for teacher candidates who hold a Preliminary license, serve in a school and are either hired as teachers of record or are serving an apprenticeship in a classroom under the direct supervision of a teacher who holds an appropriate license. Candidates seeking licensure under Route Three shall meet the following requirements:
   (a) Possession of a Preliminary license in the field and at the level of the license sought.
   (b) An approved program for the license sought.

D. **Route Four** is the Performance Review Program for Initial licensure process for teacher candidates who hold a Preliminary license, are hired as teachers of record, and are working in a district that does not have an approved program for the Initial license. This route is not available for the Early Childhood, Elementary, Library, and several special education licenses.

E. **Route Five** is for candidates who have completed an educator approved preparation program outside Massachusetts.

[2] For complete information about the Massachusetts Routes to Licensure, contact the Department.

STAGES OF LICENSURE

A. **Preliminary License:** (valid five years of employment).
   1. Possession of a bachelor's degree.
   2. Passing score on the Communication and Literacy Skills test.
   3. Passing score on the subject matter knowledge test(s) appropriate to the license sought, based on the subject matter knowledge requirements.
   4. Competency Review for candidates seeking the following licenses: (a) Teacher of students with moderate disabilities, teacher of students with severe disabilities, teacher of the deaf and hard-of-hearing, and teacher of the visually impaired; and (b) Fields for which there is no subject matter knowledge test available.
   5. Additional requirements for the early childhood, elementary, teacher of students with moderate disabilities, and teacher of the visually impaired licenses: (a) seminars or courses that address the teaching of reading, English language arts, and mathematics; (b) seminars or courses on ways to prepare and maintain students with disabilities for

general classrooms; for example, use of strategies for learning and of behavioral management principles; and (c) passing score on the Foundations of Reading test.

6. Additional requirements for the teacher of students with severe disabilities and teacher of the deaf and hard of hearing licenses: (a) seminars or courses that address the teaching of reading, English language arts, and mathematics; and (b) seminars or courses on ways to prepare and maintain students with disabilities for general classrooms; for example, use of strategies for learning and of behavioral management principles.

7. Evidence of sound moral character.

B. **Initial License:** (valid 5 years of employment, renewable once). Formerly, the Provisional Certificate with Advanced Standing.
   1. Possession of a bachelor's degree.
   2. Passing score on the Communication and Literacy Skills test.
   3. Passing score on the subject matter knowledge test(s) appropriate to the license sought, based on the subject matter knowledge requirements. Where no test has been established, completion of an approved program will satisfy this requirement.
   4. Seminars or courses that address the Professional Standards established by the Department; (a) field-based experiences in varied settings and integrated into courses or seminars that address Professional Standards for Teachers; and (b) supervised practicum or a practicum equivalent in the field and at the level of the license sought.
   5. Evidence of sound moral character.

C. **Professional License:** (valid five years, renewable). Formerly, the Standard Certificate.
   1. Possession of an Initial license in the same field (with conditions).
   2. Completion of a one-year induction program with a mentor.
   3. At least three full years of employment in the role of the license.
   4. At least 50 hours of a mentored experience beyond the induction year.
   5. Completion of one of the following:
   (a) Approved district-based program for the Professional license sought;
   (b) A master's or higher graduate level program in an accredited college or university that is or includes one of the following: (i) Approved program for the Professional license sought; (ii) A master's degree program or other advanced graduate program in the academic discipline appropriate to the license sought in a graduate or professional school other than education.
   (c) For those who have completed any master's or higher degree or other advanced graduate program not described in an accredited college or university, one of the following: (i) Approved, non-degree, 12-credit program of which no fewer than nine credits are in the academic discipline appropriate to the instructional field of the Professional license sought; (ii) 12 credits of graduate level courses in the academic discipline appropriate to the instructional field of the Professional license sought; these may include credits earned prior to application for the license.
   (d) Programs leading to eligibility for master teacher status, such as those sponsored by the National Board for Professional Teaching Standards and others accepted by the Commissioner.
   (e) A Department-sponsored Performance Assessment Program, when available.

D. **Temporary License:** (valid one year, non-renewable). Formerly, the Temporary Certificate.
   1. Possession of a valid teaching license or certificate from another state or jurisdiction of a type comparable to at least an Initial license in Massachusetts;
   2. At least three years of employment under such valid license or certificate;
   3. Has not failed any part of the applicable licensure tests required by the Department; and
   4. Evidence of sound moral character.

TEACHER LICENSES AND LEVELS

Biology	5-8; 8-12	Technology/Engineering	5-12
Business	5-12	Theater	All
Chemistry	5-8; 8-12	Visual Art	PreK-8; 5-12
Dance	All	Teacher of Students with Moderate Disabilities	

Early Childhood: Teacher of Students With and Without Disabilities PreK-2	.... PreK-8; 5-12
Earth Science 5-8; 8-12	Teacher of Students with Severe Disabilities All
Elementary 1-6	Teacher of the Deaf and Hard-of-Hearing ... All
English 5-8; 8-12	Teacher of the Visually Impaired .... All
English as a Second Language (ESL)	**Specialist Teacher Licenses and Levels:**
.... PreK-8; 5-12	Academically Advanced PreK-8
Foreign Language PreK-6; 5-12	Reading .... All
General Science 1-6; 5-8	Speech, Language, and Hearing Disorders .. All
Health/Family and Consumer Sciences ..... All	**Administrator Licenses and Levels:**
History 1-6; 5-8; 8-12	Superintendent/Assistant Superintendent .. All
Instructional Technology .... All	School Principal/Assistant School Principal
Latin and Classical Humanities 5-12	.... PreK-6; 5-8; 9-12
Library .... All	Supervisor/Director
Mathematics 1-6; 5-8; 8-12	.... Dependent on Prerequisite License
Middle School: Humanities 5-8	Special Education Administrator .... All
Middle School: Mathematics/Science 5-8	School Business Administrator .... All
Music: Vocal/Instrumental/General .... All	**Prof. Support Personnel Licenses and Levels:**
Physical Education PreK-8; 5-12	School Guidance Counselor PreK-8; 5-12
Physics 5-8; 8-12	School Nurse .... All
Political Science/Political Philosophy .. 5-8; 8-12	School Psychologist .... All
Speech .... All	School Social Worker/School Adjustment Counselor .... All

STATE OF MICHIGAN

Michigan Department of Education
Office of Professional Preparation Services
P.O. Box 30008
Lansing, Michigan 48909
Phone: 517-373-3310 / Fax: 517-373-0542
Web Site: **www.michigan.gov/mde**

INITIAL REQUIREMENTS AT A GLANCE:

Also needed are items A, B, C, E, G and M - See page 2. The fees are: (A) Provisional Certificate In-State $125.00 / Out-of-State $175.00; Additional Certification Endorsement $50.00; Provisional Renewal $75.00. A state administered Basic Skills and Subject Area certification test, the Michigan Test for Teacher Certification (MTTC), IS required for the initial teaching certificate. Michigan DOES belong to the Interstate Certification Compact, the NASDTEC Interstate Contract (Teachers only), and has additional agreements with all 50 states and the U.S. Territories. Michigan does NOT belong to the Interstate New Teacher Assessment and Support Consortium (INTASC). Coursework in Special Education IS required. *In addition to Michigan's reading methods requirement of six semester credit hours at the elementary level and three semester credit hours at the secondary level as of July 1, 2007, Michigan has approved a three semester hour diagnostic reading requirement with appropriate field experience.* Michigan no longer issues Administrative Certificates though they require the completion of 6 semester hours or 18 State Board Continuing Education Units every five years. Beginning 7/1/2004, all applicants for an initial Michigan certificate must provide evidence of completing a course in CPR/First Aid and hold a valid certificate of completion. Only American Red Cross or American Heart Association courses are acceptable. Major revisions are ongoing.

Renewal Requirements: The Provisional Certificate may be renewed twice. The first renewal requires not less than 9 semester hours of post graduate credit. The second renewal requires not less than 18 semester hours of credit in an approved program or master's degree program. For Provisional renewal (and for advancement to the Professional Certificate), a three semester hour course of study with the appropriate field experiences in the diagnosis and remediation of reading disabilities and differentiated instruction will be required. The Professional Certificate must be renewed every 5 years and may be renewed with either 6 semester hours of credit **or** 18 state approved Continuing Education Units.

Note: Michigan is emphasizing their Teacher Induction and Mentoring Program Standards which were approved by the State Board of Education on January 13, 2004. It is designed to assure that new teachers will receive the support necessary to provide a consistent, well informed, and effective teaching force for Michigan students. The program is structured around six broad performance-based standards. Contact the Department for complete details.

EQUIVALENCY OPTION - OUT OF STATE APPLICANTS
(All criteria must be met in full)

A.   An out-of-state applicant may be issued a **Professional Certificate** if the following criteria are met:
1.   Holds a valid teaching certificate from another state;
2.   Has taught successfully for three years in a position for which the out-of-state certificate was issued;
3.   Has earned, after his or her initial certification in another state, at least 18 semester credit hours in a planned course of study at a state approved institution **(or)** has earned a state board approved master's or doctoral degree; and
4.   Has met the elementary or secondary reading credit requirement established under state board rules.

B.   An out-of-state applicant who otherwise meets all of Michigan's certification requirements but has not met all of the above requirements may be issued a non-renewable, one year **Temporary Teacher Employment Authorization** allowing them the time to pass the Basic Skills and Subject Area tests of the MTTC.

STATE MINIMUM GENERAL REQUIREMENTS BY ADMINISTRATIVE RULE

A.   Forty (40) semester hours in a program of general or liberal education; and
B.   Twenty (20) semester hours in Professional Education (how students learn, education in our society, methods and materials--at the appropriate level - elementary/middle/secondary--and a minimum of six (6) semester hours of student teaching (minimum of 180 clock hours).
C.   Reading Requirements: Elementary (6 semester hours) and Secondary (3 semester hours)

PROVISIONAL CERTIFICATE
(Valid 6 years, renewable)

The Michigan Provisional Certificate is the mandatory initial Teaching Certificate. The requirements are:
A.   18 years of age;
B.   Approved Bachelor's Degree;
C.   Completion of the specific teacher preparation program of an institution (the Vocational endorsement also requires two full years--4000 hours--of recent work experience in the appropriate field--Health Occupations, Business, Distributive Education, Trades and Industry, and Home Economics);

PROFESSIONAL EDUCATION CERTIFICATE
(Valid 5 years, renewable)

The Michigan Professional Education Certificate may be issued to all candidates who have held the Provisional Certificate. The requirements are:
A.   18 semester hours of credit;
B.   Three years of successful teaching experience;
C.   Completion of 3 semester hours of reading methodology with a secondary certificate, or 6

semester hours with an elementary certificate.

Effective July 1, 2007, a three semester hour course of study with the appropriate field experiences in the diagnosis and remediation of reading disabilities and differentiated instruction will be required.

ELEMENTARY CERTIFICATE
(K - 5; 6 - 8 with Major/Minor; or K - 8 Self Contained)

A.   A major of not less than 30 semester hours or a group major of 36 semester hours and a planned program of 20 semester hours in other fields appropriate to elementary education. Six (6) semester hours must be completed in the teaching of reading; **(or)**

B.   three minors of not less than 20 hours each and the remainder in Part (a) above--planned program and teaching reading;

C.   Elementary certificates are valid for all teaching subjects in K-5, majors and minors in grades 6 - 8, and all subjects K - 8 in a self-contained classroom.

SECONDARY PROVISIONAL CERTIFICATES
(6 - 12 in Major/Minor)

A.   Major of 30 semester hours or group major of 36 semester hours;

B.   Minor of 20 semester hours or group minor of 24 semester hours;

C.   Six semester hours in teaching of reading;

D.   Valid for subject areas in grades 6-12 where the applicant has a major or minor;

E.   Added subjects require a new major or minor recommended by the sponsoring institution.

OTHER CERTIFICATE ENDORSEMENTS

For these endorsements, the applicant must complete a planned program of 18 semester hours (middle school must include six semester in reading, including reading in the content areas and developmental reading; (a) Early Childhood; (b) Bilingual language area; (c) General Elementary; (d) Middle School; (e) other areas appropriate to secondary grades.

SCHOOL GUIDANCE COUNSELOR CREDENTIALS

School Guidance Counselor Endorsement:

A.   Available as additional endorsement to candidates with a valid Michigan teaching certificate;

B.   Completion of an approved school counselor preparation program; and

C.   Passing scores on the Guidance Counselor subject area exam of the MTTC.

Preliminary Employment Authorization for School Guidance Counselors - Valid 3 yrs., Non-renewable

A.   34 semester hours of course work in an approved school guidance counseling program; and

B.   Passing scores on the Guidance Counselor subject area exam of the MTTC.

School Counselor License: Valid 5 yrs., Renewable.

A.   Master's Degree or higher from an approved School Counselor Education program meeting, minimally, all Michigan skills and content areas;

B.   passing scores on the MTTC School Guidance Counselor examination;

C.   Recommendation from an approved School Counselor Education program.

Note: *Out-of-state candidates* who have 5 years of successful experience serving in a school counseling role within the immediately preceding 7 years; and who pass the MTTC guidance counselor examination, and holds either a bachelor of science or bachelor of arts degree, and can provide a copy of the credential or approval document required by the state to serve in the school counseling role.

LIBRARIAN

A.   Hold a valid Michigan teaching certificate; and

B.   A major of not less than 30 sem. hrs. for K - 12 Librarianship, or minor of not less than 20 sem. hrs. for Teacher/Librarian certificate in Library Science.

STATE OF MINNESOTA

Department of Education
Educator Licensing Division
1500 Highway 36 West
Roseville, MN 55113
Phone: 651-582-8691 / Fax: 651-582-8809
Web Site: **http://education.state.mn.us/mde/Teacher_Support/Educator_Licensing/index.html**

INITIAL REQUIREMENTS AT A GLANCE:

Also needed will be items A, B, C, E, G, J (one copy), K, N, and O - See page 2. The fee is $57.00 plus $26.25 for state background check. Effective 9/1/01, the Praxis I Pre-Professional Skills Test (PPST) and Praxis II (PLT) scores ARE required. *Note:* minimum scores for the Praxis II are scheduled for adjustment effective 9/1/2005. The original license is valid for 1 year pending completion of the PPST. Minnesota DOES belong to the NASDTEC Interstate Agreement (Teachers and Administrators) and allow for temporary licensing of qualified out-of-state applicants (see below). Minnesota does NOT belong to Interstate New Teacher Assessment and Support Consortium (INTASC). Courses or competencies in Special Education are NOT required. A program in Human Relations IS required. Minnesota has a standards-based licensure system; evidence of proficiency and/or portfolios are helpful. For complete details, visit their web site.

Renewal Requirements: Continuing Professional Licenses are renewed every five years. **Professional Teaching License** or **Related Personnel Services Professional License**: 125 approved clock hours are required for the renewal of a teaching license. Applicant must affiliate with a Minnesota Continuing Education / Relicensure Committee when the first five-year license is issued. Applicants are under the jurisdiction of local committee guidelines for the renewal of teaching licenses. The applicant is responsible for clock hours even if they have not taught in Minnesota during the life of the license or if they are living outside of the state.
Administrative License: Submit the renewal application along with completion certificates validating 125 clock hours of participation in state pre-approved continuing education activities or transcripts.

Out of State Applicants:

If you do substitute teaching or have a teaching position in a Minnesota elementary or secondary public school, you must hold a valid Minnesota teaching license. Minnesota does not have licensure reciprocity with any other state. An application for a Minnesota license can be found under the Licensure Forms link.

Minnesota licenses are based on the recommendation of the institution where the teacher education program was completed. Programs completed in another state must have been completed at a regionally accredited college or university and must be essentially equivalent in content to programs offered by Minnesota teacher preparation institutions.

Minnesota has two additional state requirements:
1. The Minnesota Human Relations Program.
2. Praxis I and Praxis II.

Teachers who do not meet these requirements, but otherwise meet all other licensure requirements, may be granted a one-year, non-renewable license, during which time these additional requirements must be met. The non-renewable license is for one academic school year and expire on June 30.

Initial Licensure and Renewal Requirements:

Teachers and school administrators must complete a state-approved teacher education and/or administrative preparation program through a regionally accredited institution. As of September 1, 2001, you must complete the required teacher licensing tests. **Note:** Counselors, social workers, nurses, psychologists, and educational speech-language pathologist are not subject to teacher licensure testing requirements.

The certifying officer of the college or university where you completed your state-approved program must recommend you for Minnesota licensure. The certifying officer must verify that your completed programs align with the licensure area(s) and student level(s) for which you are seeking licensure. The officer must then sign and date the application to confirm that you have completed a state-approved program that led to licensure in each of the recommended fields. A recommendation is NOT required for licensure as an educational speech/language pathologist, school psychologist, school nurse, or school social worker. A recommending signature is NOT required for school counselor licensure if you completed a preparation program for school counseling accredited by the Council for the Accreditation of Counseling and Related Educational Programs (CACREP). For complete information on initial licensure, please contact the Department.

LICENSES ISSUED

A. **Professional License**, which expires five years from the June 30 nearest the date the license is issued;

B. **Administrative License**, Initial is valid two years. The Continuing license, valid for five years;

C. **Nonrenewable License**, which expires no more than three years from the June 30 nearest the date the license is issued;

D. **Temporary Limited License**, which expires on June 30 of the school year for which the license is issued, which expires one year from the June 30 nearest the date the license is issued;

E. **Limited Intern License**, which expires on June 30 of the school year for which the license is issued;

F. **Five-year Short Call Substitute Teacher License**, which expires five years from the June 30 nearest the date the license is issued;

G. **Temporary Limited Short Call Substitute Teacher License**, which expires two years from the June 30 nearest the date the license is issued; and

H. **Life License**, which does not expire.

Effective with licenses issued on or after October 16, 2000, no person may hold a license under item C or D, or any combination of licenses under items C and D, for more than three years.

GENERAL LICENSURE REQUIREMENTS

A. Bachelor's Degree from a Minnesota university, a state university or a liberal arts college accredited for preparing teachers.

B. Demonstrate the standards for effective practice for the licensing of teachers.

C. Verify the completion of an approved Board of Teaching preparation program at the appropriate level.

D. Complete a preparation program including the demonstration of specific knowledge and practices at the appropriate level for the certification desired.

LEVELS OF CERTIFICATION

A. Early Childhood Education (Birth - Gr. 3)

B. Elementary Education (K - 6). Requires a specialization for grades 5 - 8, or pre-primary (Age three and above)

C. Middle Level Licensure for Academic Specialties (5 - 8)

D. Grade Levels for Academic Specialties (5 - 12)

LIBRARY MEDIA SPECIALIST

A. Hold a bachelor's degree from a regionally accredited college or university;

B. Demonstrate the standards for effective practice for licensing of beginning teachers;

C. Completion of a Department-approved teaching preparation program for library media specialists; and

D. Complete a preparation program demonstrating specific knowledge and skills as required by the Department.

K - 12 SCHOOL GUIDANCE COUNSELOR

A. Hold a master's degree or equivalent from a regionally accredited institution as approved by the Association for the Accreditation of Colleges and Secondary Schools (AACSS); and

B. Complete an approved preparation program for school counselors approved by CACREP, or the State of Minnesota.

SCHOOL PSYCHOLOGIST

A. Complete a preparation program accredited by the National Association of School Psychologists.

ADMINISTRATIVE LICENSURE

A. An applicant for Superintendent or Principal must have three years of successful classroom teaching experience while holding a classroom teaching license valid for the position(s) in which the experienced was gained;

B. The applicant must:

Complete a specialist or doctoral program, or a program consisting of a master's degree plus 30 semester or 45 quarter credits in school administration;

Have field experience of at least 320 hours or eight weeks to be completed within 12 continuous months in elementary or secondary schools as an administrative aide to a licensed and practicing school principal, or have placement with a licensed educational administrator appropriate for the school superintendency and principalship.

A two-year nonrenewable Provisional License will be issued upon application to currently licensed elementary and secondary school principals seeking entry into a position as a K-12 principal. Evidence must be provided that the candidate is enrolled in an approved administrative licensure program for the K-12 principal.

Out of State Candidates: Persons prepared in other states may be granted an initial license by having met the Human Relations Program requirements as well as the following additional criteria:
Attended a regionally accredited institution by the (AACSS);
The program leading to licensure has been recognized by the state as qualifying the applicant completing the program for such licensure within that state;
The program leading to licensure completed by the applicant is essentially equivalent in content to approved programs offered by Minnesota institutions according to the rules; and
The institution that offers the program leading to licensure verifies that the applicant has completed an approved licensure program at that institution and recommends the applicant for a license in a licensure field at a license level.

STATE OF MISSISSIPPI

State Department of Education
Office of Educator Licensure
359 North West Street, P.O. Box 771
Jackson, Mississippi 39205-0771
Phone: 601-359-3483 / Fax: 601-359-2778
Web Site: **http://www.mde.k12.ms.us/ed_licensure/index.html**

INITIAL REQUIREMENTS AT A GLANCE:

Also needed will be items A, B, C, D, F, N, O and Q - See page 2. There is NO FEE. Scores on the Praxis I (PPST or CBT) and Praxis II (PLT or Specialty Area) ARE required. Mississippi DOES belong to the Interstate Certification Compact. They are also members of the NASDTEC Interstate Contract (all categories). Courses or competencies in Special Education ARE required.

Renewal Requirements: Class A License—Ten (10) continuing education units (CEUs) in content area(s) or job/skill related area; **OR** Three semester hours in content area or job/skill related area **AND** five CEUs in content area or job/skill related area; **OR** Six semester hours in content area or job/skill related area. **Class AA License**--Three semester hours in content or job/skill related area; **OR** Five CEUs in content area or job/skill related area. **Class AAA License**--Three semester hours in content area or job/skill related area; **OR** Five CEUs in content area or job/skill related area.

> **Class AAAA**--Three semester hours in content area or job/skill related area; **OR** Five CEUs in content area or job/skill related area.

The following endorsements are available:

Elementary .... (K-3)	Visually Impaired ..... (K-12)	Chemistry .... (7-12)
Elementary .... (4-8)	Guidance Counselor ... (K-12)	General Science .... (7-12)
Nursery Grade 1	School Psychologist ... (K-12)	Social Studies .... (7-12)
.... (N-1, added to Elementary)	Media Librarian ...... (K-12)	Mild/Moderate Disability
Mild/Moderate Disability	Business Ed .... (7-12)	.... (7-12, added to secondary or
.... (K-8, added to Elementary)	Driver Education ...... (7-12)	special subject)
Art .... (K-12)	English .... (7-12)	Agriculture .... (7-12)
Computer Applications (K-12)	French .... (7-12)	Home Economics .... (7-12)
Computer Education .. (K-12)	German .... (7-12)	
Instructional Tech. ... (K-12)	Latin .... (7-12)	
Music .... (K-12)	Russian .... (7-12)	**For All Others: Visit the**
Physical Education .... (K-12)	Spanish .... (7-12)	**Department's Web Site for a**
Emotional Disability .. (K-12)	Mathematics .... (7-12)	**complete listing of**
Gifted .... (K-12)	Psychology .... (7-12)	**Endorsements &**
Psychometrist .... (K-12)	Biology .... (7-12)	**Supplementals.**
Speech Language ..... (K-12)	Physical Science .... (7-12)	

STANDARD EDUCATOR LICENSE - APPROVED PROGRAM ROUTE

A Standard Educator license is granted to applicants meeting all licensing requirements and completing a state approved or NCATE approved teacher education program from a regionally/nationally accredited institution of higher learning. All Standard Licenses are valid 5 years and renewable.

CLASS A LICENSE:
A. Bachelor's degree in Teacher Education from an accredited institution of higher learning;
B. Praxis II (Principles of Learning and Teaching Test) **OR** NTE (Professional Knowledge Test - only if taken prior to 8/1/97); and
C. Praxis II (Specialty Area Test) **OR** NTE (Specialty Area Test.)

CLASS AA LICENSE:
A. Meet the requirements for a Standard Class A License; and
B. Master's degree in the endorsement area in which license is being requested.

CLASS AAA LICENSE:
A. Meet the requirements for a Standard Class A License; and
B. Specialist degree in the endorsement area in which license is requested.

CLASS AAAA LICENSE:
A. Meet the requirements for a Standard Class A License; and
B. Doctoral degree in the endorsement area in which license is requested.

STANDARD EDUCATOR LICENSE - ALTERNATE ROUTE
Mississippi Alternate Path to Quality Teachers (MAPQT)

A. Undergraduate bachelor's degree (non-education) from a nationally/regionally accredited institution of higher learning. Individuals who have graduated from college 7 years or more must have a minimum of a 2.0 overall GPA. Individuals who have graduated from college for less than 7 years must have a minimum of a 2.5 overall GPA or a 2.75 GPA in major;
B. Passing scores on Praxis I (Reading, Writing, Math); and
C. Passing score on Praxis II, Specialty Area Test with a score within one standard error of measurement.

Successful completion of the above requirements qualifies an applicant for a Special One-Year

Alternate Route License.

E.   During the first year of employment, teacher must complete the following:
1. New Teacher Practicums - weekend sessions Fall & Spring focusing on: (a)Classroom Management; (b) Peer Coaching; (c) School Law; (d) Data Analysis and using test results to improve instruction; and (e) Other topics as needed.
2. New Teacher Training Modules (interactive video training)
3. Local district evaluation
4. Local school district should provide an intensive induction program and provide a mentor for new teachers.

Passing score on the Praxis II, Specialty Area Test, and successful completion of the requirements in 1 - 4 above qualifies an applicant for a Standard Five-Year License.

F.   Teachers who have not achieved a passing score on the Praxis II, Specialty Area Test after the first year of teaching must:
1. Retake the Praxis II, Specialty Area Test during the second year they hold a Special One-Year Alternate Route License;
2. Continue work on an Instructional portfolio during the second year of teaching;
3. Complete additional content specific college coursework in area of weakness.

Teachers who pass the Praxis II, Specialty Area Test at the end of the second year will be issued a Standard Five-Year License.

G.   Teachers who have not passed the Praxis II, Specialty Area Test at the end of the second year of employment must:
1. Retake the Praxis II, Specialty Area Test during the second year they hold a Special One-Year Alternate Route License;
2. Continue work on an Instructional portfolio. Classroom videos must accompany the written portfolio;
3. Complete additional content specific college coursework in area of weakness;
4. Local district should conduct an evaluation of teacher.

H.   Teachers who have not achieved a passing score on the Praxis II, Specialty Area Test by the end of the third year of teaching, but has a score within one standard error of measurement of the passing score, shall submit his/her Instructional Portfolio to the State Board of Education. The Board will have the portfolio evaluated by an external team. If the portfolio is recommended for approval by the external team, the teacher may be issued a Standard Five-Year License.

STANDARD LICENSE - LIBRARY/MEDIA

CLASS A LICENSE:
EITHER:
Complete a bachclor's degree program or higher in Library/Media
Praxis I (Pre-Professional Skills Test-PPST)
Praxis II (Principles of Learning and Teaching
Praxis II (Specialty Area for Library/Media)
OR:
Hold a five year educator license
Complete an approved Library/Media program
OR:
Hold a five year educator license
Praxis II (Specialty Area for Library/Media)

CLASS AA, AAA, or AAAA LICENSE:
Meet requirements for a Five Year Class A license; and
Completion of an approved master's, specialist, or doctorate in library/media from a state approved or regionally/nationally accredited institution of higher learning.

STANDARD EDUCATOR LICENSE - GUIDANCE AND COUNSELOR

CLASS AA LICENSE:
EITHER:

A. Hold a standard teaching certificate;
B. Complete a master's degree program in guidance and counseling **(OR)**
  Hold a master's degree in another area and complete an approved program for guidance and counseling; and
C. Praxis II - Specialty Area for Guidance Counselor **(OR)**
  Praxis II - Specialty Area for Guidance Counselor **(OR)**
D. Complete an approved master's degree program for guidance and counseling which includes a full year internship **(OR)**
  Hold a master's degree in another area and complete an approved program for guidance and counseling which includes a full year internship;
E. Praxis I - Pre-Professional Skills Test (PPST); **(OR)**
  Praxis I - Computer Based Assessment (CBT); **(OR)**
F. Praxis II - Specialty Area Test

Renewal: Three semester hours in content or job/skill related area **(OR)**
  Five CEUs in content or job/skill related area

CLASS AAA LICENSE:
A. Meet the requirements for a Class AA License; and
B. Specialist degree in guidance and counseling.

Renewal: See Class AA renewal requirements.

CLASS AAAA LICENSE:
A. Meet the requirements for a Class AA License; and
B. Doctoral degree in guidance and counseling.

Renewal: See Class AA renewal requirements.

STANDARD EDUCATOR LICENSE - SCHOOL PSYCHOLOGIST

CLASS AAA LICENSE:
A. Complete an approved Specialist's degree program in school psychology or a degree program approved by NASP;
B. Praxis I - Pre-Professional Skills Test (PPST); **(OR)**
  Praxis I - Computer Based Assessment (CBT); **(OR)**
C. Praxis II - Specialty Area Test for Psychology

Renewal: Three semester hours in content or job/skill related area **(OR)**
  Five CEUs in content or job/skill related area

CLASS AAAA LICENSE:
A. Meet the requirements for a Class AAA License; and
B. Doctoral degree in psychology.

Renewal:
  See Class AAA renewal requirements.

ADMINISTRATOR LICENSE - APPROVED PROGRAM ROUTE*

The Non-Practicing administrator license is issued to an educator NOT currently employed in an administrative position. The Entry Level Administrator License is issued to an educator employed as a beginning administrator. The Standard Career Level Administrator License is issued to a practicing administrator who has completed all entry-level requirements. Applicants for ALL Administrator licenses must hold a 5-year educator license and have 3 years of instructional experience.

NON-PRACTICING ADMINISTRATOR (Class AA, AAA, or AAAA) - Validity based upon validity period of license currently held.

A.   Completion of an approved master's, specialist, or doctoral degree in educational administration/leadership from a state-approved or regionally/nationally accredited institution of higher learning; and

B.   Successful completion of SLLA Licensure Assessment -Educational Testing Service (ETS.)

Renewal: Three semester hours in content or job/skill related area **(OR)**
Five CEUs in content or job/skill related area.

ENTRY LEVEL ADMINISTRATOR (Class AA, AAA, or AAAA) - Valid 5 years (Non-Renewable)

A.   Completion of an approved master's, specialist's, or doctoral degree in educational administration/leadership from a state-approved or regionally/nationally accredited institution of higher learning; and

B.   Successful completion of SLLA Licensure Assessment (ETS)

Renewal: Non-Renewable, candidate has five (5) years to complete requirements to convert to Standard Career Level License which include the following: Completion of School Executive Management Institute (SEMI) Entry-Level Requirements

STANDARD CAREER LEVEL ADMINISTRATOR LICENSE (Class AA, AAA, or AAAA) - Valid 5 years, Renewable.

A.   Completion of an approved master's, specialist's, or doctoral degree in educational administration/leadership from a state-approved or regionally/nationally accredited institution of higher learning;

B.   Successful completion of SLLA Licensure Assessment (ETS); and

C.   Completion of School Executive Management Institute (SEMI) Entry-Level Requirements.

Renewal: Completion of the following renewal requirements will also renew all existing standard educator licenses for the applicant:

70 School Executive Management Institute (SEMI) credits; **(OR)**
6 hours of coursework; **(OR)**
Completion of 35 SEMI credits AND three hours of coursework; and
Complete a specialist or doctoral degree in educational administration/leadership.

* NOTE: An ALTERNATE ROUTE for Entry Level Administrator Licenses is also available. Contact the Department or visit their web site for further information.

STATE OF MISSOURI

Department of Elementary & Secondary Education
Teacher Education and Certification
205 Jefferson
Jefferson City, Missouri 65102-0480
Phone: 573-751-0051 or 573-751-3847
Web Site: **http://dese.mo.gov/divteachqual/teachcert/**

INITIAL REQUIREMENTS AT A GLANCE:

Also needed are items A, B, C, E, G, J (electronically), K, M, O, and Q - See page 2. There is a $35.00 fee for the Career Continuous Professional Certificate. Effective 10/1/07, a $52.50 fingerprint fee is required as well as a Missouri "Open Records" check for $9.00. A state administered certification test is NOT required. Praxis II Specialty Area Test ARE required. Applicants must have maintained an overall GPA of 2.5 **and** a 2.5 GPA in Major and 2.5 GPA in Professional Education. Missouri DOES maintain reciprocity agreements with Kansas, Iowa, Illinois, and Oklahoma. Also, Missouri offers reciprocity for comparable certificates to out-of-state license holders. Please contact the Department for complete information. Missouri DOES belong to the NASDTEC Interstate Contract (Teachers, Support Professionals, Administrators, and Vocational Educators) and the Interstate New Teacher Assessment and Support Consortium (INTASC). A course in special education IS required for all teaching certificates. Licensing revisions are ongoing.

NOTE: Effective 8/28/2008, Missouri will allow persons who hold a certificate from the American Board for Certification of Teacher Excellence (ABCTE) to be eligible for a regular Missouri teaching certificate in the following areas: English/Language Arts; Biology; Chemistry; General Science; Mathematics; Physics; and U.S./World History. By law, ABCTE certificate-holders are NOT eligible for a regular Missouri license in the areas of early childhood education, elementary education or special education.

Renewal Requirements: One credit, or 15 clock hours of annual professional development is required each year.

CURRENT LICENSE CLASSIFICATIONS
(Since August, 2003)

The **Initial Professional Certificate (IPC)** is valid for four years and assigned to new graduates of teacher education programs and individuals with less than four years of teaching experience who meet the minimum requirements and qualifications. To advance to the next level during the valid dates of the classification, a teacher must meet the following requirements: (a) participation in a district-provided and approved mentoring program for two years; (b) successful completion of 30 contact hours of professional development which may include college credits; (c) participation in a Beginning Teacher Assistance program; (d) successfully participate in a performance-based teacher evaluation; (e) complete four years of approved teaching experience; and (f) have a local professional development plan.

The **Career Continuous Professional Certificate (CCPC)** is valid continuously depending on an individual meeting the following: (a) The requirements at the IPC level (four years of experience); (b) successful, yearly completion of 15 contact hours of professional development which may include college credits; and (c) have a local professional development plan,

OR

Two of the three following items: (a) ten (10) years of teaching experience; (b) a master's degree; or (c) National Board certification.

Provisional Classification refers to a two-year non-renewable certificate issued to teachers who do not meet all of the requirements for Professional Certificates. If additional coursework is needed to meet the minimum requirements, the deficiencies may not exceed 12 semester hours. Individuals enrolled in an alternative program for educators may qualify for a provisional classification.

Administrative Classification refers to the certification of Elementary School (K-8), Middle School (5-9), Secondary Principals (7-12); Superintendents (K-12); Special Education Administrators (K-12) Secondary Career Director and Postsecondary Career Director certificates are included in this classification. Missouri requires the completion of an advanced degree with a major emphasis in Educational Administration from an approved college or university. Missouri also requires the recommendation for certification from the designated recommending official of an approved college or university. This recommendation must be part of the Application for the Certificate.

Student Services Classification includes certification for all areas of Pupil Personnel Services: Counselor K-8, Counselor 7-12, Psychological Examiner K-12, School Psychologist K-12, Speech-Language Pathologist, Vocational Adult Education Supervisor, Post-secondary Vocational Counselor Certificate, Placement Coordinator Certificate, and Vocational Student Services. Missouri requires the completion of a Master's degree with a major emphasis in Guidance and Counseling from an approved college or university. Missouri also requires the recommendation for certification from the designated recommending official of an approved college or university. This recommendation must be part of the Application for Counselor's Certificate.

Temporary Authorization Classification is a one-year certificate that may be requested jointly by a school district and an individual who holds a baccalaureate degree with a minimum overall grade point average of 2.5 on a 4.0 scale. An individual may hold more than one temporary certificate, it is renewable yearly, and enables a person to teach while earning the necessary requirements for a professional classification, including: (a) successfully passing the Praxis tests; (b) yearly completion of nine semester hours toward professional certification; (c) participation in a mentoring program; and (d) Successful participation in a performance based teacher evaluation.

The **Temporary Authorization Certificate** does not include elementary (1-6); early childhood; early childhood special education (B-3); blind and partially sighted (K-12); and/or deaf and hearing impaired (K-12) areas. Applicants for the areas of driver's education, English for speakers of other languages, gifted and special reading must already hold a certificate of license to teach or must seek a certificate of license to teach in a stand-alone area.

Doctoral Route to Classification must be applied for by a Missouri public school district and an individual who has earned a doctoral degree from a college or university accredited by a regional accreditation agency. The certificate is limited to the major area of the applicant's post-graduate study, must be in a subject area for which there is a Missouri teaching certificate, and the individual must pass a specified test.

Alternative Routes to entering the teaching profession are available at some colleges/ universities for college graduates who have not completed a teacher education program. This certification is offered through an approved college/university and includes specific qualifications for acceptance. It also requires employment with a district prior to being accepted into the college's alternative program.

EARLY CHILDHOOD CERTIFICATE
(Birth Through Grade 3)

I. GENERAL REQUIREMENTS:
- A. A baccalaureate degree from a college or university having a teacher education program which addresses the competencies required for this certificate and is approved by the Missouri Department of Elementary and Secondary Education or from a college or university having a teacher education program approved by the state education agency in states other than Missouri;
- B. Must have recommendation of designated official for teacher education in the college or university;
- C. Must have a grade point average of 2.5 on a 4.0 scale overall and in the major area of study;
- D. Must complete the content knowledge or specialty area test designated by the State Board of Education with a score equal to or greater than the Missouri qualifying score;
- E. Completion of professional requirements as determined by the recommending college or university, which may exceed these minimum requirements; and
- F. Individuals who completed their teacher education program outside of the United States shall provide documentation of completion of approved course work.

II. PROFESSIONAL REQUIREMENTS:

A minimum requirement of forty-eight (48) semester hours. The lists following the major areas of professional studies are to be regarded as areas of study and/or content and not necessarily as course titles:
- A. Foundations of Teaching (Minimum requirement of six (6) semester hours);
- B. Child Development (Minimum requirement of nine (9) semester hours);
- C. Teaching the Young Child (Minimum requirement of twenty-one (21) semester hours);
- D. Home-School-Community Relations (Minimum requirement of six (6) semester hours);
- E. Program Management (Minimum requirement of six (6) semester hours);
- F. Pre-Student Teaching (Minimum requirement of ninety (90) contact hours. Fifteen (15) contact hours equals one (1) semester hour):
  Pre-student teaching must include a minimum of thirty (30) contact hours in each of the three (3) different age levels (infant/toddler, pre-K/Kindergarten, and primary K-3). This pre-student teaching may be included as part of courses identified in areas B-E above or be offered as a separate course(s).

III. STUDENT TEACHING:

The individual participates and applies the competencies in a variety of supervised student teaching experiences. Interactions with children and families from a variety of backgrounds shall be an integral part of the student teaching; and Student Teaching will require a minimum of twelve (12) semester hours spent with two (2) different age levels (infant/toddler, pre-K/Kindergarten, primary K-3). Each of the two (2) student teaching experiences requires a minimum of five (5) semester hours.

ELEMENTARY CERTIFICATE
(Grades 1-6)

I. GENERAL REQUIREMENTS:
   See Early Childhood Certificate General Requirements.

II. PROFESSIONAL REQUIREMENTS:
   A minimum of sixty (60) semester hours of professional preparation. Competency must be demonstrated in each topic listed to the satisfaction of the teacher preparation institution.
   A.   Foundations for Teaching (Minimum requirement of ten (10) semester hours);
   B.   Teaching Methods (Minimum requirement of fifteen (15) semester hours); and
   C.   Clinical Experiences (Minimum requirement of ten (10) semester hours): A minimum of two (2) semester hours of field experiences prior to student teaching and a minimum of eight (8) semester hours of student teaching in elementary grades are required. Teachers meeting certification requirements for Early Childhood or Middle School teaching certificates will be exempt from this clinical experience requirement. A fully certificated secondary teacher with two (2) or more years of secondary teaching experience may satisfy this Revised May 2003 requirement through the completion of a two (2) or more semester hour practicum at the elementary level; and
   D.   Elementary School Courses:
       1.   Courses appropriate for Elementary grades: a. Mathematics (two (2) courses, minimum total of five (5) semester hours); b. Economics; c. Geography; d. Health; and e. Art or Music; and
       2.   Area of Concentration: The student must have a total of at least twenty-one (21) semester hours in an area of concentration.

MIDDLE SCHOOL EDUCATION CERTIFICATE
(Grades 5-9)

I. GENERAL REQUIREMENTS:
   See Early Childhood Certificate General Requirements.

II. PROFESSIONAL REQUIREMENTS:
   A minimum of fifty-three (53) semester hours in professional education. Competency must be demonstrated in each area listed to the satisfaction of the teacher preparation institution.
   A.   Foundations for Teaching (Minimum requirement of twelve (12) semester hours): 1. The Pupil/Society—A minimum of eight (8) semester hours with knowledge acquired and competency developed to the satisfaction of the teacher preparation institution and 2. The School/Society—A minimum of four (4) semester hours with knowledge acquired and competency developed to the satisfaction of the teacher preparation institution;
   B.   Middle School Concentration (Minimum requirement of thirty-one (31) semester hours): 1. Middle School Methods (Minimum requirement of ten (10) semester hours); and 2. Subject Area Requirements (Minimum requirement of twenty-one (21) semester hours): Subject area certification in grades 5-9 will be granted upon the basis of a minimum of twenty-one (21) semester hours with appropriate distribution as determined by the teacher preparation institution and/or the Department of Elementary and Secondary Education; and
   C.   Clinical Experience (Minimum requirement of ten (10) semester hours): A minimum of two (2) semester hours of field experience prior to student teaching and a minimum of eight (8) semester hours of student teaching in grades 5-9 is required. Teachers meeting requirements for Early Childhood, Elementary, or Secondary certification must complete a practicum with middle level students. This practicum may be integrated within

appropriate required courses.

SECONDARY EDUCATION CERTIFICATE
(Grades 9-12)

I. GENERAL REQUIREMENTS:
> See Early Childhood Certificate General Requirements.

II. PROFESSIONAL REQUIREMENTS:
> A minimum requirement of twenty-six (26) semester hours in professional education as follows:
>
> A.   Foundations of Teaching (Minimum requirement of eight (8) semester hours): 1. The Pupil/Society--A minimum of six (6) semester hours with knowledge acquired and competency developed to the satisfaction of the teacher preparation institution; and 2. The School/Society--A minimum of two (2) semester hours with knowledge acquired and competency developed to the satisfaction of the teacher preparation institution;
>
> B.   Secondary Methods and Techniques (Minimum requirement of eight (8) semester hours): A minimum of eight (8) semester hours with knowledge acquired and competency developed to the satisfaction of the teacher preparation institution
>
> C.   Clinical Experiences (Minimum requirement of ten (10) semester hours): Certification in grades 9-12 should include clinical experience at the secondary level. A minimum of two (2) semester hours prior to student teaching** and a minimum of eight (8) semester hours of student teaching in grades 9-12 is required, except that K-9 or K-12 certification must also include K-6 experience in student teaching. A fully certified elementary or middle school teacher with two (2) or more years of elementary or middle school teaching may satisfy this requirement through the completion of a two (2) or more semester hour practicum at the secondary level.

*   Denotes minimum requirement of two (2) semester hours.
**   Denotes minimum requirement of eight (8) semester hours.

STATE OF MONTANA

Office of Public Instruction
Educator Licensure
P.O. Box 202501
Helena, Montana 59620-2501
Phone: 406-444-3150 / Fax: 406-444-3924
Web Site: **http://www.opi.mt.gov/cert/**

INITIAL REQUIREMENTS AT A GLANCE:

Also needed will be items A, B, C, D (or State Board approval), E, H and K - See page 2. The fee is $36.00. There is a recent credit requirement if applicant's degree is over 5 years old. The original certificate is valid for 5 years. Montana DOES belong to the Interstate Certification Agreement Contract and the NASDTEC Interstate Contract (Teachers, Administrators, and Vocational Educators). Montana will also accept National Board Certification (NBPTS) as evidence of eligibility. Course work in Special Education is NOT required. For complete certification requirements, contact the Office.

Renewal Requirements*:
Class 1 Professional Teaching and Class 3 Administrative: 60 Office of Public Instruction (OPI*) renewal units
Class 2 Standard Teaching: College credit and OPI renewal units: 3 semester credits and 15 OPI renewal units; or 4 semester credits; or 4 quarter credits and 20 OPI renewal units; or 5 quarter credits and 10 OPI renewal units; or 6 quarter credits.
Class 4C Vocational: Same as Class 2 Standard Teaching License
* 1 semester credit = 15 OPI renewal units. 1 quarter credit = 10 OPI renewal units. 1 hour of

attendance at a workshop = 1 OPI renewal unit.

LICENSE CLASSES

Class 2 - Standard Teacher's License - Valid five years. Renewable.
Requirements: Bachelor's degree with a completed and accredited professional educator preparation program; **and** verify completion of an accredited professional educator preparation program in an area approved for endorsement in Montana; **and** successfully complete a supervised teaching experience either as part of an accredited professional educator preparation program or successfully complete one year of teaching experience in a state accredited elementary and/or secondary school district.

Class 1 - Professional Teacher's License - Valid five years. Renewable.
Requirements: Hold a Class 2 Standard Educator License or meet the qualifications of the Class 2 Standard Educator License; **and** master's degree or one year of study consisting of at least 30 graduate semester credits beyond the bachelor's degree in professional education or an endorsable teaching area(s) from an accredited college or university; **and** verification of three years of successful teaching experience or the equivalent.

Class 3 - Administrative License - Valid five years. Renewable.
A.   **Basic Education License:** Master's degree in an accredited school administration program or the equivalent, and qualify for a Class 1, 2, or 5 license.
B.   **Principal:** Verification of three years of successful teaching experience at the desired grade level.
C.   **Superintendent:** Verification of one year of administrative experience and program.

Class 4 - Vocational Education License - Valid five years. Renewable.

Requirements: 10,000 hours of verified work experience. Applicant will be issued a Class 4A, 4B, or 4C license depending on education.

Class 5 - Alternative License - Valid three years. Non-renewable.
A.   Bachelor's degree and major preparation toward full licensure, but have minor discrepencies such as a lack of recent credits or program deficiencies.
B.   Recipient of the Class 5 Alternative must sign and file with the Superintendent of Public Instruction a plan of professional intent leading to full licensure within three years of the date of the alternative license.

Class 6 - Specialist License (Psychologist / School Counselor) - Valid five years. Renewable.
Requirements: Master's degree; supervised internship.

Class 7 - American Indian Language Specialist License - Valid five years. Renewable.
Requirements: Each Tribe establishes criteria and recommends individuals meeting requirements.

MINIMUM QUALIFICATIONS

A.   18 years of age or older; Of good moral and professional character; Have completed the teacher education program of a unit of the Montana University System or an essentially equivalent program at an accredited institution of equal rank and standing as that of any unit of the Montana University System, and your training must be evidenced by at least a bachelor's degree and a certification of the completion of the teacher education program (except for Class 5 and Class 4 Licenses.

B.   You must take the following oath or affirmation before an officer authorized by law to administer oaths (generally a notary public): "I solemnly swear (or affirm) that I will support The Constitution of the United States of America and The Constitution of the State of Montana."

MONTANA ENDORSEMENTS

Teaching (Class 1 & 2):   **Teaching (Cont'd):**   Aviation

Agriculture
Art K-12
Biology
Business Education
Business Education
Chemistry
Computer Science K-12
Drama
Earth Science
Economics
Elementary Education
English
ESOL K-12
Family and Consumer Sciences
French K-12
Geography
German K-12
School Counseling K-12
Health
History
History-Political Science
 Industrial Arts
Journalism
Latin K-12
Library K-12
Marketing

Mathematics
Music K-12
Other Language K-12
P.E. and Health K-12
Physical Science
Physics
Political Science
Psychology
Reading K-12
Russian K-12
Science
Social Studies
Sociology
Spanish K-12
Special Education P-12
Speech Communication
Speech-Drama
Technology Education
Trade and Industry, and
Traffic Education K-12

**Career and Vocational &
Technical (Class 4):**
Agricultural Mechanics
Auto Body
Automotive Technology

Building Maintenance
Building Trades
Computer Information Systems
Culinary Arts
Diesel Mechanics
Drafting
Electronics
Graphic Arts
Health Occupations
Heavy Equipment Operator
Horticulture
Industrial Mechanics
Machining
Metals
Small Engines
Welding

Administrative (Class 3):
Elementary Principal
Secondary Principal
Principal K-12
Superintendent and Supervisor
.... K-12

Specialist (Class 6):
School Psychologist
School Counselor

STATE OF NEBRASKA

Department of Education
Teacher Certification
301 Centennial Mall South, PO Box 94987
Lincoln, Nebraska 68509
Phone: 402-471-0739 / 402-471-2496 (electronic forms or materials) / Fax: 402-471-9735
Web Site: **http://www.nde.state.ne.us/TCERT/**

INITIAL REQUIREMENTS AT A GLANCE:

Also needed will be items A, B, C, E, G, J (Nebraska Form), K, and N - See page 2. Fee is $55.00. Nebraska now requires criminal history background checks and fingerprints for all first time certification applicants. There is an additional $40.00 fingerprint fee. Scores on the Praxis I (PPST) or Praxis I (CBT) ARE required. The PPST may be waived for a candidate with 3 years teaching experience and who has completed an approved teacher education program. For further information, contact the department. Nebraska DOES belong to the NASDTEC Interstate Contract (Teachers only) and also maintains certification compacts with the states of Arkansas, Illinois, Iowa, Kansas, Michigan, Missouri, Oklahoma, South Dakota and Wisconsin. Nebraska is a member of the Interstate New Teacher Assessment and Support Consortium (INTASC). Coursework in Special Education ARE required for most certificates *and* a Human Relations training course.

Renewal Requirements: Fee $55.00. Two years of teaching experience, **or** six semester hours of credit (may be undergraduate) within five years of application date. If an old certificate has expired by more than five years, 15 semester hours of credit are required to renew.

PROVISIONAL CERTIFICATES

Two Year Provisional Certificate: A regional exchange agreement has been signed by Iowa, Kansas, Minnesota, Missouri, Nebraska, North Dakota, Ohio, Oklahoma, South Dakota, and Wisconsin. If you graduated from a college in one of the above states **and** hold a valid, regular teaching certificate from one of the qualifying states **and** are lacking the Basic Skills Competency Test, Special Education Competencies, or Human Relations Training - as described in this manual, a *Two-Year Provisional Certificate* is available upon application. This type of certificate is valid in any school system in Nebraska. All deficiencies must be corrected within two years to permit *any* subsequent Nebraska certification other than a State Substitute Certificate.

One Year Provisional Certificate: This Provisional Certificate can be issued for the following reasons:

The basic skills competency test requirement has not been met; **and/or**

The special education requirement has not been met: **and/or**

The recency requirement has not been met and you need to complete college credit hours; **and/or**

A baccalaureate degree has been completed and the necessary portion of an appropriate approved program has been completed.

INITIAL TEACHING CERTIFICATE
Elementary and Secondary
(Valid 5 years, renewable)

A. Bachelor's Degree from an accredited institution with a regularly approved program for the preparation of teachers.

B. Good scholarship, sound mental and physical health, good citizenship and moral character.

C. Completion of an approved program for the grade level, the subject, the field or the area for which the applicant is specifically prepared to teach.

D. Six (6) semester hours of credit within the past three years and the recommendation of the institution.

E. Human Relations Skills Training from an approved institution (A list of qualifying courses will be provided upon request);

F. Must have 3 sem. hrs. credit in specified Special Education.

STANDARD AND PROFESSIONAL TEACHING CERTIFICATES

A. Standard Certificate: (Valid 7 years, renewable)
1. Applicants must hold an Initial Certificate; and
2. Have 2 years successive teaching experience.

B. Professional Certificate: (Valid 10 years, renewable)
1. Master's or higher degree; and
2. 6 semester hours of approved credit within 3 years of the date of application

(OR)

3. 2 years of successful teaching experience on a Standard Certificate.

SPECIAL SERVICES CERTIFICATES

A. Provisional Certificate - (Valid 1 year, non-renewable)
1. Submission of a written request for the certificate;
2. See Initial Teacher Certificate, items A, B and E;
3. Completion of at least ¾ of a program in school psychology, or completion of a bachelor's degree in speech-language pathology; and
4. Submission of a statement of intent to fulfill the remaining requirements (if needed.)

B. Standard Counseling Certificate - (Valid 7 years, renewable)
1. See Initial Teacher Certificate, items A, B and E;
2. Completion of a program in school psychology or speech pathology;
3. Hold or qualify for a school psychology endorsement; and
4. Six sem. hrs. of credit, within three years of the application, which meets all or part of the requirements for an endorsement.

STANDARD ADMINISTRATIVE CERTIFICATE
Elementary Principal
Secondary Principal
Curriculum Supervisor

An application for any Regular Nebraska Certificate requires the completion of an approved administrator training program. To be eligible for a Regular Nebraska Administrative Certificate you need to meet the following statutory requirements: Fingerprinting requirement; Basic Skills Competency; Human Relations Training; and Special Education Competencies.

PROFESSIONAL ADMINISTRATIVE CERTIFICATE
Superintendent

Two years of teaching experience in conjunction with an appropriate certificate. Recommendation from an approved institution which certifies:

A. An approved Master's Degree program for educational administration and/or supervision or 36 semester hours of graduate credit in an approved six-year program for educational administration and/or supervision;
B. Six year certificate for Superintendent Endorsement;
C. area of specialization for which the equivalent has been prepared;
D. standards which are normally required for full recommendation; and
E. six semester hours of graduate course work completed within the past three years.

STATE OF NEVADA

Nevada Department of Education
Teacher Licensing Office
9890 South Maryland Parkway, Suite 231, Rm. 234
Las Vegas, Nevada 89183
Phone: 702-486-6458 or 702-486-6457 (voice mail)/ Fax: 702-486-6450
(or)
700 East Fifth Street
Carson City, NV 89701
Phone: 775-687-9115 / Fax: 775-687-9101
Web Site: **http://nvteachers.doe.nv.gov/**

INITIAL REQUIREMENTS AT A GLANCE:

Also needed will be items A, B, E, G (from HR office), H, I, J, K, M, N and O (required for Provisional License) See page 2. The fee is $161.00 for up to 2 endorsements and $50.00 for additional endorsements. A state administered certification test is NOT required. Scores on the Praxis I and Praxis II may be required of *all* applicants. Scores on the National Teacher's Examination test are NOT required. Nevada DOES belong to the NASDTEC Interstate Certification Agreement (All areas). Nevada DOES belong to the Interstate New Teacher Assessment and Support Consortium (INTASC). *Final authority for all certification equivalencies rests with the Nevada DOE.* All applicants must have a course in the United States Constitution, Nevada Constitution, and Nevada School Law. Courses or competencies in Special Education are NOT required. Revisions are ongoing. For complete licensing requirements contact the Department or visit their web site.

Renewal Requirements: Six semester credit hours (or equivalent). Renewals every five (5) years for holders of a Bachelor degree, six (6) years for holders of a Masters degree, and 10 years for holders of a Doctoral degree. Application fee of $80.00 to renew a license.

LEVELS AND LICENSES

93

Levels: Birth-Kindergarten, Elementary (K - 8), Middle School, Secondary Academic, Secondary Vocational and *Special Education*

Licenses:
A. **Initial:**
Valid 5 years, Renewable (with 6 credit hrs.)
B. **Professional:**
1. Valid 6 years with Master's Degree, Renewable (with 6 credit hours)
2. Valid 8 years with Specialist's Degree, Renewable with evidence of professional growth
3. Valid 10 years with Doctoral Degree, Renewable with evidence of professional growth
C. **Special Endorsements:** Administrators, School Counselors, Library Media Specialist, etc.

BIRTH - KINDERGARTEN [1]

To receive a special license or endorsement to teach pupils from birth through kindergarten, a person must hold a bachelor's degree or graduate degree from an accredited college or university and must:

A. Have completed a program of preparation to teach such pupils that is approved by the board; **or**
B. Hold a license to teach such pupils that was issued by another state and approved by the commission; **or**
C. Hold an elementary license, a middle school or junior high license, or a secondary license that is endorsed with a major in child care; **and**
    1. Have experience teaching pupils under 6 years of age that consists of:
        a) Eight semester hours of student teaching; **or**
        b) One year of verifiable experience teaching pupils in a program of early childhood education conducted by a public school, a public agency or a private school that is licensed pursuant to chapter 394 or NRS at the conclusion of which the person was eligible for re-employment; **or**
        c) An equivalent field experience or practicum conducted by an accredited college or university; **and**
        d) Have completed at least 12 semester hours of courses in early childhood education, of which six semester hours must consist of courses in any of the following subjects: Early childhood curriculum; Emergent language and literacy; **or** Play theory and creativity; **and**
        e) Any additional semester hours must consist of courses in any of the subjects listed above or in any of the following subjects: Child development from birth to age 8; Diversity in young children; Introduction to early childhood education; Positive discipline and guidance for young children; **or** Working with families with young children.

[1] There is also an endorsement for Birth - Second Grade.

ELEMENTARY CERTIFICATES[1]

A. **Initial Elementary License:**
1. Bachelor's degree from an accredited college or university;
2. Completion of a state Board of Education approved program of preparation for teaching in elementary grades;
3. Professional education coursework 32
Including the following:
    (a) Supervised student teaching (K-8) 8
    (b) Teaching methods, not including reading 9
    (c) Literacy or language arts 9
    (d) Classroom management, or English as a second language, or technology, or evaluation of pupils, or child development, or special education, or social and cultural issues 6

B. **Professional Elementary License:** (Valid 6 or more years, Renewable)
1. Complete the requirements for an Elementary License;
2. Master's degree; and
3. 3 years of elementary teaching experience

Individual elementary subject area endorsements are available and usually require 12 additional credit hours of preparation.

SECONDARY CERTIFICATES

A. **Requirements for Teaching Endorsements in Recognized Teaching Fields:**
1. Comprehensive fields of concentration (in semester hours)
   a. Majors 36
   b. Minors 24
2. Single subject majors and minors
   a. Majors 30
   b. Minors 16

B. **Secondary License:** Requirements as follows:
1. Bachelor's degree and completion of an approved program of preparation for secondary school teaching;
   (OR)
2. Required courses for a teaching major from a regionally accredited institution;
   (AND)
3. Professional secondary or occupational education 22
   Including:
   a. Supervised teaching and/or teaching internship 8
   b. A course in methods and materials in specialization
      (AND)
   c. If the endorsement is in occupational education:
      (i) Professional occupational courses 9
      (ii) Two years of verifiable work experience in area(s) of endorsement
      (iii) Hold a valid occupational license in the area of endorsement if the license is required by state law to provide services to the general public

C. **Professional Secondary License:** (Valid 6 years or more, Renewable)
1. Complete requirements for Secondary License;
2. Master's degree; and
3. 3 years of secondary teaching experience.

LIBRARY MEDIA SPECIALIST

To receive an endorsement as a school library media specialist, a person must have a valid elementary, secondary or special teaching license, excluding a business and industry endorsement, and:

Have completed a program for school library media specialists which has been approved by the board or a regional accrediting association;

Hold a master's degree in library science, with specialization in school librarianship, from a school accredited by the American Library Association; or

Have completed 21 semester hours of course work in the following subjects: (1) Organization and administration of a school library; (2) The cataloging and classification of materials for a library; (3) Reference, bibliography and information skills; (4) The use and selection of educational media for a library; (5) Children's and young adults' literature; (6) Computers in the library; (7) A supervised practicum in an elementary or secondary school library.

PROFESSIONAL SCHOOL LIBRARY MEDIA SPECIALIST

To receive an endorsement as a professional school library media specialist, a person must:

Hold a master's degree in any field;

Have met all the requirements for an endorsement as a school library media specialist, and have completed an additional 9 semester hours in curriculum and instruction, educational technology or information technology; and

Have 3 years of experience, in state-approved schools or accredited private schools, as a librarian or school library media specialist.

SCHOOL COUNSELOR ENDORSEMENTS[2]

To qualify for an endorsement to serve as a school counselor, a person must hold a master's of education in school counseling, master's of art in school counseling, master's of science with a major in school counseling or a more advanced degree with a major in school counseling. The degree required by this section must be conferred by a regionally accredited college or university.

[2] For a complete listing of School Counselor requirements, visit Nevada's web site.

AUTHORIZATION TO SERVE AS SCHOOL COUNSELOR WITHOUT ENDORSEMENT

The superintendent of public instruction may authorize a person who has not received an endorsement to serve as a school counselor in a school district or charter school if the school district or charter school demonstrates that a person with an endorsement is not available for employment. To receive an authorization, a person must:

A. Hold a current license issued by the superintendent of public instruction, excluding a business and industry endorsement;

B. Hold a master's degree in a field related to school counseling or an advanced degree in a field related to school counseling;

C. Have completed at least:
1. Two years of teaching experience at any grade level in kindergarten through grade 12;
2. Two years of school counseling experience at any grade level (K-12); or
3. A practicum, internship or field experience in school counseling at any grade level in kindergarten through grade 12 in addition to the practicum, internship or field experience that is completed pursuant to paragraph (e);

D. Be admitted into a regionally accredited graduate-level program in school counseling;

E. Complete at least 280 hours of an initial practicum, internship or field experience in school counseling at any grade level (K-12); **and**

F. Have completed at least 24 graduate credits in the following areas of study:

The process of individual counseling; the process of group counseling; Testing and educational assessments, as applicable to a school setting at any grade level in kindergarten through grade 12; Legal and ethical issues in counseling; Developing careers and choosing occupations; Organization and administration of school counseling programs; Multicultural counseling; Child and family counseling, as applicable to a school setting at any grade level (K-12); **and**

One of the following: The use of technology in education; Exceptional children; Human growth and development; or Substance abuse counseling.

The superintendent shall not authorize a person to serve as a school counselor as described in this section for more than 3 years. Such an authorization may be issued only once per person.

SCHOOL PSYCHOLOGIST
(K - 12)

To qualify for an endorsement to serve as a school psychologist, a person must:

A. Hold a graduate degree from an accredited college/university with a concentration in school psychology;

B. Have successfully completed the course work in prescribed Areas of Study[3];

C. Have earned 60 semester hours of graduate credits in prescribed in either Required Areas of Study or Optional Areas of Study[3]; and

D. Have completed an internship in school psychology as outlined in Requirements for a Practicum[3];
    (OR)

E. Hold a certificate as a nationally certified school psychologist issued by the National School Psychology Certification System of the National Association of School Psychologists;
    (OR)

F. Have completed a program approved by the board which prepares a person to be a school psychologist.

[3]   For a complete listing of School Psychologist requirements, visit Nevada's web site.

SCHOOL MEDIA SPECIALIST
(K - 12)

To receive an endorsement as a school library media specialist, a person must have a valid elementary, secondary or special teaching license, excluding a business and industry endorsement, and must:

A. Have completed a program for school library medal specialists which has been approved by the board or a regional accrediting association;

B. Hold a master's degree in library science, with specialization in school librarianship, from a school accredited by the American Library Association; or

C. Have completed 21 semester hours of course work in the following subjects:
   1. Organization and administration of a school library;
   2. The cataloging and classification of materials for a library;
   3. Reference, bibliography and information skills;
   4. The use and selection of educational media for a library;
   5. Children's and young adults' literature;
   6. Computers in the library; and
   7. A supervised practicum in an elementary or secondary school library

Professional Endorsement: To receive an endorsement as a professional school library media specialist, a person must:

A. Hold a master's degree in any field;

B. Have met all the requirements for an endorsement as a school library media specialist, and have completed an additional 9 semester hours in curriculum and instruction, educational technology or information technology; and

C. Have 3 years of experience, in state-approved schools or accredited private schools, as a librarian or school library media specialist

ADMINISTRATIVE ENDORSEMENTS
Professional administrator of a school;
Professional administrator of a program; and
Supervisor of curriculum and instruction.

Only a professional administrator of a school may be employed by a school district as: Superintendent of schools; Assistant superintendent of schools; Associate superintendent of schools; Principal; Vice principal; Supervisor; Administrative assistant; or Supervisor or coordinator of: A program of nursing; A program of psychology as it is applied in a school; A program of speech therapy; A program of physical therapy; A program of occupational therapy; or any other program area.

Typically, a person must hold an endorsement as an Administrator of a Program if they supervise or coordinate a program of: Nursing; Psychology as it is applied in a school; Speech therapy; Physical therapy; or Occupational therapy.

A person is not required to hold an endorsement as an administrator of a school before performing services as an assistant superintendent, principal or vice principal if he holds a diploma designated as a "life diploma" by the institution that granted the diploma in the field in which they are employed. The Administrator of a School endorsement may only be obtained by holders of the Elementary, Secondary, or a Special license to teach in Nevada.

STATE OF NEW HAMPSHIRE

State Department of Education
Bureau of Licensure and Credentialing
101 Pleasant Street
Concord, New Hampshire 03301
Phone: 603-271-2408 / Fax: 603-271-4134
Web Site: http://www.ed.state.nh.us/education/doe/organization/programsupport/boc.htm

INITIAL REQUIREMENTS AT A GLANCE:

Also needed will be items A, B, C, D, E, G, N and O - See page 2. Additional documentation includes a resume, a certificate of health, and letters of work experience for superintendent candidates. The fee is $130.00 with a renewal fee of $130.00. New Hampshire now requires a criminal record check at the time of hire. The original certificate is valid for 3 years. New Hampshire DOES belong to the Northeast Regional Common Market and maintains agreements with Pennsylvania, New Jersey and D.C., as well as the NASDTEC Certification Contract (Teachers and Support Professionals). Courses or competencies in Special Education are NOT required. Revisions are ongoing.

Renewal Requirements: Renewable every 3 years. New rules requires a minimum of 75 clock hours for recertification in one field; an additional 30 clock hours for each additional endorsement. (If you have more than three endorsements you are able to request an extension of time.) An individual may drop an endorsement, except for General Special Education, and add it back at a later date by presenting 30 hours of professional growth and a $10.00 fee. The General Special Education endorsement must be maintained if an individual holds a special education categorical endorsement.

BASIC SKILLS COMPETENCE

All candidates for initial New Hampshire teacher certification must demonstrate basic skills competence in reading, writing, and mathematics by *passing all three tests* in either the Praxis I Pre-Professional Skills Test (PPST) or Computer Based Test (CBT). The following requirements apply to all five certification alternatives. Minimum passing scores as follows:

	PPST	CBT
Reading*	174	174
Writing	172	172
Mathematics	172	172

* A composite score option is available with minimums of Reading (172), Mathematics (170), Writing (170), and a total of at least 518.

Additionally, candidates must pass the Praxis II content assessments in the areas of Biology, Chemistry, Earth/Space Science, English/Language Arts, General Science, Middle School Mathematics, Physical Science, Physics, Secondary Mathematics, and Social Studies.

CERTIFICATION SUBJECT AREAS

Administrators:	Teachers:	Career and Technical Ed:
Superintendent	Biology 7-12	Agriculture, Food, and Natural
Assistant Superintendent	Chemistry 7-12	Resources
Business Administrator	Earth/Space Science 7-12	Architecture and Construction
Curriculum Administrator	General Science 5-9	Arts, Audio-Visual Technology
Principal	Physical Science 7-12	and Communications
Associate Principal	Physics 7-12	Business Management and
District Administrator	Art	Administration
Special Education	Comprehensive Agriculture	Education and Training
Administrator	Comprehensive Business	Finance
Career and Technical Director	Comprehensive Family and	Government and Public
	Consumer Science	Administration
Educational Specialists:	Comprehensive Marketing	Health Science
School Psychologist	Comprehensive Technology	Hospitality and Tourism
Associate School Psychologist	Computer Technology	Human Services
Guidance Director	Early Childhood	Information Technology
Guidance Counselor	Elementary ...... K-6 and K-8	Law and Public Safety
Library Media Specialist	English .... 5-12 and 5-8	Manufacturing
Media Supervisor	English for Speakers of Other	Marketing, Sales and Services
Reading Specialists	Languages	Science, Technology,

Social Worker Speech-Language Specialists SAIF **Special Education:** Early Childhood Special Education General Special Education Acoustically Handicapped Emotionally Disturbed Learning Disabilities Mental Retardation Physically Handicapped Visually Handicapped	Mathematics .... 7-12 and 5-8 Music Nursery/Kindergarten Physical Education Social Studies ... 5-12 and 5-8 Theatre **World Languages:** Greek, Latin, Arabic, Chinese, French, German, Italian, Russian, and Spanish	Engineering and Mathematics Transportation, Distribution and Logistics **Other Instructional Areas:** Educational Interpreter/ Transliterator Paraeducator I Paraeducator II

PROFESSIONAL CERTIFICATES

Professional Certificates:

A. **Beginning Educator Certificate** - Valid 3 years, Renewable
   Applicants must have:
   1. Completed an approved program of professional preparation in education (as outlined below); and
   2. Been recommended by designated official of preparatory institution.
   3. Upon recommendation of Superintendent of Schools, a Beginning Educator may be eligible for an Experienced Educator Certificate at the end of the three year period.

B. **Experienced Educator Certificate** - Valid 3 years, Renewable
   Applicants must have:
   1. Met all requirements for previous levels of certification; **(OR)**
   2. Successfully completed an approved graduate program that extends clinical experience to a full year with supervision.

ALTERNATIVES FOR CERTIFICATION IN NEW HAMPSHIRE

The New Hampshire State Board of Education recognizes that persons may become qualified as educators through a variety of educational and life experiences. Therefore, the following alternatives to becoming a certified **Beginning Educator** in New Hampshire are made available to applicants.

ALTERNATIVE 1: **APPROVED PROGRAMS IN NEW HAMPSHIRE**[1]

The New Hampshire State Board of Education approves programs of professional preparation in education and the chairperson of the Education Department of each institution recommends certification to the Bureau of Credentialing.

ALTERNATIVE 2: **STATES OTHER THAN NEW HAMPSHIRE**[1]

The State of New Hampshire and the majority of states and territories of the United States have entered into an agreement concerning certification. This agreement is called the Interstate Certification Compact, usually referred to as "reciprocity."

ALTERNATIVE 3: **DEMONSTRATED COMPETENCIES AND EQUIVALENT EXPERIENCE**[1]

Designed for candidates who have gained the competencies, skills, and knowledge through means other than Alternative 1 or Alternative 2. The Alternative 3 is a process which includes both written examination and oral review. Candidates may request teaching, administrative or educational specialist certification on the basis of demonstrated competencies and equivalent experiences.

ALTERNATIVE 4: **INDIVIDUALIZED PROFESSIONAL DEVELOPMENT PLAN (RESTRICTED)**[1]

A certification process restricted to critical shortage areas, certain vocational areas, and to business administrators. A superintendent may employ a candidate who meets eligibility requirements. The superintendent of schools, or his/her designee, shall then develop an Individualized Professional Development Plan leading to full certification. Entry level requirements for all areas are available from the Bureau. A list of critical shortage areas for the following school year is published by the Bureau each

May.

ALTERNATIVE 5: **SITE BASED CERTIFICATION PLAN**[1]

An on-the-job training option which allows an individual to attain certification in elementary and secondary teaching areas if he/she has bachelor's degree, (a 2.50 GPA overall and at least 30 credits in the area they wish to pursue certification), and if a local school district is willing to assume the responsibility for training and supervising the teacher candidate. A superintendent may hire an individual who possesses a statement of eligibility issued by the Bureau of Credentialing.

[1] For additional information on Alternative Certifications, contact the Bureau or visit their web site.

LIBRARY MEDIA SPECIALIST

Effective 7/23/2003, the following requirements shall apply to the certification of a library media specialist in grades K-12[2]:

A.   Bachelor's degree; and

B.   A candidate for certification as a library media specialist shall demonstrate skills in the following areas, competencies, and knowledge through a combination of academic and supervised practical experiences in the following areas:

Administration; Ethical, legal, and responsible use of information; Collection development; Teaching and learning; and Literature

[2] For complete requirements, contact the Bureau or visit their web site.

GUIDANCE COUNSELOR / SCHOOL PSYCHOLOGIST ENDORSEMENTS

A.   **Guidance Counselor Endorsement:** Valid 3 years, Renewable
   1.   Beginning Educator Certificate requires a master's degree in guidance and counseling.
   2.   Experienced Educator Certificate requires 3 years of successful experience and 50 clock hours of staff development.

B.   **School Psychologist Endorsement:** Valid 3 years, Renewable
   1.   Beginning Educator Certificate requires a Ph.D. in school psychology leading to an approved program in school psychology, leading to a Certificate of Advanced Graduate Study (CAGS) or Doctorate.
   2.   Experienced Educator Certificate requirements same as for Guidance Counselor above.

PRINCIPAL / SUPERINTENDENT ENDORSEMENT

A.   **Principal Endorsement:** Valid 3 years, Renewable
   1.   Beginning Educator Certificate requires a New Hampshire certificate with teaching endorsement; a Master's Degree; approved Education Administration program; and a recommendation from a New Hampshire college or university.
   2.   Experienced Educator Certificate requirements same as for Guidance Counselor above.

B.   **Superintendent Endorsement:** Valid 3 years, Renewable
   1.   Have completed a state board of education approved educational administration program at the certificate of advanced graduate study (CAGS) or doctorate level; OR
   2.   Have acquired the competencies, skills and knowledge through experience in comparable leadership positions in education or other professions including:

Supervision and evaluation of program and staff effectiveness; staff development; planning for individual needs, goal setting, decision making; the change process; organizational management, including such techniques as staffing, program and personnel evaluation, office procedures and record-keeping, decision-making and negotiations; total budget process and cost analysis relative to program effectiveness; communications and human relations; community and school partnership development, including continuing education; the law and education; curriculum theory and development; school facility design and utilization; and reporting procedures and practices.

STATE OF NEW JERSEY

Department of Education
Office of Teacher Licensure
PO Box 500
Trenton, New Jersey 08625-0500
Phone: 609-292-2070 / Fax: 609-292-3768
Web Site: **http://www.state.nj.us/njded/educators/license/**

INITIAL REQUIREMENTS AT A GLANCE:

Also needed will be items A, B, E, G (when applicable,) H, I, M and N - See page 2. Fees: $170 for instructional *Certificates of Eligibility* (which include the issuance of a Provisional or Standard Certificate requiring tests); $150 for those not requiring tests;$200 for Administrative certificates; $95 for a Standard Certificate requiring a test and $75 when no test is required. Scores on Praxis II Subject Assessment tests or the National Teacher's Examination Programs Specialty Area tests ARE required. Some requirements have changed (see table below.) The Standard Certificate is valid for LIFE. New Jersey DOES belong to the Interstate Certification Compact and the NASDTEC Interstate Contract (Teachers only). A course in Special Education is NOT required. Applicants must pass an examination in physiology and hygiene, including the effects of narcotics and alcohol.

Renewal Requirements: Professional development for all active instructional and educational services school personnel whereby they must complete 100 clock-hours of State-approved continuing professional development and/or in-service training every five years.

Revised Praxis II Testing Requirements:

Effective 12/1/2007, the State Board adopted new Praxis tests and respective qualifying scores for some certificates. These include tests and scores for Early Childhood, replacement or updated tests for a number of the sciences, and basic skills tests in reading, writing, and mathematics for vocational certificates whose applicants do not possess a bachelor's or associate's degree. These tests are generally required of applicants, however, there will be grandfathering for students enrolled in approved teacher preparation programs:

Test	Test #	Score
Biology: Content Knowledge test	0235	152
Chemistry: Content Knowledge test	0245	152
Early Childhood: Content Knowledge test	0022	159
General Science: Content Knowledge test	0435	152
Earth Science: Content Knowledge test	0571	153
Physics: Content Knowledge test	0265	141
PPST: Reading test	0710	175
PPST: Writing test	0720	173
PPST: Math test	0730	174

GENERAL REQUIREMENTS[1]
(All Instructional Certificates)

A. Bachelor's Degree from an accredited college or university;

B. Passing score in Praxis Program Specialty Area test(s) for secondary teachers and in the Content Knowledge test for elementary teachers;

C. Completion of a major in the liberal arts or sciences for elementary education. Completion of a major in the subject teaching field for and initial endorsement in a subject field. For additional endorsements, completion of at least 30 semester hours in a coherent major in the subject teaching field; and

D. Completion of a Provisional Teacher Program (alternate route to certification) or an approved college teacher preparation program.

[1] Minimum grade point average (GPA) has been raised from 2.5 to 2.75 for beginning teachers who

graduate after September 1, 2004.

PROVISIONAL TEACHER PROGRAM
(All Grade Levels)

Major revisions were adopted in January, 2004 establishing a sequential 3-step licensure process as follows:

A.   **CERTIFICATE OF ELIGIBILITY (CE):**
This certificate provides an applicant with the opportunity to seek employment. It is NOT a teaching license.
1.   Bachelor's (or Master's) Degree;
2.   Secondary School candidates (N-12): a major in the subject teaching field (e.g., Biology, English, Mathematics), or, Elementary School candidates (N-8): a major in the liberal arts or sciences; and
3.   Completion of the DOE's test requirements.
(OR)

B.   **CERTIFICATE OF ELIGIBILITY WITH ADVANCED STANDING (CEAS):** See A.1 (1-3) above.
Additionally, requires the completion of a state approved college teacher training program culminating in supervised student teaching.

C.   **PROVISIONAL CERTIFICATE:** Valid 2 years.
1.   Applicant must hold a CE or a CEAS (see above);
2.   Applicant has accepted an offer of employment; and
3.   Employing school district or approved non-public school has agreed to provide a Beginning Teacher Induction Program leading to standard certfication.

   ALTERNATE ROUTE TO PROVISIONAL CERTIFICATION:
An alternate route to a provisional certificate is also available. For complete information, visit the web site or contact the Department.

D.   **STANDARD CERTIFICATE:** Valid for life.
Successful completion of a district/school induction program while serving under a provisional certificate for the first year of employment **OR** a state approved college teacher preparation program and one year of full time teaching under a valid state license.

E.   **EMERGENCY CERTIFICATE:** Valid 1 year.
This is a substandard one-year license issued only in limited fields of educational services.

F.   **COUNTY SUBSTITUTE CREDENTIAL:** Allows the holder to temporarily perform the duties of a fully licensed and regularly employed teacher.

CERTIFICATES AND ENDORSEMENTS

For a complete listing of New Jersey certificates and endorsements, please visit:
http://www.state.nj.us/njded/educators/license/endorsements/endorsements3.htm

SCHOOL LIBRARY MEDIA SPECIALIST

   The school **Library Media Specialist Endorsement** is required for any person who serves as a school library media specialist in grades preschool through 12.
A.   To be eligible for the endorsement, a candidate must hold a master's degree from a regionally accredited college or university and complete one of the following:
   1. A graduate curriculum approved by the Department as the basis for issuing this certificate;
   OR
   2. A program of graduate studies consisting of at least 36 semester-hour credits in a coherent sequence of studies.
B.   To be eligible for the **Standard** Educational Services Certificate with a **School Library Media Specialist Endorsement**, a candidate shall:

1. Meet the requirements above; **AND**

2. Hold a **Standard** New Jersey Instructional Certificate or complete a year-long school-based residency program in a school library media center under a **Provisional Certificate** and college-level study in educational theory, curriculum design and integration, teaching methodology, student/learning development, and behavior management. A certified school administrator, principal or supervisor shall provide supervision during the candidate's provisional year.

C.   An **Emergency Certificate** may be issued to a candidate who meets the following requirements:

1. Matriculation in an approved school library media program; and

2. Completion of a minimum of 12 graduate-level semester-hour credits in school library media.

D.   Candidates in possession of a written evaluation completed by the office prior to January 20, 2004 will have until January 20, 2009 to complete the requirements set forth in the written evaluation.

E.   The following individuals are eligible to receive the standard school media specialist endorsement:

1. Those holding a permanent New Jersey school librarian or standard educational media specialist endorsement; and

2. Those holding a standard New Jersey instructional certificate or a valid out-of-State instructional license who have completed a graduate degree program in a regionally accredited institution with specialization in library science, school library media, or equivalent media areas.

F.   Individuals holding the school librarian or educational media specialist endorsement may serve in any position requiring the school library media specialist endorsement.

G.   Individuals in possession of a written evaluation completed by the office prior to January 20, 2004 will have until January 20, 2009 to complete the approved program or the requirements set forth in the written evaluation.

SCHOOL COUNSELOR ENDORSEMENT

The school counselor endorsement authorizes the holder to perform school counseling services in grades preschool through 12.

A.   To be eligible for the **Standard Educational Services Certificate** with a school counselor endorsement, a candidate must hold a master's or higher degree from a regionally accredited college or university, and complete one of the following:

1. A Department-approved graduate curriculum in school counseling; or

2. A minimum of 48 graduate semester hour credits

B.   A candidate who has completed a master's or higher degree from a regionally accredited college or university whose school counseling program meets the standards of the Council for Accreditation of Counseling and Related Educational Programs (CACREP) will be issued a **Standard School Counselor Certificate**.

C.   The Office may issue an **Emergency Certificate** upon the request of the county superintendent to a candidate who meets the following requirements:

1. A bachelor's degree from a regionally accredited college or university; and

2. Fifteen graduate semester hour credits in guidance/counseling.

D.   Applicants in possession of a written evaluation completed by the office prior to January 20, 2004 will have until January 20, 2009 to complete the requirements set forth in the written evaluation.

SCHOOL PSYCHOLOGIST ENDORSEMENT

The school psychologist endorsement authorizes the holder to serve as a psychologist in grades preschool through 12.

A.   To be eligible for the **Standard** Educational Services Certificate with a **School Psychologist Endorsement**, a candidate must hold a master's or higher degree from a regionally accredited college or university and complete the following:

1. A Department-approved graduate curriculum or a minimum of 60 semester-hour graduate credits;

2. A practicum of 300 clock hours that consists of a sequence of closely supervised on-campus and field-based activities designed to develop and evaluate a candidate's mastery of distinct professional skills consistent with program and/or course goals;

3. An externship of 1,200 clock hours. A minimum of 600 clock hours must be completed in a school setting with school age children. The remaining 600 clock hours may be completed in a

school or clinical setting or may be completed under an emergency certificate while concurrently participating in an approved college or university school psychology program. Externship experiences completed in a school setting must be supervised by a person holding a standard New Jersey or out-of-State school psychologist certificate; and

4. Persons who completed a master's or higher degree in clinical psychology from a regionally accredited college or university and can present official documentation of 600 clock hours of experience as a psychologist working with children in a clinical setting may meet the school psychology externship and practicum requirements by completing a 900 clock hour school psychology externship in a New Jersey school, with school age children, under a New Jersey emergency certificate.

B.   School districts desiring authorization for the employment of an extern under **Emergency Certification** should submit a request to the county superintendent for preliminary approval. If the county superintendent grants preliminary approval, the emergency certificate will be forwarded to the applicant.

C.   Candidates who completed a master's or higher degree in clinical psychology from a regionally accredited college or university with a minimum of 60 semester hours that include study in the required areas and can present official documentation of 600 clock hours of experience as a psychologist working with children in a clinical setting may meet the school psychology externship and practicum requirements by completing a 900 clock hour school psychology externship in a New Jersey school, with school age children, under a **School Psychologist Emergency Certificate**.

D.   The Office will issue a Standard New Jersey School Psychologist Certificate to holders of a currently valid Nationally Certified School Psychologist (NCSP) license.

E.   The Office may issue an **Emergency Certificate** upon the request of the county superintendent to a candidate who meets the following requirements:

1. A bachelor's degree from a regionally accredited college or university; and

2. Official college transcripts showing successful completion of a minimum of 40 semester-hour graduate credits applicable towards standard school psychologist certification in approved areas. This must include study and practicum experience in the required areas of cognitive assessment, personality assessment and school consultation.

ADMINISTRATIVE CERTIFICATE[2]

To be eligible for the standard administrative certificate with a school administrator endorsement, the candidate shall:

Possess a **Provisional Certificate**; and

Complete a one to two-year State-approved residency program while employed under provisional certification in a public school district. The residency program shall:

Take place in a functioning public school district environment, and will require the candidate to develop a thorough understanding of New Jersey Standards: the Core Curriculum Content Standards; the Professional Standards for Teachers. Candidates shall demonstrate that understanding by promoting excellence in teaching and learning and providing educational leadership to the district;

Be conducted in accordance with a standard agreement issued by the Department and entered into by the Department, the employing school district, the candidate and the residency mentor. No residency program may be undertaken without a valid agreement;

Be administered by a State-appointed mentor, an experienced administrator who has completed a State-approved orientation, and who shall supervise and verify completion of all required experiences and training by the candidate. The mentor and the local board shall, at the start of the residency, submit to the Department a written recommendation on State-developed forms concerning any areas of professional experience that should be waived and any additional teaching or other special experiences, if any, that the individual candidate should complete before achieving standard certification. Department review and subsequent approval shall consider the candidate's past work experience and recommended standards-based performance goals during residency, and shall be specified in the standard written agreement; and

Provide professional experiences, training and instruction as defined in the Professional Standards for School Leaders and in the areas of district planning and policy formulation; board of education operations and relations; supervision of district wide programs of curriculum, instruction and student services; collegial management, participatory decision-making and professional governance; the roles, supervision and evaluation of central office staff and school

104

principals; district financial, legal and business operations; management of district operations; school facilities; labor relations and collective bargaining; government and community relations; and school law.

2 For complete Administrative certification details, contact the Department.

STATE OF NEW MEXICO

Department of Education
Professional Licensure Bureau
300 Don Gaspar Street
Santa Fe, New Mexico 87501-2786
Phone: 505-827-6587 / Fax: 505-827-4148
Web Site: **http://www.ped.state.nm.us/div/ais/lic/index.html**

INITIAL REQUIREMENTS AT A GLANCE:

Also needed are items A, B, C, E, G, J and Q - See page 2. The fee for the initial license is $65.00. There is a $29.25 fingerprint card and background check fee. Effective 7/1/01, a state administered licensure test is NOT required for out-of-state teachers who have completed an equivalent test to the New Mexico test, or have verifiable experience in their state. New Mexico DOES belong to the NASDTEC Interstate Contract (Teachers and Administrators).Courses or competencies in Special Education are NOT required.

Renewal Requirements:
Teachers:
Level 1 Provisional Licenses are valid for 5 years. Completion of a one-year supervised mentorship and passage of a Professional Development Dossier (PDD). The fee for higher levels is $185.00 and includes the cost for processing candidate dossiers.
Level 2 Professional Licenses are valid for 9 years. Verification of satisfactory demonstration of teaching competencies by the employing district is required. The fee for the same level renewal is $35.00. If advancing to Level 3 with a master's degree, passage of a PDD is required. The fee for the higher levels is $185.00 and includes the cost of processing dossiers.
Level 3A Instructional Leader Licenses are valid for 9 years. Verification of satisfactory demonstration of teaching competencies by the employing district is required. The fee for same level renewal is $35.00.
Administrators:
Level 3B Educational Administrative Licenses are valid for 9 years. Verification of satisfactory demonstration of administratione

OUT-OF-STATE TEACHER AND ADMINISTRATOR LICENSE APPLICANTS

Possess a bachelor's and/or master's degree from a regionally accredited college or university; possess a valid standard certificate/license/authorization issued by another state/country, or National Board Certification; have completed an educator preparation program; have passed teacher exams; and have completed satisfactory teaching experience.

Teachers:
Bachelor's degree with exam scores or less than 3 years of teaching experience - Level 1
Bachelor's degree with 3 or more years of teaching experience - Level 2
Master's degree with 6 or more years of teaching experience - Level 3A

Administrators:
Master's degree and 7 years of teaching experience and/or administrative experience.

LEVELS OF LICENSURE
Applicable to All Levels

I.	**Level 1 License** - Valid for five years. Renewable only if never used or for years not used up to five years if notarized letter provided.
- A.	Bachelors degree;
- B.	General education requirements: 54 semester hours (see individual level licenses;)
- C.	Professional Education requirements as determined by the Public Education Dept. (see individual level licenses;) and
- D.	Teaching field study appropriate to license.

II.	**Level 2 License** (*Continuing instructional*) - Valid for nine years. Renewable.
- A	Meet all Level 1 requirements; and
- B.	Completed Professional Development Dossier (PDD)
- C.	Verification by local superintendent that applicant has met all Public Education Dept.'s prescribed competencies.

III.	**Level 3-A License** (*Instructional Leadership*) - Valid for nine years. Renewable.
- A.	Meet all Level 2 requirements;
- B.	PPD and Masters degree **OR** National Board Certification; and
- C.	Verification by local superintendent that applicant has met all Public Education Dept.'s prescribed competencies.

IV.	**Level 3-B License** (*Administration and Management*) - Valid for nine years. Renewable.
- A.	Meet all Level 3-A requirements;
- B.	Master's degree;
- C.	Administrative internship/apprenticeship completion; and
- D.	18 graduate semester hours in educational administration mandated by Public Education Dept. requirements.

LICENSURE IN ELEMENTARY EDUCATION
(Grades K-8)

I.	**APPLICABILITY:**
This regulation governs licensure in elementary education for those persons seeking such licensure on or after July 1, 1989.

II.	**REQUIREMENTS:**
Persons seeking Level 1 licensure in elementary education pursuant to the provisions of this regulation shall meet the following requirements:
- A.	Bachelor's degree from a regionally accredited college or university and including, for those students first entering a college or university beginning in the fall of 1986, the following (in semester hours):
  1.	English 12
  2.	History 12
    (including American history and western civilization)
  3.	Mathematics 6
  4.	Government, economics or sociology 6
  5.	Science 12
    (including biology, chemistry, physics, geology, zoology, or botany)
  6.	Fine arts 6
- B.	Credits from a regionally accredited college or university which include (in semester hours):
  1.	Professional education: elementary course work approved by the Public Education Dept.
    . . . . 30 - 36
    Including:
    - a.	completion of the Public Education Dept.'s approved functional areas and related competencies in professional education, and;
    - b.	a mandatory student teaching component.
  2.	One teaching field such as mathematics, science(s), language arts, reading, or social studies (or other content related areas) 24-36
- C.	Passage of the New Mexico Teacher Assessments **(OR)**

Hold a valid certificate issued by the National Board for Professional Teaching Standards for the appropriate grade level and type.

LICENSURE IN SECONDARY EDUCATION
(Grades 7-12)

I.   **APPLICABILITY:**

This regulation governs licensure in secondary education for those persons seeking such licensure on or after July 1, 1989.

II.   **REQUIREMENTS:**

Persons seeking Level 1 licensure in secondary education pursuant to the provisions of this regulation shall meet the following requirements:

A.   See Elementary Licensure II, A;

B.   Credits from a regionally accredited college or university which include:

1.   Professional education: Secondary course work approved by the Public Education Dept. 24-30
Including:

a.   completion of the Public Education Dept.'s approved functional areas and related competencies in professional education, and;

b.   a mandatory student teaching component.

2.   One teaching field such as mathematics, science(s), language arts, reading, or social studies (or other content related areas), twelve (12) hours of which must be in upper division courses as defined by the college or university 24-36

C.   See Elementary Licensure, II, C.

LIBRARY MEDIA SPECIALIST[1]

Persons seeking an endorsement in library media to a New Mexico educator license must complete the following core requirements:

A.   Hold a minimum of a baccalaureate degree from a regionally accredited college or university,

B.   Have completed an approved educator preparation program that includes at least 14 weeks of supervised student teaching, **and**

C.   Pass the Public Education Dept.'s required licensure examination.

Additionally, the following are the broad competencies for entry-level library media specialists:
Professionalism (Ethics, Professional Development, and Advocacy);
Communication and Collaboration;
Collection Development and Management;
Shared Instructional Leadership;
Technology Information Management;
Organization; and
Administration

[1]   For complete information about the requirements and competencies, visit their web site.

LICENSURE IN SCHOOL COUNSELING
(Grades K-12)

I.   **REQUIREMENTS:**

A.   Bachelor's degree from a regionally accredited college or university; **AND** either B1 or B2 below **OR** C.

B.   Either:

1.   Master's degree in school counseling from either New Mexico college or university, or a regionally accredited college or university with competencies in the area of school counseling;
(OR)

2.   Master's degree in a discipline other than school counseling and 36-42 graduate

hours in school counseling including a practicum in a school setting.

C.   Passage of exam.

(OR)

C.   National certified school counselor credential issued by the National Board for Certified Counselors.

LICENSURE IN EDUCATIONAL ADMINISTRATION
(GRADES K-12)

I.   **REQUIREMENTS:**

In addition to qualifications for Level 2 or Level 3-A teacher licensure, persons seeking licensure in educational administration shall additionally meet the following requirements:

A.   Bachelor's degree and Master's degree from a regionally accredited college or university and including, for those students first entering a college or university beginning in the fall of 1986, an apprenticeship. The apprenticeship must either:

    1.   be completed at a college or university with an educational administration program approved by the Public Education Dept. and consist of a minimum of 180 clock hours to include time at the beginning and end of the school year. A passing grade on the apprenticeship will verify completion of this requirement **(OR)**

    2.   be completed under the supervision of a local school superintendent or a private school official at the school and consist of a minimum of 180 clock hours to include time at the beginning and end of the school year. The local school superintendent will verify that the apprenticeship has met the Public Education Dept.'s adopted competencies for educational administration. Such verification will be considered completion of this requirement; and

    3.   Passage of exam.

B.   A valid Level 2 teaching license if coursework for administration was started *before* April, 2003, or a valid Level 3-A teaching license if administrative coursework started *after* April, 2003. A Level I license will not meet this requirement. Candidate must teach under the Level 3A license for one full school year before qualifying for the administration license.

C.   Eighteen (18) semester hours of graduate credit in an educational administration program approved by the Public Education Dept. The eighteen semester hour program must address the Public Education Dept.'s approved functional areas and related competencies in educational administration. Colleges and universities may offer these hours through their educational administration, public administration, business administration, or other appropriate departments.

D.   See Elementary Licensure, II, C.

STATE OF NEW YORK

New York State Education Department
Office of Teaching Initiatives
5N Education Building
89 Washington Avenue
Albany, New York 12234
Phone: 518-474-3901 / Fax: 518-473-0271
Web Site: **http://www.highered.nysed.gov/tcert/**

INITIAL REQUIREMENTS AT A GLANCE:

Also needed will be items A, B (original,) E, G, I, J and K - See page 2. The fee is $100.00. Fingerprinting fee: $94.25. Satisfactory scores on the Liberal Arts and Sciences Test (LAST) portion and the Assessment of Teaching Skills Written (ATS-W) test of the New York State Teacher Certification Examination ARE required. New York DOES belong to the NASDTEC Interstate

Contract (Teachers, Support Professionals, and Vocational Educators). New York participates in the Interstate New Teacher Assessment and Support Consortium (INTASC). Course(s) or competencies in special education ARE required. All teaching certificates require preparation for teaching minority cultures, students from both sexes, students from homes where English is not the primary language, handicapped students, and gifted students. Workshops on the identification of suspected child abuse and prevention of school violence are required. Contact the Office for further information on workshop requirements.

Major revisions took effect on 02/02/2004. See excerpts of the certification requirements below. Please contact the Office of Teaching Initiatives web site for further details.

Continuing Requirements: 175 clock hours of approved professional development are required. Fees: $100.00 (Basic); $50.00 for college recommended. NYSTCE test fees vary by test.

Certificate Requirements
Requirements for First (Initial) Certificate: **(Except for career and technical subjects within fields of agriculture, business and marketing, family and consumer sciences, health, a technical area or a trade):**
Baccalaureate teacher preparation program completion for first certificate
May qualify through interstate reciprocity
Three examinations: LAST, ATS-W, and CST (Except for Speech and Hearing Disabilities)
National Board certification qualifies candidate for initial certificate
Validity of First (Initial) Certificate:
Valid for 5 years, 1 year extension possible with 24 semester hours of approved graduate study
May not be renewed
May be reissued, with completion of additional professional development
Requirements for Professional Certificate:
Master's degree
Three years teaching experience
No examinations required (CST required for speech and Language Disabilities)
One-year mentored teaching experience
Validity of Professional Certificate:
Validity maintained through completion of professional development
Professional Development Requirement: **Key Features:**
175 hrs required for all professional certificate holders;   75 hrs required for level III teaching assistants. Five-year cycle. Pro-rated requirements for those not teaching in public schools. Follows districts' professional development plans. Due process provisions for certificate holders not meeting requirements. Reporting requirement for schools and individuals. Provision for restoration of suspended certificate

CERTIFICATE TYPES AND DURATIONS

A. Initial: *Valid 5 years with the possibility of a one-year time extension.* The Initial certificate is the entry-level classroom teaching and school building leader certificate, and is issued for a specific subject/grade level (e.g. Biology 7-12).

B. Professional: *Continuously valid upon completion of required professional development hours on a*

5-year cycle. The Professional certificate is the second-level classroom teaching certificate, and is issued to a holder of an Initial certificate with the completion of educational, experience, and school leader requirements for the Professional certificate.

C. Transitional: The Transitional certificate is a credential issued in specific situations to candidates who have not yet met the requirements for an Initial classroom teaching certificate, but who have an employment and mentoring commitment from a public school district and who may be enrolled in an intense, time-shortened preparation program.

D. Teaching Assistant: The Teaching Assistant certificate authorizes individuals to provide direct instructional services to students under the general supervision of a certified teacher. There are four levels issued: Level I, Level II, Level III, and Pre-Professional.

E. Provisional: *Valid for 5 years.* The Provisional certificate is the entry-level certificate in New York State for certification in pupil personnel service titles.

F. Permanent: *Continuously valid with no further requirements.* The Permanent certificate is the second-level certificate in pupil personnel service titles and administrative and supervisory service titles, and is issued to holders of a Provisional certificate with the completion of educational, experience, and testing requirements for the Permanent certificate.

INITIAL EARLY CHILDHOOD EDUCATION (Birth-grade 2)
CHILDHOOD EDUCATION (1-6)
MIDDLE CHILDHOOD EDUCATION (5-9)
(Valid 5 Years)

Pathway: Approved Teacher Preparation Program
Requirements:
A. Completion of a NYS Registered program in Early Childhood Education (Birth -2), Childhood Education (Grades 1-6), or Middle Childhood Education - Generalist (5-9)
B. Institutional recommendation - Childhood Education (Grades 1-6)
C. New York State Teacher Certification exam - Liberal Arts and Sciences test (LAST)
D. New York State Teacher Certification exam - Elementary Assessment of Teaching Skills (ATS-W)
E. Content Specialty Test (CST) - Multi-subject
F. Fingerprint clearance.

PROFESSIONAL CERTIFICATE
(Continuously valid with Professional Development)

A. Hold a valid Initial Certificate - Childhood Education (Grades 1-6)
B. Master's degree
C. Graduate coursework content core - Liberal Arts and Sciences - 12 S.H.
D. Paid, full-time classroom teaching - 3 Yrs.
E. Mentored experience - 1 Yr.
NOTE: The Professional certificate remains continuously valid, provided that the certificate holder completes the professional development requirement. With the issuance of a Professional certificate, a 5-year professional development cycle is established and the required professional development must be completed within each succeeding 5-year cycle in order for the certificate to remain valid.

INITIAL SPECIALIST IN MIDDLE CHILDHOOD EDUCATION (5-9)
ADOLESCENCE EDUCATION (7-12) - *Issued in Specific Subject Areas*
(Valid 5 years)

A. Bachelor's Degree from a regionally accredited institution;
B. General Education Core . . . . **30 sem hours**
C. Content Core (Minimum grades: Undergraduate: C; Graduate: B minus) . . . . **30 sem hours**

Must include studies specific to the subject of the certificate sought.

D.   Pedagogy Core . . . . **21 sem hours**
       Same required **Core** coursework as for Elementary Certificate above;

E.   40 days college supervised teaching or as an employed teacher within the range of grades and subject area of the certificate sought; and

F.   Satisfactory scores on the Liberal Arts and Sciences Test; the Assessment of Teaching Skills-Written (appropriate to the grade level); and the Content Specialty Test (appropriate to the grade level) from the New York State Teacher Certification Examination Program.

PROFESSIONAL SECONDARY CERTIFICATE
(Continuously valid with Professional Development)

Same as **Professional Childhood Certificate**, except on secondary level.

INITIAL LIBRARY MEDIA SPECIALIST (all grades)

A.   Bachelor's Degree from a regionally accredited institution;

B.   General Education Core . . . . **30 sem hours**

C.   Content Core (Minimum course grades: Undergraduate: C; Graduate: B minus) . . **30 sem hours**
       To include graduate level study in library science (including instructional and assistive technology);

D.   Pedagogy Core . . . . **21 sem hours**
       Same required **Core** coursework as for Elementary Certificate above;

E.   40 day college-supervised practicum (20 days in an elementary school and 20 days in a secondary school).

F.   Satisfactory scores on the Liberal Arts and Sciences Test; Assessment of Teaching Skills-Written; and the Content Specialty Test for Library Media Specialists from the New York State Teacher Certification Examination Program.

PROVISIONAL SCHOOL COUNSELOR (All Grades)
(Valid 5 years)

A.   Completion of program registered and approved by the Department, (or)

B.   Evidence that requirements below have been met:
      1.   Bachelor's Degree from a regionally accredited institution;
      2.   30 semester hours of graduate study in the field of school counseling from an approved institution; and
      3.   A supervised practicum in school counseling.

PERMANENT SCHOOL COUNSELOR CERTIFICATE
(Valid for Life)

A.   Satisfaction of the requirements for provisional certificate;

B.   Addition 30 semester hours of graduate study in school counseling;

C.   Master's degree from an approved institution; and

D.   2 years of elementary and/or secondary school experience in pupil personnel services.

PROVISIONAL SCHOOL ADMINISTRATOR AND SUPERVISOR
Initial School Building Leader (SBL) Certifcate *

Pathway: Approved Teacher Preparation Program
This pathway refers to programs specifically designed and registered with the New York State Education Department to qualify students for New York State teacher, pupil personnel, or administrative certification. A listing of these pre-approved programs is available through our Inventory of Registered Programs. Candidates applying under this pathway are recommended by their college or university for a certificate in the subject area(s) of the registered program. Specified non-coursework requirements, such as the New York State Teacher Certification Examinations and fingerprint clearance, must also be satisfied.

Requirements:

A. Completion of a NYS Registered Program by 09/01/2007 - School Administrator/Supervisor
B. Institutional Recommendation - School Administrator/Supervisor
C. Additional Education - Masters Degree
D. Paid, full-time Admin experience - 2 Yrs
E. Paid, full-time Admin/PPS/Classroom Teaching experience - 3 Yrs
F. Fingerprint Clearance
G. Citizenship Status - INS Permanent Residence or U.S. Citizenship

Pathway: Certificate Progression

This pathway is for individuals who hold a valid New York State entry-level certificate (such as an Initial or Provisional certificate). They may progress to the advanced-level credential (such as a Professional or Permanent certificate) by meeting the requirements for that certificate.

Requirements:

A. Hold a Valid Provisional Certificate - School Administrator/Supervisor
B. Additional Education - Masters Degree
C. Paid, full-time Admin experience - 2 Yrs
D. Workshop - Child Abuse Identification
E. Workshop - School Violence Intervention and Prevention
F. Fingerprint Clearance
G. Citizenship Status - INS Permanent Residence or U.S. Citizenship

* For complete SBL requirements, visit contact the Office of Teaching Initiatives web site and search on "Administration and Pupil Personnel Services".

STATE OF NORTH CAROLINA

Department of Public Instruction
Licensure Section
6365 Mail Service Center
Raleigh, North Carolina 27699-6365
Phone: 919-807-3300 / 800-577-7994 (in-state) / Fax: 919-807-3350
Web Site: **http://www.ncpublicschools.org/licensure/**

INITIAL REQUIREMENTS AT A GLANCE:

Also needed will be items A, B (original for each degree earned), C, E, G, I, O, and P - See page 2. The fee is $85.00. Passing scores on the Praxis II are required for licensure, but not necessarily with the application. The Initial License is valid for three years. A continuing license is valid for five years. North Carolina DOES belong to the Interstate Certification Compact and the NASDTEC Interstate Contract (Teachers, Support Professional, Administrators, and Vocational Educators). North Carolina is a member of the Interstate New Teacher Assessment and Support Consortium (INTASC). Course(s) or competencies in Special Education ARE required.

Renewal Requirements: Requires completion of 15 Renewal Units (RUs) where 1 semester hours equals 1.5 RUs, or 10 semester hours every five years. Locally sponsored training programs and conferences can be approved for RUs as well. The renewal fee is $55.00.

LICENSURE CATEGORIES

Standard Professional 1 (SP1) Licenses are valid for three years. To be issued a SP1 License, an individual must have:

A.   completed a state approved teacher education program from a regionally accredited college or university, or

B.   completed another state's approved alternative route to licensure, met the federal requirements to be designated as "Highly Qualified," and earned a bachelor's degree from a regionally accredited college.

Standard Professional 2 (SP2) Licenses are valid for five years. Teachers who are fully licensed and "Highly Qualified" (as defined in the NCLB Act) in another state who have three or more years of teaching experience in another state AND who meet NC's Praxis testing requirements OR have National Board Certification are issued the SP2 license.

MEDIA COORDINATOR

REQUIREMENTS:

A.   completion of an approved program for a media coordinator at the master's degree level or above,

    (OR)

B.   completion of an approved program after July 1, 1984, allows a provisional license upon employment with requirements to update to master's degree level, or obtain a provisional media coordinator license

C.   Praxis Library Media Specialist test

GUIDANCE COUNSELOR
(Valid 5 years, renewable)

REQUIREMENTS:

A.   Master's Degree or higher earned degree from a regionally accredited college or university with an approved program in guidance and/or school counseling;

B.   Minimum required score on the Praxis test; and

C.   Recommendation from the preparing institution.

SCHOOL PSYCHOLOGIST
(Valid 5 years, renewable)

REQUIREMENTS:

A.   Sixth year approved program and Praxis specialty area test.

ADMINISTRATION

PRINCIPAL REQUIREMENTS:

A.   Master's Degree from a regionally accredited institution including the completion of an approved program in administration;

B.   Minimum required scores on the School Leaders Licensure Assessment (SLLA) administered by ETS; and

C.   Recommendation from the preparing institution.

SUPERINTENDENT REQUIREMENTS:

A.   6th year, advanced degree minimum plus 1 year service as principal.

B.   While a superintendent's license is preferred, under some circumstances a local board of education may employ a superintendent without a license. Contact the Licensure Section for details.

North Dakota Department of Public Instruction
Education Standards and Practices Board
2718 Gateway Avenue, Suite 303
Bismarck, North Dakota 58503-0585
Phone: 701-328-9641 / Fax: 701-328-9647
Web Site: **http://www.nd.gov/espb/**

INITIAL REQUIREMENTS AT A GLANCE:

Also needed will be items A, B, C, E, H, I, J, K, N and O - See page 2. Current fees: $30.00 (application packet fee); $70.00 (initial license); $175.00 (transcript review fee for out-of-state candidates). There is a $52.00 fingerprint fee. Passing scores on the Praxis I PPST are required after 7/1/2002. The original certificate is valid for 2 years. North Dakota DOES belong to the Interstate Certification Compact and the NASDTEC Interstate Contract (Teachers). North Dakota is not a member of Interstate New Teacher Assessment and Support Consortium (INTASC). Courses and/or competencies in Special Education ARE required. A minimum overall GPA of 2.5 is required for all applicants.

Renewal Requirements: Fee: $125.00. **Teachers** - A five-year renewal may be issued with 18 months of full-time successful teaching experience in the state. Each renewal of the five-year certificate requires four (4) semester hours of work. **Elementary Principal** - 4 semester hours of teacher training in fields of administration, supervision, or subject matter fields; and successful professional performance. **Secondary Principal** - Six workshops or conferences, plus 2 semester hours of course work in related administrative field; **OR** 4 semester hours of related administrative course work. **Superintendent** - Four (4) semester hours of additional work or two (2) semester hours additional work plus attendance at state, regional, or national conferences, and successful recommendation by supervisor.

LICENSURE TYPES AND LEVELS[1]

Initial License (Two-Year): Issued to first-time applicants who have met all of the ND requirements for licensure but have not taught or been under a contract for 18 months. The requirements include the completed application form, official transcripts showing a bachelor of science degree in education, recommendation by the college of education, three signed recommendations, completed fingerprint cards and all fees.

Regular (Five-Year): Issued to individuals who have met all of the requirements for a ND Educator's Professional License and have successfully taught 18 months (full-time equivalent) in the state of North Dakota. Individuals must be under contract at least thirty days of the five-year period and complete four semester hours of re-education.

30-Year (Life): A license issued to a teacher who has held a ND license for 30 years. Expiration: none

Level I - the individual still has educational or employment requirements to meet before receiving the regular Level II license, or that they are not currently maintaining contracted employment.
Note: Life Certificates will appear as a Level I since they do not report their status thru renewals.

Level II - the individual has met all of the basic requirements for a regular North Dakota Educators' Professional License. Full text of the rules and standards are available from the office of the Education Standards and Practices Board (ESPB).

Level III - the individual has earned advanced degrees beyond the bachelors level (masters, specialist, or doctoral), or National Board for Professional Teaching Standards (NBPTS) advanced licensure.

For a complete listing of licensure types and levels, visit North Dakota's web site.

ELEMENTARY SCHOOL
(K-8, 1-8 and 5-8)

North Dakota Educator's **Professional Certificate**: (Valid 2 years, Renewable)
A.   Bachelor's Degree from an accredited college approved to offer teacher education. An overall GPA of 2.5 minimum in a state approved program; and
B.   Professional requirements (credits in professional education including student teaching, semester hours) 34

SECONDARY SCHOOL
(K-12)

North Dakota Educator's Professional Certificate: (Valid 2 years, Renewable as in Elementary)
A.   Same as Elementary School A and B except professional hours are 26; and
B.   Certifiable major and/or minor.

LIBRARY MEDIA SPECIALIST[2]

A.   Bachelor's degree;
B.   Valid North Dakota Educator's Professional License; and
C.   Complete coursework in library media from a state-approved program.

[2]   North Dakota also has credentials for Librarian and Library Media Director. For details, contact the Board or visit their web site.

SCHOOL COUNSELOR

Professional Credential - Elementary, Secondary or K - 12 (First year on a provisional basis):

A.   Master's Degree with specified core guidance courses and practicum.
B.   two (2) years of teaching experience or related human services experience.
C.   valid North Dakota Educator's Professional License.

SCHOOL PSYCHOLOGIST[3]

A.   Master's degree in school psychology from an accredited institution; and
B.   Supervised practicum or internship of 350 clock hours in a school setting.

[3]   If applicant does not hold a valid elementary or secondary education certificate, they may qualify for a restricted license.

ELEMENTARY PRINCIPAL

Elementary School Principal's Credential (valid 5 years):

A.   Master's Degree with graduate work in elementary education (sem. hrs.) 20
      (Must include elementary education, elementary supervision, elementary curriculum, as well as content fields);
B.   North Dakota Educator's Professional Certificate;
C.   Major, Minor, or endorsement in elementary education; and
D.   Three years of teaching or administration at the elementary level.

SECONDARY PRINCIPAL

Secondary School Principal's Credential:
A.   Master's Degree with major or equivalent in secondary school administration from an approved

institution;
B.   Major or equivalent (sem. hrs.) 20
C.   Four (4) years of successful teaching and/or administrative experience at secondary level; and
D.   North Dakota Professional Educator's Certificate.

SUPERINTENDENT

A.   Master's Degree in school administration;
B.   North Dakota Educator's Professional Certificate;
C.   Credits (sem. hrs.) in administration for both elementary and secondary school fields 20
D.   Four (4) years of successful experience, two in administrative position, in a accredited system.

STATE OF OHIO

Ohio Department of Education
Office of Educator Licensure
25 South Front Street, Mail Stop 105
Columbus, Ohio 43215-4183
Phone: 614-466-3593
Web: **http://www.ode.state.oh.us/GD/Templates/Pages/ODE/ODEDefaultPage.aspx?page=1**

INITIAL REQUIREMENTS AT A GLANCE:

Also needed are items A, B, C (for in-state applicants,) E, G, J (with complete background check*), K, and O - See page 2. The fee for a licensing is $12 / year. Submission of fingerprints for a state and national background check IS required with a $15.00 fee. Passing scores on the Praxis II PLT and Specialty Area tests ARE required. Ohio DOES belong to the Interstate Certification Compact. Special Education coursework IS required. For a complete review of current standards, contact the Department or visit their web site.

* NOTE: All individuals teaching under a professional teaching certificate must undergo a background check upon a date prescribed by the State Board of Education and every five years thereafter. Sept. 5, 2008, was selected as the initial date by which professional certificate holders (eight year, permanent, and permanent non-tax) must submit fingerprints for background checks.

Renewal Requirements:
First Time Renewal: The Professional Teacher License is valid for five years and may be renewed by individuals currently employed in a school or district upon verification that the following requirements have been completed since the issuance of the license to be renewed:
1.   6 sem. hrs. of course work related to classroom teaching and/or the area of licensure; or
2.   Eighteen Continuing Education Units (CEUs - one hundred and eighty contact hours) or other equivalent activities related to classroom teaching and/or area of licensure as approved by the local professional development committee of the employing school or school district.
Second Renewal: The second renewal of the Professional Teacher License shall require:
1.   Completion of a master's degree, or thirty semester hours of graduate credit in classroom teaching and/or an area of licensure.
2.   A minimum of six semester hours, eighteen CEUs or equivalent activities.
      The requirement of a master's degree or thirty semester hours shall pertain to any individual who is admitted to a licensure program at an approved college or university after the effective date of this rule, and to any individual who is admitted to a licensure program prior to the effective date of this rule and who completes said program after July 1, 2002.

Ohio bases their teacher licenses on performance-based standards. With a renewable, five-year license system, the state will no longer award permanent certificates. To renew a license, a teacher must develop a professional development plan that is then approved by a local professional development committee.

Coursework, continuing education units, or other equivalent activities related to the license areas or to classroom teaching will also be required - as well as a master's degree or 30 semester hours of graduate credit to renew a license the second time after 10 years. The requirement of a master's degree or 30 semester hours pertains to any applicant admitted to a licensure program at an approved institution after July 1, 1998, and to any applicant admitted to a licensure program prior to January 1, 1998, and who completes the program after July 1, 2002.

Entry Year Program (Performance Standards):

A. An Entry Year Program shall include the performance-based assessment of the entry year teacher or principal, and a formal program of support, including mentoring to foster professional growth of the individual, that agrees with the required performance-based assessment.

B. Beginning July 1, 2002, school districts, chartered community schools, and chartered non-public schools, are required to provide a formal structured program of support, including mentoring, to all entry year teachers and principals.

C. Upon documentation of successful completion of the Entry Year Program, which includes the performance-based assessment and formal program of support, based on standards established by the Ohio Department of Education, the individual shall be deemed to have met the requirements for professional licensure.

D. School districts, chartered community schools, and chartered nonpublic schools, shall provide entry year teachers and principals full salary as determined by the appropriate placement on the school district or school salary schedule.

PROVISIONAL LICENSES: Valid 2 years, renewable (required for Entry Year Program).

A. **Provisional Teacher License:** (May be used for substitute teaching) shall be issued to individuals who:
1. Hold a degree required by the license
2. Have successfully completed an approved program of preparation;
3. Are deemed to be of good moral character;
4. Have successfully completed all examinations prescribed by the State Board;
5. Have demonstrated skill integrating educational technology in the instruction of children;
6. Have been recommended by the dean or head of teacher education at an institution approved to prepare teachers; and
7. Have completed:
   a. A minimum of six semester hours in the teaching of reading, including at least one separate three semester hour course in the teaching of phonics for the early childhood license, and
   b. A minimum of six semester hours in the teaching of reading, including at least one separate three semester hour course in the teaching of phonics for the middle childhood license.

B. **Provisional Principal License:** Valid as long as Professional Teacher License is maintained.
1. Hold a Master's Degree; and
2. As for Teacher License (See A2, A3, A4, A6);

PROFESSIONAL LICENSES: Valid 5 years, renewable.

Issued to individuals holding the appropriate provisional license and a bachelor's degree, deemed to be of good moral character and who has completed an approved program of teacher preparation, an Entry Year Program, and a examination prescribed by the State Board.

PROFESSIONAL EARLY CHILDHOOD LICENSE
(PK - 3, Ages 3 - 8)

A. Valid for teaching children who are typically developing, at-risk, gifted, and who have mild/moderate educational needs;

B. A minimum of 12 cumulative semester hours in the teaching of reading at the appropriate level shall be required for this license.

PROFESSIONAL MIDDLE CHILDHOOD LICENSE

(Grades 4 - 9, Ages 8 - 14)

A.   Preparation in the humanities (including the arts) and areas of concentration in at least two of the following: reading and language arts, mathematics, science, and social studies;

B.   Same as Early Childhood (B) above.

PROFESSIONAL ADOLESCENCE TO YOUNG ADULT LICENSE
(Grades 7 - 12, Ages 12 - 21)

A.   Academic major or its equivalent with sufficient advanced course work in all areas to be taught;

B.   Licenses shall be issued in the following teaching fields: (1) Earth Sciences; (2) Integrated language arts; (3) Integrated mathematics; (4) Integrated science; (5) Integrated social studies; (6) Life sciences; and (7) Physical sciences.

PROFESSIONAL MULTI-AGE LICENSE
(Grades PK - 12, Ages 3 - 21)

A.   At least one academic major or its equivalent with advanced coursework in all areas to be taught.

B.   Licenses shall be issued in the following teaching fields: 1. Dance; 2. Drama/theater; 3. Foreign language; 4. Health; 5. **Library/Media**; 6. Music; 7. Physical education; and 8. Visual arts.

ADDITIONAL ENDORSEMENTS
(Valid for Age/Grade Levels Indicated)

A.   Bachelor's degree;

B.   Of good moral character;

C.   Successfully completed an approved program of preparation;

D.   Successfully completed and examination prescribed by the State Board; and

E.   Been recommended by the dean or head of teacher education at an approved institution.

F.   The following endorsements apply: (1) Adapted physical education (limited to license); (2) Adult education (full time programs); (3) Computer / Technology; (4) Driver education (limited to an adolescence or multi-age teacher license; (5) Early education of handicapped children (this will be phased out); (6) Pre-kindergarten (Ages 3 - 5); (7) Reading; (8) Occupational Work Experience and Occupational Work Adjustment (Under professional Middle, Adolescence, or Vocational License); (9) Teaching English to speakers of other languages/bilingual; (10) Transition to work (with Intervention specialist or vocational license); and (11) Vocational work-site teacher/coordinator (limited to professional vocational license.

PROFESSIONAL PUPIL SERVICES LICENSE
(School Counselor / Psychologist / Social Worker)

Shall be issued to an individual deemed to be of good moral character who has successfully completed an approved program of preparation and who is recommended by the dean or head of teacher education, and who has completed an examination prescribed by the State Board and who has evidenced the education and experience requirements specified below:

School Counselor:

A.   Master's degree, two years of successful teaching experience under a standard teaching certificate, or provisional or professional teacher license, and successful completion of an internship consisting of six hundred contact hours in a school setting; **OR**

B.   Master's degree, successful completion of an internship consisting of six hundred contact hours in a school setting, and a one-year induction under the supervision of a licensed school counselor; **OR**

C.   Master's degree and three years experience as a licensed school counselor in another state.

School Psychologist:

A.   Master's degree, **AND**

B.   An approved program of preparation; recommendation by the dean or head of teacher education; successful completion of an examination prescribed by the State Board of Education; and evidence of the education and applicable experience requirements; **AND**

C. Successful completion of a nine month, full-time internship in an approved school setting as described in the Ohio internship in school psychology guidelines.

School Social Worker:

A. Master's degree in social work, **AND**

B. An approved program of preparation; recommendation by the dean or head of teacher education; successful completion of an examination prescribed by the State Board of Education; and evidence of the education and applicable experience requirements; **AND**

C. One year of successful experience in a chartered school or school district under a professional license; or one year of social work experience under a current license issued by the Ohio Counselor and Social Worker Board; or a graduate level social work practicum of at least ten weeks in a chartered school or school district; **AND**

D. Current license to practice social work issued by the Ohio Counselor and Social Worker Board;

PROFESSIONAL ADMINISTRATOR LICENSE
(Principals / Superintendent)

Ohio is creating an aligned, standards-based education system in which all of Ohio's students achieve at the highest levels. There are five standards delineated:

Standard 1: Continuous Improvement - Principals help create a shared vision and clear goals for their schools and ensure continuous progress toward achieving the goals.

Standard 2: Instruction - Principals support the implementation of high-quality standards-based instruction that results in higher levels of achievement for all students.

Standard 3: School Operations, Resources and Learning Environment - Principals allocate resources and manage school operations in order to ensure a safe and productive learning environment.

Standard 4: Collaboration - Principals establish and sustain collaborative learning and shared leadership to promote learning and achievement of all students.

Standard 5: Parents and Community Engagement - Principals engage parents and community members in the educational process and create an environment where community resources support student learning, achievement and well-being.

Superintendent: License shall be added to a valid professional teacher license of an individual who holds a principal or administrative specialist license and shall be valid for teaching in the areas designated on the license; for supervising programs for ages three through twenty-one and pre-kindergarten through grade twelve; OR for administrative duties in a school system. The following requirements shall be met prior to issuance of the superintendent license:

A. Three years of successful experience in a position requiring a principal or administrative specialist license; and

B. Completion of an approved preparation program for superintendents.

STATE OF OKLAHOMA

Oklahoma Department of Education
Professional Standards Section
2500 N. Lincoln Boulevard, #212
Oklahoma City, Oklahoma 73105-4599
Phone: 405-521-3337 / Fax: 405-521-3337
Web Site: **http://sde.state.ok.us/Teacher/ProfStand/default.html**

INITIAL REQUIREMENTS AT A GLANCE:

Also needed will be items A, B, C, E, G and K - See page 2. The fees are $10.00 (Residency program); $30.00 (Initial Certificate;) and $10.00 (all others.) Passing scores on the Oklahoma Teacher Certification Test ARE required. Scores on the National Teacher's Examination test are NOT required. Oklahoma DOES belong to the Interstate Certification Compact and has extended compacts with Missouri, Iowa, Nebraska, Kansas, South Dakota and Illinois,

Renewal Requirements: A $10.00 fee

Teaching Experience:	Prof. Development Points:	College Hours:
3 years	--	--
2 years	45	0
	30	1
	15	2
	0	3
1 year	60	0
	45	1
	30	2
	15	3
	0	4
0 year	75	0
	60	1
	45	2
	30	3
	15	4
	0	5

TEACHING LICENSES AND CERTIFICATES

Secondary Subject Matter Specializations:
Business Education, Driver/Safety Education, English, Family and Consumer Sciences, Journalism, Mathematics, Science, Social Studies, Speech/Drama/Debate, Career and Technology Education*, with Subject matter in Agricultural Education, Marketing Education, Technology Education, Business, Family and Consumer Sciences.

NOTE: For complete information concerning competencies in the specializations listed above, contact the Commission or visit their web site.

* Competency for Occupational Agriculture, Occupational Family and Consumer Sciences, Trade and Industrial Education, and Career and Technology Health Occupations will be verified by passing a state or national licensure examination developed specifically to the occupation and/or occupational testing approved by the Oklahoma Department of Vocational and Technical Education.

GENERAL COMPETENCIES FOR LICENSURE AND CERTIFICATION[1]

1. The teacher understands the central concepts and methods of inquiry of the subject matter discipline(s) he or she teaches and can create learning experiences that make these aspects of subject matter meaningful for students.
2. The teacher understands how students learn and develop, and can provide learning opportunities that support their intellectual, social and physical development at all grade levels including early childhood, elementary, middle level, and secondary.
3. The teacher understands that students vary in their approaches to learning and creates instructional opportunities that are adaptable to individual differences of learners.
4. The teacher understands curriculum integration processes and uses a variety of instructional

strategies to encourage students' development of critical thinking, problem solving, and performance skills and effective use of technology.

5. The teacher uses best practices related to motivation and behavior to create learning environments that encourage positive social interaction, self-motivation and active engagement in learning, thus, providing opportunities for success.

6. The teacher develops a knowledge of and uses a variety of effective communication techniques to foster active inquiry, collaboration, and supportive interaction in the classroom.

7. The teacher plans instruction based upon curriculum goals, knowledge of the teaching/learning process, subject matter, students' abilities and differences, and the community; and adapts instruction based upon assessment and reflection.

8. The teacher understands and uses a variety of assessment strategies to evaluate and modify the teaching/learning process ensuring the continuous intellectual, social and physical development of the learner.

9. The teacher evaluates the effects of his/her choices and actions on others (students, parents, and other professionals in the learning community), modifies those actions when needed, and actively seeks opportunities for continued professional growth.

10. The teacher fosters positive interaction with school colleagues, parents/families, and organizations in the community to actively engage them in support of students' learning and well-being.

11. The teacher shall have an understanding of the importance of assisting students with career awareness and the application of career concepts to the academic curriculum.

12. The teacher understands the process of continuous lifelong learning, the concept of making learning enjoyable, and the need for a willingness to change when the change leads to greater student learning and development.

13. The teacher understands the legal aspects of teaching including the rights of students and parents/families, as well as the legal rights and responsibilities of the teacher.

14. The teacher understands, and is able to develop instructional strategies/plans based on the Oklahoma core curriculum.

15. The teacher understands the State teacher evaluation process, "Oklahoma Criteria for Effective Teaching Performance," and how to incorporate these criteria in designing instructional strategies.

[1] Specific competencies are defined for each teaching certificate have been recompiled and revised as of February, 2002. For a complete current summary, contact the Department or visit their web site.

LIBRARY MEDIA SPECIALIST CERTIFICATION COMPETENCIES

The candidate for licensure and certification:

1. Defines a program of information literacy and integrates it into the curriculum.

2. Defines a school library media program emphasizing information problem-solving skills and integrates it into the curriculum.

3. Motivates and guides students and faculty in recognizing literature as an essential base of cultural and practical knowledge and in reading for pleasure as well as for information.

4. Communicates effectively with students, faculty, staff, administrators, parents, other colleagues, and the general public.

5. Applies basic principles of evaluating and selecting resources and equipment to support the education goals of the school.

6. Uses resources to support the personal, developmental, and curricular needs of students, and the instructional development needs of the faculty.

7. Recognizes the value of new technologies for information and instruction and assists faculty and students in their use.

8. Implements policies and procedures for effective and efficient acquisition, cataloging, processing, circulating, and maintaining equipment and resources to ensure access.

9. Develops, implements, and evaluates school library media programs, including management of personnel, resources, and facilities.

10. Serves as a learning facilitator within schools and as a leader of faculty, administration, and students in the development of effective strategies for teaching and learning.

11. Demonstrates a commitment to professionalism.

SCHOOL COUNSELOR CERTIFICATION COMPETENCIES

The candidate for licensure and certification:
1. Uses an understanding of human development to provide a comprehensive, developmental guidance and counseling program.
2. Understands the impact of environmental influences on students' development and achievement, and helps students develop strategies to resolve or cope with situations that may hinder learning.
3. Demonstrates an appreciation of human diversity by providing equitable guidance and counseling services for all students and by promoting a climate of mutual respect that helps students value themselves and others.
4. Uses effective leadership skills to plan, implement, and evaluate a comprehensive, developmental guidance and counseling program to address the needs of all students.
5. Provides guidance and counseling services to address the needs and concerns of students and to help students develop skills to use in future situations.
6. Facilitates the educational and career development of individual students to help all students achieve success.
7. Uses formal and informal assessment to provide information about and to students, to monitor student progress, and to recommend changes to the student's educational environment.
8. Consults with parents and school personnel, provides professional expertise, and establishes collaborative relationships that foster a support system for students, parents and the school community.
9. Establishes strong and positive ties with the home and the community to promote and support students' growth in school and beyond the school setting.
10. Has a knowledge of professional ethical codes, the importance of professional development, and the need to work with colleagues to advance the profession.

Standard Certificate: (Valid 5 years, renewable)
The candidate must pass the Oklahoma state competency examination (OR) possess a Nationally Certified School Counselor Credential.

SCHOOL PSYCHOLOGIST CERTIFICATION COMPETENCIES

The candidate for licensure and certification:
1. Understands and integrates into practice the principles of professional school psychology.
2. Demonstrates knowledge and skills in a comprehensive range of assessment, diagnosis, evaluation, and eligibility or intervention determination within the multi-disciplinary team process.
3. Demonstrates knowledge and skills in prevention, intervention, consultation, and counseling.
4. Demonstrates knowledge and skills in effective communication and collaboration.
5. Demonstrates knowledge and application of statistics, research methodologies/designs, measurement, and program evaluation.
6. Understands and integrates into practice psychological foundations.
7. Understands and integrates into practice educational foundations.

Standard Certificate: (valid 5 years, renewable)
Pass state approved competency exam (OR) Possess a Nationally Certified School Counselor Credential.

PRINCIPAL AND SUPERINTENDENT CERTIFICATION COMPETENCIES

Most administrative competencies apply to both the principalship and the superintendency. The depth of understanding, knowledge, or demonstrated expertise would vary by certification and/or job assignment (elementary principal vs. superintendent, for instance). For example, the elementary principal should have a better understanding of beginning reading theory, the superintendent a more comprehensive understanding of school finance. Some knowledge in all areas would improve the effectiveness of the administrative candidate regardless of assignment.
Prerequisites:
At least 2 years of successful teaching, supervisory, or administrative experience in public schools; At least a masters degree; and Passing the required competency examinations.

The candidate for licensure and certification:
1.   Administrator candidates shall have knowledge and skills to establish programs to meet the concerns and needs of students, families and the community. Skills needed to address the concerns and needs of students and families would include, but not be limited to, understanding: (a) philosophical and cultural values; (b) legal and regulatory applications; (c) policy and governance; (d) public relations; and (e) political infrastructure.
2.   Administrator candidates shall possess leadership knowledge and skills including, but not limited to: (a) group dynamics and group processes; (b) information collection; (c) problem analysis; (d) judgement and/ethics; (e) organizational oversight; (f) implementation; (g) delegation; (h) district culture; and (i) collaboration among colleagues and institutions.
3.   Administrator candidates shall be able to connect research and practice. This intersection between research and practice would include, but not be limited to: (a) instruction and learning environment (instructional leadership); (b) discipline practices: (c) curriculum design; (d) student guidance and development; (e) professional/staff development; (f) measurement and evaluation; and (g) resource allocation.
4.   Administrator candidates shall consider the developmental levels and needs of all school-age children. Administrators shall exhibit an appreciation of the diversity students bring to the classroom, thus increasing mutual understanding and better meeting the educational needs of children. Furthermore, administrators shall demonstrate a theoretical and practical understanding of the role that their own attitudes, biases, and preconceptions play in their interactions with students, colleagues, and the larger community.
5.   Administrator candidates shall have an awareness of human resource management and development including the Oklahoma administrator/teacher evaluation criteria.
6.   The administrators shall have knowledge and skills to manage the physical resources to ensure a safe, efficient, and effective learning environment.
7.   The administrator candidate shall have knowledge and skills necessary to manage the financial and business operations of a school district.

STATE OF OREGON

Teacher Standards & Practices Commission
465 Commercial St. NE
Salem, OR 97301
Phone: 503-378-3586 / Fax: 503-378-4448
Web Site: **http://www.tspc.state.or.us/**

INITIAL REQUIREMENTS AT A GLANCE:

Also needed will be items A, B, C, E, G, J, K, N (PPST - Praxis I or CBEST), O (Praxis II), and a First Aid Card and an Anti-discrimination statement – See page 2. Fees for Oregon education graduates - $100.00; all other applicants - $120.00. There is a $62 fingerprint processing fee. All Initial Teaching Licenses require passing scores on the California Basic Educational Skills Test (CBEST), OR the Praxis I PPST *AND* an affidavit attesting to knowledge of Oregon's Civil Rights laws. The above tests are waived if the applicant has completed a doctor's degree through a regionally accredited institution. The above tests are postponed for 18 months when Initial license for out-of-state application is issued. The original license is valid for three (3) years, Oregon DOES belong to the NASDTEC Interstate Contract (Teachers, Support Professionals, and Administrators). Oregon IS a member of the Interstate New Teacher Assessment and Support Consortium (INTASC). Courses or competencies in Special Education are NOT required for out-of-state applicants. Revisions in School Psychologist requirements are planned in 2007-2008.

Renewal Requirements: $100.00 fee. Candidate must complete one of the two following options:
1. One year of full-time or two consecutive years of one-half time or more appropriately assigned successful teaching experience, or 180 days (full-time equivalent days if less than half-time) of teaching, which can include substitute experience in the Oregon Schools; or volunteer or instructional assistance experience. All experience must be verified on the *Professional Educational Experience*

> *Report Form;*
> 2. Nine quarter hours of preparation completed through an approved institution. The preparation must be germane to your license or meet State Board Priorities.
> **Note**: A combination of Oregon school experience and credit may be used in which one quarter hour equals twenty days of teaching.

Licenses are available with the following *Authorization* Levels: **Early Childhood Education** (Age 3-Grade 4); **Elementary (in an Elementary School)** (3-8); **Middle Level** (5-9); and **High School** (7-12).

SPECIALTY AREA ENDORSEMENTS

Specialty Endorsements Requiring One Authorization Level: foreign languages, health, home economics, technology education, math, agricultural science & technology, general business education, marketing-professional technical education, language arts, speech, drama, biology, integrated science, chemistry, physics, social studies, and early intervention special education.

Specialty Endorsements Requiring at least Two Authorization Levels: art, ESOL, ESOL/Bilingual, music, physical education, adaptive physical education, reading, and special education.

Specialty Endorsements Requiring all Four Authorization Levels: educational media, communications disorders, hearing impaired, and visually impaired.

INSTRUCTIONAL LICENSES

Initial I Teaching - Valid 3 years. May be renewed twice for 3 years upon completion of an additional 3 semester or 4.5 quarter hours of graduate level coursework at a regionally accredited institution and germane to the requirements of the Level II Teaching license. An educator must qualify for the Initial II Teaching license or optional Continuing Teaching license upon 10 years following issuance of the first Initial I Teaching license. If necessary, a one year unconditional extension may be requested to complete the qualifications for the Initial II Teaching license within the 9 year renewal period.
Requirements: Bachelor's or higher degree from a regionally accredited institution; completion of an approved bachelor's or post-bachelor's teacher education program including passage of subject matter exams, basic skills, civil rights knowledge, **and** recent experience.

Initial II Teaching Licence - Valid 3 years. Renewable.
Requirements: If original Initial I license was based on a bachelor's level teacher education program, educator must verify completion of 45 quarter hours of graduate preparation in the areas prescribed by the commission or have a master's degree from a regionally accredited institution. If the original Initial I license was based on a fifth-year or master's level program, the educator must verify 9 quarter hours of graduate preparation since the Initial license was issued which are germane to the license through a regionally accredited institution.

Initial License for Out-of-State Candidates - First Application (Valid 18 months and non-renewable). Candidate must qualify for the Initial I license within the 18 month period.
Requirements: Hold a bachelor's or higher degree from a regionally accredited institution in the US or foreign equivalent approved by the commission AND completion of an approved initial teaching license program or hold an unrestricted teaching license in any US state or territory or foreign program evaluated as satisfactory by an Oregon approved teacher education institution, and not yet passed subject matter exams, basic skills, and civil rights knowledge.
　　This license also requires recent educational experience meaning either within three years of completion of required coursework in an approved teaching program, OR during the effective period of a comparable license AND within three years of the last public or private regionally accredited years of experience on such a license. If more than three years have elapsed, then 6 semester or 9 quarter hours of coursework through a regionally accredited institution must be completed.

Continuing Teaching License (Valid 5 years. Renewable) - Completion of a master's or higher degree from a regionally accredited institution; **(AND)** demonstrate advanced competencies by completing one of the following:

    A. Complete a TSPC-approved Continuing Teaching License program offered by an Oregon College or University; **(OR)**

    B. Hold a doctorate degree in education from a regionally accredited institution; or the foreign equivalent of such degree approved by the commission; **(OR)**

    C. Obtaining certification from the National Board of Professional Teaching Standards; **(OR)**

    D. Have a Certificate of Clinical Comptetence awarded by the American Speech and Hearing Association for those holding a communications disorders endorsement; **(OR)**

    E. Hold a Professional Certificate issued by the State of Washington;

AND have taught 5 years at least half-time on any non-provisional license appropriate for the assignment.

Substitute Teaching - Requirements: Bachelor's degree related to teaching at one or more levels through a regionally accredited college or university; completion of an approved teacher education program in any state in an institution approved to prepare teachers, **or** possession of an unrestricted license for full-time teaching in any state. This is valid at any level for replacing a teacher who is temporarily unable to work.

Limited Teaching - After being offered employment, apply for this license jointly with your new employer if you have an associate's degree or the equivalent in formal post-secondary education and wish to teach at any level a highly specialized subject for which the commission does not issue a specific endorsement.

Professional-Technical Teaching - After being offered employment, apply for this license jointly with your new employer if you have a combination of education and experience judged adequate by the employer's instructor appraisal committee for teaching in a professional-technical program approved by the Oregon Department of Education.

PERSONNEL SERVICE LICENSES: SCHOOL COUNSELOR AND SCHOOL PSYCHOLOGIST LICENSES

Transitional School Counselor License - (Valid 3 years. Non-renewable. Must qualify for Initial I School Counselor License upon expiration)
Requirements: Master's or higher degree in counseling, education, or related behavioral science, including, but not limited to social work, or psychology from a regionally accredited institution in any state AND have completed an approved graduate program in school counseling in any state or hold an unrestricted license for school counseling in any state but have not passed subject matter exams, basic skills, teaching experience or teaching practicum requirements, civil rights knowledge and recent educational experience.

Initial I School Counselor License (Valid 3 years. Renewable twice) –
Requirements: (1) two academic years of experience as a full-time licensed teacher in a public school or regionally accredited private school in any state; or have completed a practicum in teaching at any level as part of an initial graduate program or separately; (2) hold a master's or higher degree in counseling, education, or related behavioral science from a regionally accredited institution; (3) completed an initial graduate program in school counseling; (4) obtained passing scores on CBEST or Praxis 1 PPST. The test may be waived with a regionally accredited doctor's degree; (5) obtained a passing score on the Praxis exam for school counselor or verify 5 years of experience counseling full time in a public or regionally accredited private school; and (6) meet the recent educational experience requirement.
Renewal: May be renewed two times for three years upon completion of an additional 3 semester or 4.5 quarter hours graduate level coursework through a regionally accredited college or university germane to the license for each renewal. Must qualify for the Initial II School Counselor License or the optional Continuing School Counselor License upon expiration of 9 years following issuance of the first Initial I School Counselor License.

Initial II School Counselor License (Valid 3 years. Renewable) –
Requirements: Must have completed an additional 6 semester or 9 quarter hours graduate level academic credit germane to the license from a regionally accredited college or university since issuance of the first Initial I School Counselor License. May be renewed repeatedly for three years each renewal based on one year of licensed educational experience or completion of 6 semester or 9 quarter hours, as above, during the life of the license.

Continuing School Counselor License (Valid 5 years, Renewable).
Requirements: Completion beyond the initial graduate program in school counseling, an advanced program in counseling competencies consisting of at least 9 quarter hours of graduate credit; practica in counseling early childhood or elementary students, and middle or high school students. Exceptionally, waive of advanced program with a regionally accredited doctor's degree in Education or Vocational or Clinical Counseling; and three years of successful experience counseling at least half time in the Oregon schools.
Renewal: See Initial II School Counselor License.

SCHOOL PSYCHOLOGIST LICENSES

Initial School Psychologist (Valid 3 years, Renewable once)– Apply if you have a master's or higher degree in behavioral science or their derivative therapeutic professions from a regionally accredited institution and completed as part of a master's degree or separately an initial graduate program in school psychology at an approved institution; completed a clinical practicum in a public service agency serving persons of school age, and either practica covering all student age levels or one academic year of varied and mentored experience; passing scores on CBEST or PPST or completion of a doctor's degree through an accredited institution; and either a passing score on the Praxis exam in school psychology or verification of five years of successful licensed school psychologist experience in the public or private regionally accredited schools; and meet the recent educational experience requirement.
NOTE: The degree, program, and practicum requirements specified above can be satisfied by obtaining certification from the National Association of School Psychologists.

Continuing School Psychologist (Valid 5 years, Renewable). Completion of an advanced program in psychologist competencies consisting of at least 9 quarter hours of graduate credit. Exceptionally, the advanced program in psychologist competencies may be waived by obtaining a regionally accredited doctor's degree in educational or clinical or counseling psychology **or** hold a current National School Psychologist Certificate from the National Association of School Psychologists; and three years of school psychologist experience in the Oregon schools.
Renewal: See Initial II School Counselor Renewal above.

ADMINISTRATIVE LICENSES

Transitional Administrator Licence (Valid 3 years. Non-renewable) Must qualify for Initial Administrator License upon expiration.
Requirements: Completion of both a master's degree or higher from a regionally accredited institution in the US or the foreign equivalent approved by the commission in the arts and sciences or an advanced degree in the professions AND an approved Initial Administrator program or hold an unrestricted license for school administration; have 3 academic years as a full time licensed educator on any license appropriate for the assignment in a public school or regionally accredited private school in the US but not have passed subject matter exams, Oregon school law and finance and civil rights knowledge; and recent educational experience.

Initial Administrator License (IAL) - Valid 3 years, Renewable twice*.
Requirements: Three years of academic experience as a full time licensed educator; obtained a master's or higher degree in the arts and sciences or an advanced degree in the professions from a regionally accredited institution; completed 18 semester or 27 quarter hours graduate credit in a state-approved school administrator program; received a passing score on tests of knowledge of Oregon school law and finance and civil rights and meet recent educational experience requirements.
Renewal: May be renewed repeatedly for three years with completion of an additional 6 semester or 9 quarter hours of graduate preparation towards requirements for the Continuing Administrator License

during the life of each license.

* If the holder of an IAL becomes a superintendent at any time during the life of the license, then the Continuing Administrator License must be obtained within 3 years following the next renewal of the IAL.

Continuing Administrator: Valid 5 years. Renewable.
Requirements: Completion beyond the master's degree and initial graduate program in school administration an advanced program in administrative competencies consisting of 18 semester or 27 quarter hours of graduate credit or its equivalent. Exceptionally, waiver may be obtained with a regionally accredited doctor's degree in School Administration or educational leadership; a passing score on a test of professional administrative knowledge approved by the commission; and three years of half time or more on any school administrator license in a public or regionally accredited private school setting.
Renewal: May be renewed repeatedly for five years each renewal period based on at least one year of licensed experience or completion of 6 semester or 9 quarter hours of preparation germane to the license during the life of the license.

Transitional Superintendent: Valid three years. Non-renewable. Must qualify for Continuing Superintendent upon expiration.
Requirements: Master's or higher degree in the arts and sciences or an advanced degree in the professions from a regionally accredited institution; hold a valid superintendent's license from any state in the US based upon completion of an approved program and have been employed as a superintendent for five years or more on that license before holding an Oregon license.

Continuing Superintendent: Optional license. Valid 5 years. Renewable.
Requirements: Completion beyond the advanced administrator program; at least an additional 18 quarter hours in an advanced superintendent program or a doctorate degree in school administration or educational leadership through an approved institution and three years experience as a superintendent in a public school, education service district, or regionally accredited private school system in any state.
Renewal: See Continuing Administrator

STATE OF PENNSYLVANIA

Department of Education
Bureau of School Leadership and Teacher Quality
Division of Certification Services
333 Market Street
Harrisburg, Pennsylvania 17126-0333
Phone: 717-787-3356 / Fax: 717-783-6736
Web Site: **http://www.teaching.state.pa.us/teaching/site/default.asp**

INITIAL REQUIREMENTS AT A GLANCE:

Also needed will be items A, B, C, E, G, I (or Employment Visa), H, I, N, O and Q - See page 2. The fee is $15.00. FBI Background check is $40.00. Scores from the PPST *and* appropriate Praxis II Specialty Area Tests ARE required (must have been taken within the five years prior to application). Revised testing requirements became effective 9/1/01 (see D.1. below). Instructional and Education Specialist certificates are valid for six (6) teaching years. Pennsylvania DOES belong to the Interstate Certification Compact (Teachers), the NASDTEC Interstate Contract (Teachers, Support Professionals, Administrators and Vocational Educators) and the Interstate New Teacher Assessment and Support Consortium (INTASC). Competency with Special Needs Students IS required. Changes are ongoing.

Renewal Requirements: 24 post-baccalaureate credits to move from Level I to Level II. Six credits or 180 hours of continuing education every six years thereafter. Fee: $40.00 for in-state applicants and $80.00 for out-of-state applicants.

INSTRUCTIONAL LEVEL I CERTIFICATE

A. Bachelor's Degree from an approved institution.
B. Completion of an approved certification program of studies with a major in the area for which certification is requested. *Effective 9/1/2003*, all applicants will be required to have maintained a 3.0 GPA and have had a minimum of 6 semester credit hours in both math and English.
C. Satisfaction in meeting a condition (or key) allowing Pennsylvania to evaluate your credentials: (1) recommendation by the institution where teacher education program has been completed; (2) presentation of a comparable certificate.

NOTES:

1. All individuals applying for an initial **Instructional I certificate** are required to take the PPST Reading, PPST Writing, PPST Mathematics, Fundamental Subjects: Content Knowledge (all K-6 and K-12 areas) in addition to the appropriate subject assessment test(s). All individuals seeking dual certification will be required to be examined in both areas of specialization, and all persons who already have a valid Pennsylvania **Instructional I or II certificate** and wish to add another area to that certificate will be required to take the appropriate subject assessment test.
2. All persons holding Pennsylvania professional educator certification must complete continuing education requirements every five years in order to keep their certificates active.

INSTRUCTIONAL LEVEL II (PERMANENT) CERTIFICATE

A. Three (3) years of successful teaching in Pennsylvania on a Pennsylvania Instructional Level I certificate;
B. Twenty-four (24) semester hours of post-baccalaureate collegiate study. Any or all of which may be satisfied through in-service programs approved by the department;
C. Completion of a State-approved induction program; and
D. Satisfactory assessment/evaluations for six semesters.

INSTRUCTIONAL CERTIFICATES

The instructional Certificate is issued to a person whose primary responsibility shall be direct contact with learners in teaching-learning situations. The following are the grade levels and areas for which certificates are issued.

K - 12	Business/Computer Information Tech.	7 - 12	Biology
K - 12	Art	K - 12	Chinese
7 - 12	Chemistry	7 - 12	Cooperative Education
7 - 12	Communication	7 - 12	Driver Education
7 - 12	Marketing-Distributive Education	N - 3	Early Childhood
7 - 12	Earth & Space Science	K - 6	Elementary
7 - 12	English	K - 12	Environmental Education
K - 12	French	7 - 12	General Science
K - 12	German	K - 12	Greek
K - 12	Health	K - 12	Health/Physical Education
K - 12	Hearing Impaired	K - 12	Hebrew
K - 12	Family and Consumer Science	K - 12	Technology Education
K - 12	Italian	K - 12	Japanese
K - 12	Korean	K - 12	Latin
K - 12	Library Science	K - 12	Lithuanian
7 - 12	Physics	7 - 12	Mathematics

K - 12	Portuguese	K - 12	Music
K - 12	Russian	K - 12	Polish
K - 12	Spanish	K - 12	Reading Specialist
K - 12	Speech/Language Impaired	K - 12	Sanskrit
K - 12	Vietnamese	7 - 12	Social Studies
N - 12	Special Education	K - 12	Ukrainian
7 - 12	Social Sciences	K - 12	Visually Impaired
K - 12	Agriculture	7 - 12	Citizenship Education

SCHOOL LIBRARY CERTIFICATION

Any one who desires school library certification must affiliate with a college having state-approved certification in that area and pursue certification through that college's or university's program. Pennsylvania colleges and universities will prescribe courses for certification. The Pennsylvania Department of Education does not prescribe credit hours or courses.

Pennsylvania teaching certificates with endorsement in school librarianship may be issued to graduates of Pennsylvania colleges and universities who have:
A. Completed a school librarianship preparation program;
B. Received a competency recommendation from the preparing institution;
C. Completed the test requirements for professional certification in Pennsylvania;
D. Passed the Praxis test (a set of rigorous and carefully validated assessments administered by the Educational Testing Service that provides accurate, reliable information for use by state education agencies in making licensing decisions); and
E. Met all other requirements provided by law.

SCHOOL COUNSELOR
(Elementary K-6 or Secondary 7-12)

A. Completion of an Approved Program in school counseling at a college or university;
B. If prepared **Out-of-State** the candidate must have completed a preparation program for Elementary or Secondary Counselor at an out-of-state institution which has approval by the respective state department of education as a teacher preparing college or university and has secured the recommending signature of that institution.
Effective 9/1/01: Praxis, PPST and School Counselor Test.

PRINCIPAL
(K-12)

A person prepared as a school administrator may be eligible for certification as a Principal K-12 provided that the applicant:

A. Has completed an approved program of graduate study preparing him/her to direct, operate, supervise, and administer the organizational and general educational activities of a school. (Preparation completed out-of-state must meet Pennsylvania standards for certification.)
B. Is recommended for certification as a principal by the authorized certification officer of the institution where such education was obtained, or holds a comparable certificate from another state (for out-of-state graduates only).
C. Provides a chief school administrator's verification of the completion of five years of satisfactory professional school experience on a state-issued certificate appropriate for the assignment.
D. Has provided evidence of satisfactory achievement on assessments prescribed by the Department.
E. Is able to meet all other requirements provided by law.

SUPERINTENDENT

The Department will issue the appropriate Letter of Eligibility for consideration for appointment as a

District Superintendent or Assistant Superintendent to an applicant who shall:

Either:

A. Have completed a Pennsylvania approved graduate-level program of educational administrative study minimally approximating two full academic years for the preparation of chief school administrators; **OR**

B. Have been prepared through an out-of-state graduate-level program equivalent to those approved in this Commonwealth.
AND

C. Have received the recommendation of the preparing institution for certification as a chief school (district-level) administrator or, if prepared through an out-of-state institution, holds a comparable certificate issued by another state for professional service in the public schools of that state; **AND**

D. Have provided evidence of six years of teaching or other professionally certificated service in the basic schools for the Assistant Superintendent's Letter of Eligibility, and for the Superintendent's Letter of Eligibility three of those six years must have been in a supervisory or administrative capacity.

STATE OF RHODE ISLAND

Department of Education
Office of Educator Quality and Certification
255 Westminster Street
Providence, Rhode Island 02903
Phone: 401-222-4600 / Fax: 401-222-6178
Web Site: http://www.ride.ri.gov/ride/teachadmin.aspx

INITIAL REQUIREMENTS AT A GLANCE:

Also needed will be items A, B, C, D, E, G, and O - See page 2. The initial certification processing fee is $25.00. Issuance/Renewal of 5 year Professional Certificate is $100. Fee for a two-year Professional Certificate is $300.00. A state administered certification test is NOT required. Passing scores on the Praxis II Principles of Learning and Teaching (PLT-Elem and PLT-Sec) test ARE required and a Certificate of Eligibility will not be granted until they are received. The original certificate is valid for three (3) years. Rhode Island DOES belong to the Interstate Certification Compact and the Northeast Regional Credential Compact. Rhode Island also belongs to the NASDTEC Interstate Contract for all licensed categories and the New Teacher Assessment and Support Consortium (INTASC). A course in Special Education IS required for all certificates. Major changes are scheduled for 2009/2010.

Renewal Requirements: Individual Professional Development Plans (I-Plan) are developed to guide renewal through a three step process: I-Plan approval; I-Plan implementation; and submission of final documentation. Completed Individual I-Plan proposals and I-Plans are reviewed. 150 contact hours of qualifying Professional Development (PD) Activities for a five-year plan (although 15 hours = one PD credit, you must document at least five hours of sustained, not necessarily consecutive work, in one area).

CERTIFICATE AND ENDORSEMENT TYPES
Effective 1/1/2005

Certificate of Eligibility for Employment (CEE) (valid for 3 years): A CEE is a certificate issued to an individual who has satisfied all requirements for certification but who has not secured regular employment in Rhode Island. The CEE is valid for service as a substitute teacher.

Professional Certificate (valid for 5 years): A professional certificate is a certificate issued to an individual who holds regular employment in the schools of Rhode Island.

Two (2) Year Professional Certificate: A two (2) year professional certificate is a certificate that can be issued to individuals who completed teacher preparation but who do not meet current requirements or who have not completed requirements for renewal of their certificate. This certificate allows the individual to assume regular employment or to continue regular employment for a two-year period with the stipulation that all requirements for professional certification are completed within two (2) years. This certificate can only be issued once to an individual and is not renewable.

Endorsements: An endorsement is a provision added to a specific teaching certificate that expands on the validity of the certificate; e.g. a physical education teacher can be endorsed to be an adapted physical education teacher by satisfying the requirements of this endorsement area.

Emergency Permit (valid for one (1) year): A one (1) year emergency permit can be issued to individuals who do not meet requirements for the professional certification to assume regular employment in a specific school district in Rhode Island. The one (1) year emergency permit is issued at the request of a local school superintendent after he/she has documented that the services of a fully certified educator are unavailable.

EARLY CHILDHOOD CERTIFICATE
(Grades P - 2)

I. Certificate of Eligibility for Employment (CEE) – valid for three (3) years.

The initial certificate in Rhode Island for all areas of certification is a CEE. The CEE is used to seek regular employment in the public schools of Rhode Island for the field identified on the CEE. The CEE is also valid for service as a substitute teacher. If regular employment is not secured in the three (3) year period, the CEE can be renewed every three (3) years (see Note One below) until regular employment is secured. To be issued a CEE in early childhood education an individual needs to satisfy all of the following:

A. Bachelor's Degree from an accredited or an approved institution of higher education as defined in these regulations

B. Graduate of an approved program for the preparation of early childhood school teachers within the previous five (5) years from the date of application. Applicants who have not completed an approved program can be certified by transcript analysis by presenting evidence of six (6) semester hours of student teaching (SEE NOTE TWO) in the early childhood grades and not less than twenty-four semester hours of course work to include work in each of the following areas; Child Growth and Development, Curriculum and Methods in Early Childhood Education, Reading Readiness and Developmental Reading, Health and Nutrition for the Young Child; Child, Family, and Community Relationships; and Identification of and Service to Special Needs Children.

C. Applicants who have not been previously certified in the State of Rhode Island must achieve a score of 171 on the Early Childhood (0021) and 169 on the Early Childhood Content Knowledge Test (0022).
The Elementary Content Knowledge Test (0014) with a score of 145 and the Elementary Content Areas Exercises Test (0012) with a score of 148 also meet the test requirement for this area of certification.

II. Professional Certificate – valid for five (5) years

A. The professional certificate is issued to individuals who secure regular employment in the public schools of Rhode Island. Upon securing regular employment in Rhode Island, the CEE is used to request a five (5) year professional certificate. When applying for a five (5) year professional certificate the applicant must submit the CEE along with documentation from the employing authority that regular employment has been secured in the certification area of the CEE. Upon securing regular employment, the educator must write and get approved a five (5) year Individual Professional Development Plan (I-Plan).

B.   The professional certificate may be renewed every five (5) years upon the successful completion of an (I-Plan) that has been approved by the I-Plan Review Panel. Individuals who have not served as an early childhood education teacher in Rhode Island for the five (5) year period are entitled to an extension to the professional certificate (SEE NOTE THREE) at the end of each five (5) year period without the completion of an I-Plan.

NOTE ONE (1): Individuals who do not renew their CEE or Professional Certificate within six (6) months from the date of expiration may be required to complete additional requirements under new regulations to re-instate the expired certificate.

NOTE TWO (2): The student teaching requirement may be waived for an applicant who has had two or more documented years of successful teaching experience in an approved early childhood setting. Certified teachers who have had two or more years of teaching experience and who seek early childhood certification may fulfill the student teaching requirement by completing a one-year supervised internship at the early childhood level. After completing the necessary course work for the early childhood certificate, and arranging through the local community for a one-year internship, the Superintendent of Schools may request the issuance of a one-year professional certificate. The Department of Education must approve the internship in advance and the supervisor must have at least 3 years of teaching experience. Upon successful completion of the internship, the individual will be issued a five (5) year professional certificate.

NOTE THREE (3): The five (5) year professional certificate requires the successful completion of an I-Plan every five years for renewal for individuals who have been in regular employment for the five-year term of the certificate. To be entitled to an extension of the professional certificate without the completion of an I-Plan, educators must document their employment history during the previous five (5) years. Educators holding regular employment who serve for less than 135 days during any school year are entitled to a one (1) year extension of the professional certificate for each year of service less than 135 days to complete their I-Plan. Educators who leave regular employment during the term of the professional certificate are also entitled to an extension of the professional certificate for the number of years not engaged in regular employment. Educators who return to regular employment, must modify, if appropriate, the I-Plan on record and complete the five (5) year I-Plan during the remaining term of the extended certificate.

ELEMENTARY CERTIFICATE
(Grades 1 - 6)

Certificate of Eligibility for Employment (CEE): Valid three (3) years.
A.   See Early Childhood, CEE, A.
B.   See Early Childhood, CEE, B.
C.   Applicants who have not been previously certified in the State of Rhode Island must achieve a score of 145 on the Elementary Content Knowledge Test and 148 on the Elementary Content Area Exercises Test.

Professional Certificate:
A.   See Professional Certificate, Early Childhood Certificate, A.
B.   See Professional Certificate, Early Childhood Certificate, B.

NOTE ONE (1): See Early Childhood Certificate, Note One.
NOTE TWO (2): See Early Childhood Certificate, Note One, except at the Elementary level.
NOTE THREE (3): See Early Childhood Certificate, Note Three.

SECONDARY CERTIFICATE
(Grades 7 - 12)

Certificate of Eligibility:
A.   Bachelor's Degree from an accredited or an approved institution of higher education; and
B.   Graduate of an approved program for the preparation of secondary education school teachers within the previous five (5) years from the date of application. Applicants who have not completed an approved program can be certified by transcript analysis by presenting evidence of six (6) semester

hours of student teaching (SEE NOTE TWO) in the secondary grades and not less than eighteen (18) semester hours of course work to include work in each of the following areas: Adolescent Psychology, Secondary Methods, Measurements and Evaluation, Identification of and Service to Special Needs Students, Teaching of Reading in the Content Area, and Foundations of Education.

C.   Applicants who have not previously been certified in the State of Rhode Island must achieve a score of at least 167 on the Principles of Learning and Teaching Test, 7-12 prior to being certified.

D.

Requirements*	Sem. Hrs.	Requirements*	Sem. Hrs.
Agriculture	36	Secretarial (Bus.)	36
Social (Bus.)	36	English	30
History	30	Language (Classical)	30
Language (Foreign)	30	Mathematics	30
Science (General, Biology, Chemistry, Physics)	30	Social Studies	36
Areas not Listed	18		

*   For complete information, check the Rhode Island web site.

Professional Certificate:
A.   See Professional Certificate, Early Childhood Certificate, A.
B.   See Professional Certificate, Early Childhood Certificate, B.

NOTE ONE (1): See Early Childhood Certificate, Note One.
NOTE TWO (2): See Early Childhood Certificate, Note One, except at the Elementary level.
NOTE THREE (3): See Early Childhood Certificate, Note Three.

SPECIAL SUBJECTS CERTIFICATE
(PK - 12)

Certificate of Eligibility for Employment (CEE) – valid for three (3) years
    The initial certificate in Rhode Island for all areas of certification is a CEE. The CEE is used to seek regular employment in the schools of Rhode Island for the field identified on the CEE. The CEE is also valid for service as a substitute teacher. If regular employment is not secured in the three (3) year period, the CEE can be renewed every three (3) years until regular employment is secured. To be issued a CEE in special subjects education an individual needs to satisfy all of the following:

A.   See Early Childhood, CEE, A;
B.   Graduate of an approved program for the preparation of special subjects teachers within the previous five (5) years from the date of application. Applicants who have not completed an approved program can be certified by transcript analysis by presenting evidence of six (6) semester hours of student teaching (SEE NOTE TWO) in the both the elementary and secondary grades and not less than eighteen (18) semester hours of course work to include work in each of the following areas; Human Growth and Development; Foundations of Education; Methodology (must include at least one course in the Special Subjects field); Measurement and Evaluation; Identification of and Service to Special Needs Students; and the Teaching of Reading in the Content Area.
C.   Applicants who have not previously been certified in the State of Rhode Island must achieve a score

of at least 167 on the Principles of Learning and Teaching test, K-6 or the Principles of Learning and Teaching test 7-12. Only one test is required.

D.

Requirements[1]	Sem. Hrs.	Requirements[1]	Sem. Hrs.
Art	36	Dance	24
Health	24	Phys. Education	24
Home Econ.	36	Tech. Education	36
Library/Media	36	Music	36
Theatre	24	Special Subjects	18*

* A teaching certificate will be issued in any special subject field not listed above provided the candidate has met all requirements listed under Parts A and C of Section I and has 18 semester hours of credit in the special subject field for which certification is sought.

Professional Certificate: Valid 5 years.
A. See Professional Certificate, Early Childhood Certificate, A.
B. See Professional Certificate, Early Childhood Certificate, B.

NOTE ONE (1): See Early Childhood Certificate, Note One.
NOTE TWO (2): See Early Childhood Certificate, Note One, except at the Special Subjects level.
NOTE THREE (3): See Early Childhood Certificate, Note Three.

[1] Individuals who desire to secure certification in special subjects education by means of transcript evaluation will be required to submit evidence that they have completed appropriate academic course work. The Certification Office will publish an updated list annually of academic content areas required for each special subjects area of certification. This list of courses will take into consideration the desired distribution and appropriate level of academic course work which must be completed by individuals desiring to teach in the special subject grades.

SCHOOL COUNSELOR

The School Counselor certificate is valid for service as a school counselor in grades PK-12 in the public schools of the State of Rhode Island.

Certificate of Eligibility for Employment (CEE) - Valid for three years:
A. See Early Childhood, CEE, A;
B. An advanced degree in an approved program in school counseling within 5 years from the date of application or a Master's Degree from an accredited or an approved institution as defined in these regulations and completion of twenty-four (24) semester hours of graduate level coursework in school counseling which must include course work in Introduction to Pupil Personnel Service, Techniques of Counseling, Psychological and Educational Assessment, Vocational and Educational Placement and a minimum of a 3 semester hour internship in school counseling;
C. Eligibility for a Rhode Island Teacher's Certificate; and
D. Two years of documented teaching experience at the elementary or secondary level.

Professional Certificate: (Valid for five years, renewable):
A. See Professional Certificate, Early Childhood Certificate, A.
B. The professional certificate may be renewed every five (5) years upon the successful completion of an (I-Plan) that has been approved by the I-Plan Review Panel. Individuals who have not served as

a school counselor in Rhode Island for the five (5) year period are entitled to an extension to the professional certificate (SEE NOTE TWO) at the end of each five (5) year period without the completion of an I-Plan.

NOTE ONE (1): See Early Childhood Certificate, Note One.
NOTE TWO (2): The five (5) year professional certificate requires the successful completion of an I-Plan every five years for renewal for individuals who have been in regular employment for the five-year term of the certificate. To be entitled to an extension of the professional certificate without the completion of an I-Plan, educators must document their employment history during the previous five (5) years. Educators holding regular employment who serve for less than 135 days during any school year are entitled to a one (1) year extension of the professional certificate for each year of service less than 135 days to complete their I-Plan. Educators who leave regular employment during the term of the professional certificate are also entitled to an extension of the professional certificate for the number of years not engaged in regular employment. Educators who return to regular employment, must modify, if appropriate, the I-Plan on record and complete the five (5) year I-Plan during the remaining term of the extended certificate.

SCHOOL PSYCHOLOGIST

Certificate of Eligibility: (Valid for three years, renewable):
A.   Advanced degree in an approved program in school psychology; and
B.   12 semester hours of appropriate courses including Foundations of Education, Introduction to Education of the Exceptional Child, Curriculum and Instruction; and Reading.

Professional Certificate: (Valid for five years, renewable):
A.   See Professional Certificate, Early Childhood Certificate, A; and
B.   The professional certificate may be renewed every five (5) years upon the successful completion of an (I-Plan) that has been approved by the I-Plan Review Panel. Individuals who have not served as a school psychologist in Rhode Island for the five (5) year period are entitled to an extension to the professional certificate (SEE NOTE TWO) at the end of each five (5) year period without the completion of an I-Plan.

NOTE ONE (1): See Early Childhood Certificate, Note One.
NOTE TWO (2): The five (5) year professional certificate requires the successful completion of an I-Plan every five years for renewal for individuals who have been in regular employment for the five-year term of the certificate. To be entitled to an extension of the professional certificate without the completion of an I-Plan, educators must document their employment history during the previous five (5) years. Educators holding regular employment who serve for less than 135 days during any school year are entitled to a one (1) year extension of the professional certificate for each year of service less than 135 days to complete their I-Plan. Educators who leave regular employment during the term of the professional certificate are also entitled to an extension of the professional certificate for the number of years not engaged in regular employment. Educators who return to regular employment, must modify, if appropriate, the I-Plan on record and complete the five (5) year I-Plan during the remaining term of the extended certificate.

ELEMENTARY PRINCIPAL[1]
(Effective August 31, 2007)

The Elementary Principal certificate is valid for service as a principal or assistant principal in the public elementary schools or middle schools of the state of Rhode Island.
I.   **CERTIFICATE OF ELIGIBILITY FOR EMPLOYMENT (CEE)** – valid for three (3) years
        The initial certificate in Rhode Island for all areas of certification is a CEE. The CEE is used to seek regular employment in the schools of Rhode Island for the field identified on the CEE. The CEE is also valid for service as a substitute teacher. If regular employment is not secured in the three (3) year period, the CEE can be renewed every three (3) years until regular employment is secured. To be issued a CEE as an elementary principal an individual needs to satisfy all of the following:
        A.   Master's Degree from an accredited institution of higher education as defined in these

regulations;

B.   Eligibility for a Rhode Island educator's certificate excluding School Business Administrator certificate;

C.   Three years of documented professional education experience in the elementary/middle grades; and

D.   Graduate of an approved program for the preparation of elementary/middle school principals within the previous five (5) years from the date of application. Applicants who have not completed an approved program can be certified by transcript analysis by presenting evidence of having completed not less than twenty-four (24) semester hours of graduate level course work to include work in each of the following areas: School/Community Relations, Elementary Curriculum Development, Organization and Administration of the Elementary School, Supervision of Instruction, Supervision and Evaluation of Professional Staff, Educational Research, Program Evaluation, Fiscal Planning and Management, and School Law (Federal and State Laws and Regulations).

E.   In addition to the twenty-four (24) semester hours of course work requirement, a supervised internship/field experience is required. The experience requirement may be satisfied through an internship at an institution of higher education with an approved administrators preparation program or through a local school district with a Department of Education approved administrators field experience program. The internship or field experience under this section can only be conducted after the candidate has completed all other requirements for certification and must:

1.   Be served under the supervision of a certified administrator;

2.   Provide for quality in-depth experience across the elementary/middle grade levels;

3.   Be aligned with nationally recognized standards for school leaders;

4.   Assess candidate performance to the standards that documents research-based knowledge of best practice in leadership, and concentrate on the core function of schools and the role of the principal in the teaching and learning process; and

5.   Require the candidate to create a learning plan based on the standards and to maintain a portfolio that demonstrates competency and culminates in a final performance assessment.

II.   **PROFESSIONAL CERTIFICATE** – valid for five (5) years.

A.   The professional certificate is issued to individuals who secure regular employment in the schools of Rhode Island. Upon securing regular employment in Rhode Island, the CEE is used to request a five (5) year professional certificate. When applying for a five (5) year professional certificate the applicant must submit the CEE along with documentation from the employing authority that regular employment has been secured in the certification area of the CEE. Upon securing regular employment, the educator must write and get approved a five (5) year Individual Professional Development Plan (I-Plan).

B.   The professional certificate may be renewed every five (5) years upon the successful completion of an (I-Plan) that has been approved by the I-Plan Review Panel. Individuals who have not served as an elementary principal in Rhode Island for the five (5) year period are entitled to an extension to the professional certificate (SEE NOTE TWO) at the end of each five (5) year period without the completion of an I-Plan.

SECONDARY PRINCIPAL[1]
(Effective August 31, 2007)

The Secondary Principal certificate is valid for service as a principal or assistant principal in the public secondary schools or middle schools of the state of Rhode Island.

I.   Certificate of Eligibility for Employment (CEE) – valid for three (3) years.

The initial certificate in Rhode Island for all areas of certification is a CEE. The CEE is used to seek regular employment in the schools of Rhode Island for the field identified on the CEE. The CEE is also valid for service as a substitute teacher. If regular employment is not secured in the three (3) year period, the CEE can be renewed every three (3) years until regular employment is secured. To be issued a CEE as a secondary principal an individual needs to satisfy all of the following:

(A - C) See Elementary Principal requirements.

136

(D - E) See Elementary Principal - applies with Secondary level experiences.

II. **PROFESSIONAL CERTIFICATE** – valid for five (5) years.
    A.   See Elementary Principal, IIA
    B.   See Elementary Principal, IIB

[1]   For complete information, see the Department's web site.

SUPERINTENDENT

This certificate is valid for service as a superintendent or assistant superintendent in the State of Rhode Island.

Certificate of Eligibility - valid for three years.
A.   An advanced degree--Doctorate, Certificate of Advanced Graduate Study, or a Master's Degree. All applicants shall present evidence of having completed not less than thirty-six (36) semester hours of graduate level course work to include work in each of the following content areas: School/Community Relations, Curriculum Construction, K - 12 Organization and Administration of the Schools, Supervision of Instruction, Supervision and Evaluation of Professional Staff, Educational Research, Program Evaluation, School Plant Planning - and School Finance;
B.   Eligibility for a Rhode Island Teaching Certificate; and
C.   Eight years of educational experience to include both teaching and administration.

Professional Certificate:
A.   As for Elementary Principal (Professional Certificate, A) above.
B.   Three years of documented service as a superintendent in Rhode Island while on provisional certification. This experience must be documented by the Chairperson of the School Committee.
C.   **NOTE**: As in Elementary Principal (Professional Certificate, C) above, but with five (5) superintendent service years.

STATE OF SOUTH CAROLINA

South Carolina Department of Education
Office of Educator Certification
3700 Forest Drive Suite 500
Columbia, SC 29204
Phone: 877-885-5280 (in-state toll-free) / 803-734-8466 / Fax: 803-734-2873
Web Site: **http://www.scteachers.org/index.cfm**

INITIAL REQUIREMENTS AT A GLANCE:

Also needed will be items A, B, C (for initial certification), D (or similar), E, G, J and O - See page 2. The fee is $75.00. Fingerprinting Fee is $29.25. Passing scores on the Praxis II - Principles of Learning and Teaching (PLT) are required for initial certification. In addition, the appropriate PRAXIS II Specialty Area Examination is required. Out of state applicants are required to provide verification of previous certification and experience. The original certificate is valid for three (3) years. South Carolina DOES belong to the Interstate New Teacher Assessment and Support Consortium (INTASC) and the NASDTEC Interstate Certification Agreement (Teachers, Support Professionals, and Administrators). Courses or competencies in Special Education are NOT required.

Renewal Requirements (2004-2005 Update): Every five years, an educator who is employed in a

South Carolina public school district or State Department of Education-approved *Renewal Credit Plan* agency and holds a position that requires South Carolina educator certification must:
A. earn a minimum of 120 renewal credits that meet the appropriate eligibility criteria for each certificate renewal option/activity;
B. maintain all required verification;
C. adhere to all district/educational agency policies related to pre-approval and processing of renewal credit; and
D. submit necessary verification to the designated district/agency administrator for review, approval, and signature.

PROFESSIONAL TEACHING CERTIFICATES
Early Childhood (PreK-3), Elementary (2-6), Middle Level[1] (5-8), Secondary (9-12)

Initial Certification: Valid three years. Renewable in one year increments (if needed).
A. Bachelor's Degree from a regionally accredited institution or an institution approved by the South Carolina Department of Education;
B. Minimum required scores on the Praxis II Principles of Learning and Teaching and the appropriate South Carolina Area Exam scores in ALL AREAS for which the applicant wishes to be certified;
C. Completion of a State Board of Education approved teacher education program; and
D. Added teaching certification areas after the original certificate must satisfy South Carolina State Board of Education requirements.

Professional Certification: Valid five years.
A. Class III Bachelor's degree
B. Class II Bachelor's degree plus 18 sem. hrs. of graduate credit
C. Class I - Master's degree
D. Class I - Master's degree plus 30 sem. hrs.
E. Class I - Doctorate (Doctorate degree having met requirements for an initial area of certification)

Temporary Certificate for Out-of-State Certified Teachers:
After June 30, 2006, temporary certificates may no longer be issued to teachers who teach core academic subjects as specified by the No Child Left Behind Act of 2001. The core academic subjects are English, reading or language arts, mathematics, science, foreign languages, civics, government, economics, history, geography, and the arts. Temporary certificates may be issued, however, in other instructional or instructional support fields not considered to be core content subjects under No Child Left Behind.

Alternative Routes to Certification:
To address critical teaching shortages, South Carolina created a conditional certification program, the Program of Alternative Certification for Educators (PACE). The purpose of the program is to enable degreed individuals who otherwise do not meet certification requirements to be hired to teach in the public schools in critical need subject areas and in critical geographic areas where teacher shortages exist. Eligible candidates are enrolled in a series of training seminars, workshops, and graduate courses that lead to their professional certification.

[1] NOTE: New regulations apply to Middle Level certification were published on 03/04/2005. For complete details, visit their web site.

SCHOOL COUNSELOR

A. Master's degree in an approved program;
B. Professional certificate at the early childhood, elementary, middle school, or secondary level; and
C. Minimum qualifying score(s) on South Carolina State Board of Education required specialty-area examination(s)

MEDIA SPECIALIST

A. Bachelor's degree
B. Professional certificate at the early childhood, elementary, middle school, or secondary level
C. Minimum qualifying score(s) on the State Board of Education required specialty-area examination(s)
D. Completion of an advanced program approved by the State Board of Education for the preparation of Media Specialists.

PRINCIPALS AND SUPERVISORS
(Elementary & Secondary)

A. Valid South Carolina teacher's professional certificate at the appropriate level;
B. Minimum qualifying score on the approved Administrator's examination adopted by the State Board;
C. Three years of teaching experience including at least one year at the appropriate level; and
D. Completion of an advanced program approved for the training of principals and supervisors.

SUPERINTENDENT

A. Hold a Master's degree;
B. Valid South Carolina teacher's or principal's professional certificate;
C. Minimum qualifying score on the approved area administrator's examination adopted by the State Board;
D. Three years experience as a PreK-12 or post secondary teacher and two years as a school or school district administrator or school business administrator; and
E. Completion of an advanced program approved for the training of school superintendents.

STATE OF SOUTH DAKOTA

Department of Education and Cultural Affairs
Office of Accreditation and Teacher Quality
700 Governors Drive
Pierre, South Dakota 57501-2291
Phone: 605-773-3134 / Fax: 605-773-6139
Web Site: **http://doe.sd.gov/oatq/**

INITIAL REQUIREMENTS AT A GLANCE:

Also needed will be items A, B, C, G, H, I, K, and O - See page 2. The fee is $30.00; $50.00 for the Advanced 10-year Certificate. There is a $20.00 transcript analysis fee. Teachers new to the profession must take one of the Principles of Learning and Teaching (PLT) tests that most closely matches their preparation. Praxis II tests are required for those persons completing a program or endorsement after July 1, 2005. South Dakota DOES belong to the Interstate Certification Compact and the NASDTEC Interstate Contract (Teachers, Administrators, and Vocational Educators) and has comprehensive certification pacts with Illinois, Iowa, Kansas, Michigan, Missouri, Nebraska, Oklahoma and Wisconsin as well as the Western States Certification Consortium (WSCC). South Dakota DOES belong to the New Teacher Assessment and Support Consortium (INTASC). Courses or competencies in Special Education ARE required as well as courses in Human Relations (3 hrs), and South Dakota Indian Studies (3 hrs.) As of 2007, major revisions have just been completed. **NOTE:** Out-of-state applicants may be issued a 5-year non-renewable certificate and must complete the Human Relations and South Dakota Indian Studies to be eligible for the renewal of a 5-year certificate.

> **Renewal Requirements:** Renewable every 5 years. Any combination of six semester hours of credit from any accredited postsecondary institution, including community colleges and technical institutes, as well as department renewal credit or CEUs may be accepted. Three of the six hours must be college transcripted.

South Dakota's **Alternative Route to Certification** is limited to content areas issued at the approved education program level. Elementary education programs will not be available in the alternative certification process beginning on July 1, 2003 and after. The three year alternative route to certification program shall consist of on-the-job classroom training during (2 semesters), mentorship during the on-the-job training, an orientation program provided by the employer, and six semester hours of education coursework in pedagogy and related fields of the education.

To be eligible for the alternative certification program, applicants must meet the following requirements:
> 1) Holds a bachelor's degree or higher, with the bachelor's degree obtained at least two-years prior to admittance into the alternative certification program;
> 2) Has maintained an overall grade point average of 2.5 grade point on a 4.0 scale or higher on the undergraduate degree transcript;
> 3) Holds a college major in the subject area to be taught or has five years experience in a related field, as determined by the department;
> 4) Has an offer of employment from a South Dakota accredited system that operates a mentoring program approved by the department;
> 5) Submits to a criminal background investigation;
> 6) Adheres to the Code of Professional Ethics; and
> 7) Completes a screening interview with school personnel and the department's program coordinator prior to being hired by a school system.

PROGRAM REQUIREMENTS - BIRTH THROUGH PRESCHOOL EDUCATION

Requirements:
> The required courses and experiences of a birth through preschool education program shall meet the National Association for Education of Young Children (NAEYC) standards, 2001 edition.
> The program shall require candidates to demonstrate the content, pedagogical, and professional knowledge and skills identified in the NAEYC standards and to demonstrate competency on multiple assessment measures.
> A birth through preschool education program shall require coursework sufficient to constitute an academic major and demonstrated competencies in the following areas of professional education:
> 1. Knowledge of the developmental characteristics of the birth through preschool learner and the student with disabilities;
> 2. Integrating technology into teaching and learning;
> 3. Completion of courses in human relations (3 hrs.) and South Dakota Indian studies (3 hrs.)

PROGRAM REQUIREMENTS - ELEMENTARY TEACHING
(Grades K - 8)

> The required courses and experiences of a K-8 elementary education program shall meet the National Association for Education of Young Children (NAEYC) standards, 2001 edition.   The program shall require candidates to demonstrate the content, pedagogical, and professional knowledge and skills identified in the NAEYC standards and to demonstrate competency on multiple assessment measures.
> A K-8 educational program shall require coursework sufficient to constitute an elementary education major and demonstrated competencies in the following areas of professional education:
> 1. Knowledge of the developmental characteristics of the elementary level learner and of the student with disabilities;
> 2. Knowledge of curriculum development that uses the South Dakota K-12 content standards as

provided in SD regulations and other established K-12 academic standards to design an instructional program that facilitates student achievement and promotes lifelong learning;

      3. Integrating technology into teaching and learning;

      4. Completion of courses in human relations (3 hrs.) and South Dakota Indian studies (3 hrs.)

      5. Verification that the candidate has completed studies and field experiences in the following:

          a. Design of curriculum and instructional strategies for middle level learners;

          b. Developmental characteristics of the middle level learner; and

          c. Concepts of middle level education or middle level learner.

PROGRAM REQUIREMENTS - MIDDLE SCHOOL / JUNIOR HIGH TEACHING
(Grades 5 - 8)

The required courses and experiences of a middle level education program shall meet the National Association for Education of Young Children (NAEYC) standards, 2001 edition.

The program shall require candidates to demonstrate the content, pedagogical, and professional knowledge and skills identified in the NMSAMTP standards and to demonstrate competency on multiple assessment measures.

A 5-8 middle level education program shall require coursework sufficient to constitute a middle school education major and demonstrated competencies in the following areas of professional education:

      1. Teaching of middle level reading;

      2. Integrating technology into teaching and learning;

      3. Knowledge of the developmental characteristics of the middle level learner and of the student with disabilities;

      4. Knowledge of curriculum development that uses the South Dakota K-12 content standards as provided in SD regulations and other established K-12 academic standards to design an instructional program that facilitates student achievement and promotes lifelong learning;

      5. Completion of courses in human relations (3 hrs.) and South Dakota Indian studies (3 hrs.)

PROGRAM REQUIREMENTS FOR SECONDARY TEACHING
(Grades 7 - 12)

All 7-12 secondary education programs shall require coursework sufficient to constitute an academic major and demonstrated competencies in the following areas of professional education:

      1. Competency in the teaching of content area literacy and instructional methods in the content area specific to the discipline;

      2. Knowledge of the developmental characteristics of the secondary level learner and of the student with disabilities;

      3. Knowledge of curriculum development that uses the South Dakota K-12 content standards as provided in SD regulations and other established K-12 academic standards to design an instructional program that facilitates student achievement and promotes lifelong learning;

      4. Integrating technology into teaching and learning;

      5. Completion of courses in human relations (3 hrs.) and South Dakota Indian studies (3 hrs.)

      6. Verfication that the candidate has completed studies and field experiences in the following:

          a. Design of curriculum and instructional strategies for middle level learners;

          b. Developmental characteristics of the middle level learner; and

          c. Concepts of middle level education or the middle level learner.

PROGRAM REQUIREMENTS FOR LIBRARY-MEDIA SPECIALIST
(PK - 12)

Requirements: A preschool through grade 12 school library media education specialist program shall comply with all standards in general education and professional education and require coursework sufficient to constitute a major. The required courses and experiences of a preschool through grade 12 school library media specialist education program shall meet the American Library Association/American Association of School Libraries (ALA/AASL) standards, 2002 edition.

The program shall require candidates to demonstrate the applicable content, pedagogical, and professional knowledge and skills identified in the ALA/AASL standards and to demonstrate competency on the required applicable multiple assessment measures. State certification may be issued after completion of a master's degree at an American Library Association accredited library school or a National Council for Accreditation of Teacher Education (NCATE) approved master's degree designed to prepare school library media specialists. For complete details, contact the Department.

PROGRAM REQUIREMENTS FOR SCHOOL COUNSELOR
(PK - 12)

Requirements: Master's degree in school guidance or counseling. The required courses and experiences of a preschool through grade 12 school counselor education program shall meet the Council for Accreditation of Counseling and Related Education Programs (CACREP) standards, 2001 edition. The program shall require candidates to demonstrate the applicable content, pedagogical, and professional knowledge and skills identified in the CACREP standards and to demonstrate competency on the required applicable multiple assessment measures. For complete details, contact the Department.

PROGRAM REQUIREMENTS FOR SCHOOL PSYCHOLOGIST
(Birth - Age 21)

Requirements: Graduate degree in school psychology. The required courses and experiences of a birth to age 21 school psychologist education program shall meet the National Association of School Psychologists (NASP) standards, 2000 edition. The program shall require candidates to demonstrate the applicable content, pedagogical, and professional knowledge and skills identified in the NASP standards and to demonstrate competency on the applicable required multiple assessment measures. State certification may be issued with documentation of current national certification by the National Association of School Psychologists. For complete details, contact the Department.

PROGRAM REQUIREMENTS FOR PRINCIPAL
(PK - 12, PK - 8, and 7 - 12)

Requirements: (1) Master's degree; (2) Three years of verified experience on a valid certificate in an accredited K-12 school, one year of which includes classroom teaching experience or direct services to students; (3) Demonstrated competence related to the age/grade span for which authorization is sought; and (4) Internship to include all job responsibilities of the principalship at the age/grade span for which authorization is sought. For a PK - 12 principal program, the internship must include time spent in at least two of the levels of elementary, junior high/middle school, or secondary school.

The required courses and experiences of a PK - 8 or 7 - 12 principal program shall meet the Educational Leadership Constituent Council (ELCC) standards, 2001 edition. The program shall require candidates to demonstrate the applicable content, pedagogical, and professional knowledge and skills identified in the ELCC standards and to demonstrate competency on the required applicable multiple assessment measures. The principal programs may be developed with multiple options to earn eligibility for a PK - 12 principal program within the same master's degree or as an additional certification-only principal program. For complete details, contact the Department.

PROGRAM REQUIREMENTS FOR SUPERINTENDENT
(PK - 12)

Requirements: (1) Completion of an education specialist or doctoral degree; (2) three years of verified experience on a valid certificate in an accredited K-12 school, one year of which includes classroom teaching experience or direct services to students; and (3) Internship that allows participation in all job responsibilities of the cooperating superintendent.

The required courses and experiences of a preschool through grade 12 career school superintendent program shall meet the Educational Leadership Constituent Council (ELCC) standards,

2001 edition. The program shall require candidates to demonstrate the applicable content, pedagogical, and professional knowledge and skills identified in the ELCC standards and to demonstrate competency on the required applicable multiple assessment measures. For complete details, contact the Department.

STATE OF TENNESSEE

Tennessee Department of Education
Office of Teacher Licensing
710 James Robertson Parkway
Andrew Johnson Tower, 9th Floor
Nashville, Tennessee 37243-0377
Phone: 615-532-4885 / Fax: 615-532-1448
Web Site: **http://www.state.tn.us/education/lic/**

INITIAL REQUIREMENTS AT A GLANCE:

Also needed will be items A, B, C, D (or State approved and regionally accredited teacher preparation program), E, G, O (some exemptions), and Q - See page 2. There is NO FEE. A state administered certification test is NOT required. Scores on the Praxis II PLT and subject area tests are required (there are exemptions). Tennessee DOES belong to the NASDTEC Interstate Compact (Teachers, Support Professionals, Administrators, and Vocational Educators) and *may* accept certificates of applicants from other NCATE member states as well. Tennessee IS a member of the Interstate New Teacher Assessment and Support Consortium (INTASC). Courses or competencies in Special Education ARE required. Performance Standards must be met to insure that teacher knows how to identify students with exceptional learning needs. Tennessee has ongoing changes to their requirements. New rules are in effect for the Alternative Licensure effective 7/1/2007. See below. Major revisions are planned for 2009. Contact the Department for complete information.

Recertification Requirements: No Fee. Must be renewed every ten years. All educators holding a Professional and Professional School Service Personnel License based on a Bachelor's degree must earn 90 renewal points. All educators holding a Professional Teacher License based on a Master's degree or higher who have not accrued five years of acceptable experience during the ten-year validity period of the license are also required to earn 90 renewal points. However if the holder of a Professional Teacher License has a Master's degree or higher, and has accrued five years of acceptable experience during the ten-year validity period of the license, no renewal points will be required, only verification of that experience.

Renewal points may be earned in a variety of ways. For example, an educator may choose to earn coursework (1 semester hour = 15 points), CEUs (1 CEU = 10 points), or participate in pre-approved professional development activities (Participant: 1 hour = 1 point or Leader/Presenter: 1 hour = 3 points, if new presentation). Contact the Department for forms and further information.

CERTIFICATE ENDORSEMENTS

The following endorsements are available in Tennessee*:

Early Childhood	Technology Engineering Education . . . . . . (5-12)
Middle Grades . . . . (4-8)	
Other Foreign Language . . . . (7-12)	**Vocational Endorsements:**
English . . . . (7-12)	Collision Repair Technology; Automotive
Theater . . . . (K-12)	Technology; Aircraft Maintenance; Carpentry;

Speech Communication . . . . (7-12)
Mathematics . . . . (7-12)
Physics . . . . (7-12)
Biology . . . . (7-12)
Chemistry . . . . (7-12)
Earth Science . . . . (7-12)
Health . . . . (K-12)
Physical Education . . . . (K-12)
History . . . . (7-12)
Government . . . . (7-12)
Geography . . . . (7-12)
Library Information Specialist . . . . (PK-12)
German . . . . (K-12 & 7-12)
Latin . . . . (K-12 & 7-12)
Spanish . . . . (K-12 & 7-12)
Russian . . . . (K-12 & 7-12)
French . . . . (K-12 & 7-12)
Other Foreign Languages . . . . (7-12) & (PK-12)
Economics . . . . (7-12)
Sociology . . . . (9-12)
Psychology . . . . (9-12)
Visual Arts . . . . (K-12)
Business Education . . . . (7-12)
Business Technology . . . . (7-12)
Marketing . . . . (7-12)
Vocal/General Music . . . . (K-12)
Instrumental Music . . . . (K-12)
Basic Business/Accounting . . . . (7-12)
Vocational Agriculture . . . . (7-12)
Agriscience . . . . (7-12)
Dance . . . . (K-12)
Technical Engineering Educ. . . . . (5-12)
Family and Consumer Science . . . . (5-12)
Driver Education . . . . (7-12)
Bible . . . . (7-12)
ESL . . . . (PK-12)

Electricity; Concrete/ Masonry; Plumbing;
Drafting/CAD; Graphic Communications;
Cosmetology; Culinary Arts; Leisure Craft
Technology; Radio/TV Broadcasting; Health
Science Occupations; Diesel Equipment
Technology; Welding and Cutting; Other T & I;
Legal and Protective Services; Jobs for Tennessee
Graduates; Aviation Ground School;
Manufacturing Technology; Electronic Media;
HVACR; Technology Infrastructure*

Coop Coordinator
Supervisor of Material
Supervisor of Attendance
Food Service Supervisor
Beginning Administration (A) . . . . (PK-12)
Beginning Administration (B) . . . . (PK-12)
Professional Administration . . . . (PK-12)
Professional Administration (B) . . . . (PK-12)
Superintendent
School Counselor . . . . (PK-12)
School Social Worker . . . . (PK-12)
School Psychologist . . . . (PK-12)
Reading Specialist . . . . (PK-12)
JROTC . . . .

Special Education:
Modified Program . . . . (K-12)
Comprehensive Program . . . . (K-12)
Vision . . . . (PK-12)
Hearing . . . . (PK-12)
Speech/Language . . . . (PK-12)
Early Childhood/Pre-K Education . . . . (PK-3)
Early Developmental/Learning . . . . (PK-K)
Gifted . . . . (PK-12)
School Audiologist . . . . (PK-12)
Speech / Language . . . . (PK-12)

* For a complete listing, visit the Department's web site

LICENSES

A. **Apprentice License:** Valid five years, Renewable. Issued to an educator who has completed an approved teacher preparation program. It is valid for five years. The holder of an Apprentice License has five years in which to teach three years in a Tennessee public or state-accredited private school. Once the Apprentice License is used for three years in an approved Tennessee school, it is no longer valid. The school district must then submit evidence of a positive local evaluation, and the license holder will advance to the Professional License.

B. **Professional License:** Valid ten years, Renewable. Issued to a teacher who has accrued a minimum of three years of acceptable experience in an approved school and has received a positive local evaluation in a Tennessee public or state-accredited private school. (The three years of experience can be a combination of in-state/out-of-state experience but the last year must be served in a Tennessee school to participate in the local evaluation process.)

C. **Out-of-State Teacher's License:** Valid five years, renewable. An Out-of-State Teacher License is issued to an applicant who meets Tennessee licensure requirements and has at least one year of acceptable teaching experience in another state. It is equivalent to an Apprentice License. Upon completion of a minimum of three years of teaching (a combination of in-state/out-of- state experience, with the last year in Tennessee) and receipt of a positive local evaluation, the license holder will advance to the Professional License.

D. **Alternative Licenses*:** Effective 7/1/2007, the following two types of alternative licenses are available in all teaching licensure areas:

Type I Alternative License - Candidates who enroll in and complete a pre-service orientation prior to beginning employment in the fall. The candidate will have met content knowledge requirements, will have been admitted to an approved Type I licensure program, will have completed the orientation component of the professional education core, and will have obtained an "intent to hire" statement and recommendation for the Type I license from the employing school system in collaboration with an institution of higher education approved to offer Type I licenses. The candidate may or may not have yet completed all required licensure exams. Type I program participants who have not attained an "intent to hire" statement from a school system upon completion of the orientation component of the program may transition to a post-baccalaureate licensure program for licensure OR they may continue to seek employment under an Alternative License Type I.

Type II Alternative License - Candidates must have met content in one of the following ways:
1. Acceptable major in the endorsement area OR
2. Document that they have at least 24 semester hours in the teaching content area OR
3. Verify that they have passed the required PRAXIS II content exam(s) for the endorsement areas sought.
Once the candidate has met one of the three ways above, additional course work in the academic major WILL NOT be required.
Teachers holding Alternative Type II licenses must demonstrate satisfactory annual progress toward completion of all licensure requirements. Teachers may teach on an Alternative Type II license no more than three years. This three-year limit MAY NOT be exceeded by switching between alternative licensure Types I and II OR by changing teaching positions OR school systems.

* For further details, contact the Department.

SCHOOL GUIDANCE COUNSELOR ENDORSEMENT
(PK - 12)

Requirements:
A. Completion of an approved preparation program in school guidance and counseling with a graduate degree.
B. Satisfy Specialty Area tests.

ADMINISTRATION / SUPERVISION
Elementary and Secondary (K - 12)

Tennessee issues two types of Administrator Licenses:

Beginning Administrator License is issued to an individual who has completed an approved graduate program in school administration at a college/university with acceptable accreditation. This program will include a practicum or a one-semester internship working through a Tennessee school system under a mentor principal. After completion of a state required test/assessment, those individuals who have completed a practicum must be recommended by the college/university for the Beginning Administrator License. Those individuals who have completed an internship program must be recommended by the college/university and the superintendent of schools to receive the Beginning Administrator License. Once the holder of the Beginning Administrator License obtains employment as a beginning principal in a Tennessee public or state accredited private school, the evaluation process can begin to advance to the Professional Administrator License.

Professional Administrator License (Valid ten years, renewable) - Issued after the holder of a Beginning Administrator License obtains employment as a principal in a Tennessee public or state-accredited private school and meets the requirements for advancement. These requirements include completion of a customized professional development program (jointly developed by principal, superintendent, college/university, and mentor), local evaluation by superintendent or designee, two years of successful experience as a principal and a recommendation by the superintendent and the college/university for the Professional Administrator License.

SUPERINTENDENT

The standard for a certificate of qualification for a superintendent shall be:

Hold any professional certificate endorsed principal and/or supervisor of instruction.
A minimum of a Master's degree with a graduate major in Educational Administration and Supervision, or, a minimum of thirty (30) graduate quarter hours (20 semester hours) in administration, supervision, and related courses. The following courses must be included: (1) School Organization and Administration; (2) Supervision; (3) Curriculum Development; (4) School Finance; (5) School Plant and Transportation; and (6) School and Community Relationships.
Five (5) years of acceptable experience which must include teaching and/or administration.

STATE OF TEXAS

Texas Education Agency
Educator Certification & Standards
1701 North Congress Ave
WBT 5-100
Austin, TX 78701-1494
Phone: 888-863-5880 / Fax: 512-469-3016
Web Site: **http://www.sbec.state.tx.us/SBECOnline/**

INITIAL REQUIREMENTS AT A GLANCE:

Also needed will be items A, B, and E (Photocopy on front and back of the certificate) - See page 2. The fee is $50.00 for a One-Year Certificate; $75.00 for a Standard Certificate; and $175.00 for out-of-state applicants (non-refundable). Fingerprinting fees: $57. The Standard Certificate is valid for five (5) years. A state administered test, the Examination for the Certification of Educators in Texas - (ExCET) IS required. Texas DOES belong to the Interstate Certification Compact. Texas DOES belong to the NASDTEC Interstate Contract (Teachers, Administrators, and Vocational). Courses in Special Education are NOT required. Major revisions are ongoing. As of 10/2007, changes are occurring in Texas certification. Contact the State Board for further information.

Recertification Requirements: Renewal requires the completion of 150 clock hours of Continuing Professional Education (CPE). Current educators holding a lifetime certificate have been exempted from the Standard Certificate renewal process.

CERTIFICATION AREAS

Pedagogy and Prof. Responsibilities ... (EC-12)
Pedagogy and Prof. Responsibilities ..... (EC-4)
Generalist .... (EC-4)
Bilingual Generalist .... (EC-4)
Bilingual Education .... (EC-4)
Bilingual Education .... (EC-4)
Generalist .... (EC-4)
Languages other than English .... (EC-12)
Pedagogy and Prof. Responsibilities ..... (8-12)
Pedagogy and Prof. Responsibilities ..... (4-8)
Generalist .... (4-8)
Bilingual Generalist .... (4-8)
Generalist .... (4-8)

Life Science .... (8-12)
Physical Science .... (8-12)
Science .... (8-12)
Technology Applications
.... (*All* Beginning Teachers)
NOTE: These Technology Applications standards are expected of ALL beginning teachers and will be incorporated into the new ExCETs for Pedagogy and Professional Responsibilities at each certification level.
History .... (8-12)
English Language Arts and Reading ..... (8-12)
Social Studies .... (8-12)

Bilingual Education	(4-8)	History	(8-12)
English Language Arts & Reading	(4-8)	Mathematics	(8-12)
Mathematics	(4-8)	Life Science	(8-12)
Science	(4-8)	Physical Science	(8-12)
Social Studies	(4-8)	Science	(8-12)
English Language Arts and Reading	(4-8)	Computer Science	(8-12)
Mathematics	(4-8)	Technology Applications	(8-12)
English Lang. Arts & Reading/Soc. Studies	(4-8)	**Master Teachers** . (EC-4, 4-8, 8-12, and EC-12)	
Mathematics/Science	(4-8)	Master Mathematics Teacher	
English Language Arts and Reading	(8-12)	Master Technology Teacher	
Social Studies	(8-12)	Master Reading Teacher	
Mathematics	(8-12)	Counselor	
Art	(EC-12)	Librarian	
Business Education	(6-12)	Principal	
Agricultural Science & Technology	(6-12)	Superintendent	

CERTIFICATE REQUIREMENTS:

A. Everyone certified to teach in Texas must hold a bachelors degree with coursework in three areas: (1) a broad general education; (2) academic specialization(s); and (3) teaching knowledge and abilities. You must complete teacher training through an approved program. You must successfully complete the appropriate teacher certification tests for the subject and grade level you wish to teach.

B. All candidates must pass examinations of professional knowledge and subject matter knowledge approved by the State Board for Educator Certification on ExCET, Texas Oral Proficiency Test (TOPT), Texas Assessment of Sign Communication (TASC) and (TASC-ASL).

CERTIFICATION OF CREDENTIALS FROM ANOTHER STATE OR U.S. TERRITORY:

An applicant who has been issued a standard certificate or credential from another state or United States territory, may apply for a Texas certificate. The credential must be equivalent to a certificate issued by the State Board for Educator Certification (SBEC), and must not have been revoked, suspended, or pending such action. SBEC will evaluate an expired credential provided it was standard at the time of issuance.

To apply for a review of credentials, all applicants must submit the following items:
A. An Application for Certification for Out-of-State Certificate Holders;
B. $175 fee (non-refundable);
C. Copies of the front and back of all educator credentials issued by another state; and
D. Official transcripts of all college credits, bearing the seal and signature of the college registrar.

An applicant who holds a standard credential from another state, and who meets specified requirements as determined by the review of credentials completed by the SBEC may be issued a One-Year Certificate in one or more subject areas. To receive a One-Year Certificate, you must indicate a specific effective date in item 26 of the application; and an additional $50 fee.

To establish eligibility for the Standard Certificate, applicants must complete all requirements specified in the certification plan prepared by the SBEC.

SCHOOL LIBRARIAN

Standard School Librarian Certification:
A. Master's degree from an accredited institution of higher education;
B. Successfully complete a school librarian preparation program;
C. Successfully complete the assessments required; and
D. Have two school years of classroom teaching experience from a public or accredited private school.

COUNSELOR

Standard School Counselor Certificate:

A.   Master's degree from an accredited institution of higher education;

B.   Two school years of classroom teaching experience in a public or accredited private school.

C.   Successfully complete the assessments required under this title; and (3) hold a master's degree from an accredited institution of higher education;

D.   Successfully complete a school counselor preparation program that meets the requirements for SBEC Standards for the School Counselor Certificate.

PRINCIPAL CERTIFICATES

Standard Principal Certificate:

A.   Hold a master's degree from an accredited institution;

B.   Successfully complete the assessments required;

C.   Have two years of creditable teaching experience as a classroom teacher;

D.   Passing scores on the Principal ExCET; and

E.   An induction period must occur during employment as an assistant principal or principal in a Texas public or private school. An individual seeking to enter the induction period more than five years after the date of issuance of the Conditional Principal Certificate must be approved by the educator preparation program that recommended him or her for the certificate.

SUPERINTENDENT CERTIFICATES

First-time Superintendents (including the first time in the state):

A.   Complete a one-year mentorship which should include at least 36 clock hours of professional development. During the one-year mentorship, the superintendent should have contact with his or her mentor at least once a month . The mentorship program must be completed within the first 18 months of employment in the superintendency in order to maintain the standard certificate.

B.   Experienced superintendents willing to serve as mentors must participate in training for the role.

Standard Superintendent Certificate:

A.   Hold a master's degree from an accredited institution;

B.   The individual shall satisfactorily complete an assessment based on the standards identified by the State Board; and

C.   The individual shall successfully complete an SBEC-approved superintendent preparation program and be recommended for certification by that program.

STATE OF UTAH

Office of Education
Educator Quality and Licensing
250 East 500 South, PO Box 144200
Salt Lake City, Utah 84114-4200
Phone: 801-538-7740 / Fax: 801-538-7973
Web Site: **http://www.usoe.k12.ut.us/cert/**

INITIAL REQUIREMENTS AT A GLANCE:

Also needed will be items A, B, C, E, G, K and O - See page 2. Fee is $50 for evaluation and licensing. There is a $69.00 fingerprint and background check fee. Qualifying scores on the Praxis II (PLT) Exam are required to move from Level I to Level II. The Level I license is valid for three (3) years. Utah DOES belong to the Interstate Certification Compact and the NASDTEC Interstate Contract (Teachers, Support Professionals, Administrators, and Vocational Educators). Utah DOES belong to the Interstate New Teacher Assessment and Support Consortium (INTASC). Courses or competencies in Special Education ARE required for all certificates.

Recertification Requirements: ($60.00 - $85.00 fee)
Level I Educators - 100 Professional Development Points over period of license. Points may come from professional development activities, workshops, or employment experience (25 points per year over previous three years). **Level 2/3 Educators** (valid license) - 200 points over the period of the license. Points may come from professional development activities and/or employment experience (35 point per year up to 3 years during license validity period). Level 2 educators have a 5 year license validity; Level 3 educators have a 7 year license validity.

ALTERNATIVE ROUTES TO TEACHER LICENSING

A program for individuals who have a bachelors degree but lack teacher preparation. The Alternative Routes to Teacher Licensure were developed to increase the number of eligible, qualified and prepared teachers. The programs offer an alternative to the traditional two year university teacher preparation.

Eligibility: To be admitted to Alternative Routes to Licensure (ARL) an individual must: Hold a bachelors degree from an accredited institution of higher education; and be employed by a Utah school district or an accredited Utah school. For complete details on ARL, contact the Section.

EARLY CHILDHOOD (K - 3), ELEMENTARY (1 - 8), ELEMENTARY (K - 6), SECONDARY (6 - 12), PRESCHOOL SPECIAL EDUCATION (Birth - Age 5), SPECIAL EDUCATION (K - 12), COMMUNICATION DISORDERS, SPEECH-LANGUAGE PATHOLOGIST, OR SPEECH-LANGUAGE TECHNICIAN LICENSES

I.   **Level 1 License** - Initial certificate - Valid 3 years. An applicant must have:
   A.   Bachelor's Degree from an accredited institution;
   B.   Completed an approved program in one of the nine license areas above which has met the Standards for program approval by the Utah State Board of Education.
      1.   An Early Childhood Education license area is required for teaching kindergarten and permits assignment in kindergarten through grade three; it is recommended for those teaching in formal programs below kindergarten level.
      2.   An Elementary Teaching license area is valid in grades one through eight. The 1 - 8 certificate permits a teacher to teach any academic area in self-contained classes in grades 1 - 6. However, the teacher must be subject specific endorsed to teach assigned subjects at the 7 - 8 grade level.
   An Elementary Teaching (K 6) license area is valid grades K through 6. The K-6 permits a teacher to teach any academic area in self-contained classes in K-6.
      4.   The Middle Level (5 - 9) license area currently in force will continue to be valid; however, a Middle Level Certificate *is no longer issued*.
      5.   A Secondary Teaching license area with subject endorsements is valid in grades 6-12. The 6-12 certificate requires a major and minor, or composite major, but the teacher cannot teach in an elementary self-contained class.
      Secondary teaching candidates must have completed an approved teaching major, or composite major, consistent with subjects taught in Utah secondary schools. The license will be endorsed for all subjects in which the candidate has at least a minor or has completed equivalent training, or has demonstrated competence in the subject(s) in accordance with criteria established by the Utah State Board of Education.
         a.   A teaching major as required for state certification includes not fewer than 30 semester hours or 45 quarter hours of credit in one subject;
         b.   A minor includes not fewer than 16 semester hours or 24 quarter hours of credit in on subject; and
         c.   A composite major includes not fewer than 46 semester hours or 69 quarter hours of credit, distributed in two or more related subjects.

6.   A <u>Special Education (Birth - Age 5)</u> license area requires the completion of an approved program which addresses early childhood special education competencies. Candidates completing an approved program will also be recommended for early intervention credentialing. Teachers holding an equivalent certificate from out of state will be required to meet the current standards when renewing or applying for Utah certification.

7.   A <u>Special Education</u> (K - 12) license area for teaching students with handicaps is issued by the Utah State Board of Education with endorsements in the following areas: (1) Mild/Moderate - permits the holder to teach students with mild/moderate learning and behavior problems; (2) Severe - permits the holder to teach students with severe learning and behavior problems; (3) Hearing Impaired - permits the holder to teach students who are deaf or hearing impaired; and (4) Visually Impaired - permits the holder to teach students who are blind or visually impaired. Special Education teaching candidates shall have completed an approved program for teaching students with mild/moderate, severe, hearing, or visual handicaps. The certificate will be endorsed for the area(s) in which the program is completed.

8.   A <u>Communication Disorders</u> license is issued by the Utah State Office of Education for teaching pupils with communication disorders. The teacher must be endorsed in audiology. This license/endorsement permits service at the elementary and/or secondary level (K-12.) Candidates shall have completed an approved program which shall have included the master's degree or 55 quarter hours earned after meeting requirements for a bachelor's degree and which shall have met the standards for program approval adopted by the Utah State Office of Education.

9.   A <u>Speech-Language Pathologist</u> (SLP) license area applies at the K - 12 levels. Candidates must have completed a Board-approved program for teaching students with speech/language impairments. Such programs include: a master's degree and certificate of Clinical Competence (CCC), or a master's degree; or an international equivalent earned in a communications disorders program after receiving a bachelor's degree from an accredited higher education institution. A candidate who has completed a Board-approved bachelor's degree program in communications disorders from an accredited institution, and acquired the competencies necessary for assignment as a graduate student intern, may receive a one-year letter of authorization from the United States Office of Education (USOE) which may be renewed up to three years. Contact the Board for complete requirements.

10.   A <u>Speech-Language Technician</u> (SLT) license area applies at the K - 12 levels. Candidates must have completed a Board-approved bachelor's degree in communications disorders at an accredited institution and additional training as required by the USOE. Addtional professional development shall be completed prior to or within the first year of receiving this area of concentration, in order to meet defined competencies. Contact the board for complete requirements.

II.   **Level 2 License** - Valid 5 years, Renewable. An applicant must have:
     A.   Completed at least three years of successful teaching under a Level I License or its equivalent;
     B.   Been recommended by the employing school district; and
     C.   Completed ancillary requirements un Utah Early Years Enhancement (EYE) program.

III.   **Level 3 License** - Valid 7 years, Renewable
Applicant must be eligible to hold a Level 2 license AND either a Doctoral degree OR National Board Certification in field.

ADDITIONAL TEACHING ENDORSEMENTS

To apply for these endorsements, you must already have a Level 1 or Level 2 License with an

Elementary or Secondary Area of Concentration. Endorsements available through this program are:

American Sign Language	Health	Mathematics - Secondary
Fine Arts Elem. Level I	Social Studies	Visual Arts
Science	Distance Learning	Elem Reading - Advanced
Career and Technical Education	Journalism	Music
Fine Arts Elem. Level 2	Speech	World Language
Sec Reading - Advanced	Driver Education	Elem Reading - Basic
Computer Science	Library Media Stage	Photography
Gifted and Talented	Craft	ESL
Sec Reading - Basic	Educational Technology	Physical Education
Dance	Mathematics - Elementary	
	Theatre	
	English	

SCHOOL COUNSELORS, SOCIAL WORKERS AND PSYCHOLOGISTS CERTIFICATION (K-12)

I. **Counseling Intern Temporary License** - An applicant must have:
    A. Been formally admitted into a state approved counselor training program;
    B. Completed all the requirements as specified in the "Standards for Approval of Programs for the Preparation of School Counselors" as adopted by the Utah State Board of Education;
    C. Completed a practicum experience which must include: test administration and interpretation, guidance curriculum planning, individual and group counseling, individual education and career planning, and use of career information delivery systems; and
    D. Been recommended for Level I certification by an institution that has a program of preparation of school counselors approved by the Utah State Board of Education.

An individual who receives a Counseling Intern Temporary License shall be able to function as a counselor for not more than one year at which time requirements for the Level I (Basic License) must be met to continue working as a certified counselor.

II. **School Counselor's Level I License** - an applicant must have:
    A. Completed all the requirements as specified in the "Standards for Approval of Programs for the Preparation of School Counselors" as adopted by the Utah State Board of Education;
    B. Have completed a practicum experience which must include: test administration and interpretation, guidance curriculum planning, individual and group counseling, individual education and career planning, and use of career information delivery systems;
    C. Under the supervision of a school counselor who holds a Level III school counselor certificate, completed an approved 600 hour field experience in a counselor education program in a school setting and demonstrated competence during field experience in the following: structured group, classroom presentations, advisement, assessment, placement and follow-up, personal counseling, consultation, referral, program management, community outreach and public relations. Only 400 hours of field experience are required if the applicant has two or more years of successful teaching or counseling experience as approved by the Utah State Office of Education Certification Section. Districts unable to provide on-site supervision may make alternative arrangements with the State Certification Office;
    D. A master's degree in school counseling or related field; and
    E. Been recommended for Level I license by an institution that has a program of preparation of school counselors approved by the Utah State Board of Education.

III. **School Social Worker's Level I License** - An applicant shall have:
    A. Completed an approved program for the preparation of School Social Workers including a

Master of Social Work degree from an accredited institution;
B.   Completed an approved school social work internship in a school setting or in an agency which includes a substantial amount of experience with children and contact with schools; and
C.   See (II. A.) and (II. E.) above.

IV.   **School Psychologist Level I License** - An applicant shall have:
A.   Completed at least an approved master's degree or equivalent certification program consisting of a minimum of 60 semester (90 quarter) hours in school psychology from an accredited institution;
B.   Completed a one academic year internship or its equivalent with a minimum of 1200 clock hours, at least 600 of which must be in a school or setting with an educational component; and
C.   Same as (II. A.) and (II. E.) above but for Psychologist.

V.   **School Counselor Professional Educator Level II License** - an applicant must have:
A.   Met all Level I requirements from an institution that has a program for the preparation of school counselors approved by the Utah State Board of Education;
B.   Completed at least three (3) years of successful experience as a school counselor under a Level I School Counselor license or its equivalent; and
C.   Been recommended by the superintendent of the employing school district.

VI.   **School Social Workers Level 2 License**
See (V. B.) and (V. C.) above but for School Social Worker.

VII.   **School Psychologist Level 2 License**
See (V. B.) and (V. C.) above but for School Psychologist.

SUPERINTENDENT
PRINCIPAL, ALL LEVELS
ASSISTANT / ASSOCIATE / VICE PRINCIPAL

Administrative/Supervisory license area - issued for five (5) years. An applicant for the Basic Administrative/Supervisory license area must:
A.   Hold a Level 2 teaching, special education, school counselor, school psychologist, or school social worker licence area;
B.   Have completed at least a fifth year of training in an approved administrative/supervisory certification program, including a master's degree in administration/supervision or related area, which shall have met the "Standards for the Approval of Programs for the Preparation of Administrators/Supervisors" adopted by the State Board of Education;
C.   Have, in addition, completed an administrative/supervisory internship of sufficient duration to permit the candidate to apply the principles and concepts of educational leadership embodied in the program;
D.   Complete, in the first year of employment as an administrator, a one school year mentoring experience established and supervised by the employing district or charter school;
E.   Have completed at least three (3) years of acceptable professional experience;
F.   Pass a Board-approved administrative test; and
G.   Have been recommended by an institution whose program of preparation has been approved by the Utah State Board of Education.

Renewals will require evidence of continued professional growth, e.g., college course work or professional experience related to administration / supervision.

STATE OF VERMONT

State Department of Education
Educator Licensing Office
1311 U.S. Route 302
Berlin, Vermont 05602
Phone: 802-828-2445 / Fax: 802-828-5107
Web Site: **http://education.vermont.gov/new/html/maincert.html**

INITIAL REQUIREMENTS AT A GLANCE:

Also needed will be items A, B, C, E, K, N and O - See page 2. The fee is $160 for Level I License; or $280 for a Level II License. A criminal background check is required, fee: $19.25. Vermont requires an applicants sworn oath. Vermont REQUIRES evidence of either (a) Vermont residency or (b) a job offer from a Vermont school prior to the issuing of licenses. They also require a notarized statement that child support and all taxes are current. A state administered certification test is NOT required. Passing scores on the Praxis I and the Praxis II are required. The original certificate is valid for two (2) years. Vermont DOES belong to the NASDTEC Interstate Contract (Teachers and Administrators), and the Northeast Regional Credential. Vermont belongs to the New Teacher Assessment and Support Consortium (INTASC). Courses in Special Education ARE required. Revisions to Knowledge and Performance Standards are ongoing and will continue through 2005. Those endorsements whose Standards have been revised are indicated below. Please contact the Department or visit the web site for further information.

Recertification Requirements: $105.00 (Level I), $245.00 (Level II). Level II License holders employed as educators in Vermont public schools, or other Vermont educational entities that are served by a local or regional standards board, shall seek a recommendation for renewal of their Level II License and endorsement(s) from their local or regional standards board. Such recommendation shall be made by the local or regional standards board if the applicant has presented a professional portfolio approved by the local or regional board; and met locally designed standards set forth in a local or regional standards board plan of operation that has been approved by the VSBPE. For complete recertification requirements, contact the Licensing Office.

GUIDELINES FOR *ALL* LICENSES

A. Documentation of the specified competencies and prerequisites for the endorsement(s) being sought;
B. Evidence of at least twelve consecutive weeks of student teaching, or an equivalent learning experience as determined by the policy of the VSBPE or by the requirements of the endorsement.
C. Demonstrated ability to communicate effectively in speaking, writing and other forms of creative expression and ability to apply basic mathematical skills, critical thinking skills, and creative thinking skills.
D. General demonstrated competencies identified by the Department.

PROVISIONAL LICENSES

Applicants for a provisional license or an endorsement shall possess a baccalaureate degree and meet at least one of the following criteria:

A. Possess any valid educator license from another state; **OR**
B. Possess any expired Vermont educator license or any expired license from another state, provided the license expired no longer than 10 years ago; **OR**
C. Have a major in the content area of the provisional endorsement sought; **OR**
D. Have successfully completed the licensure content assessment for the provisional endorsement sought.

LEVEL ONE LICENSE

Early Childhood (Birth - Grade 3) - *Standards Revised 06/21/04*
Elementary (K - 6) - *Standards Revised 04/28/04*
Middle Grades (5 - 8) - *Standards Revised 06/21/04*
Secondary (7 - 12) - *Revisions to Various Individual Endorsements*

A.   Valid three years, Renewable.
B.   Receive a Bachelor's Degree from a State Department of Education approved teacher training program in the State of Vermont.
C.   An out of state graduate who has successfully completed an approved program in a state with which Vermont has signed an Interstate Reciprocity Contract or is an experienced educator covered under the Reciprocity Contract.
D.   After two successful years under the Level One license, and upon recommendation of the local or regional standards board, the teacher may apply for a Level Two license.

LEVEL TWO LICENSE
(Valid seven years, Renewable)

A.   Successfully practiced in an endorsement area for two years, or the equivalent as determined by VSBPE policy, under a Level I License;
B.   Has an approved Individual Professional Development Plan (IPDP) for the ensuing licensure period and;
C.   Demonstrated the following characteristics: 1.ability to plan instruction, 2. ability to maintain a positive learning environment, 3. ability to conduct learning experiences for individuals as well as groups, 4. knowledge of content area, and 5. interest and motivation in continuing professional development.
D.   Satisfactorily completed an approved Technical Development Plan when required to do so for a Trades and Industry endorsement; and
E.   Documentation of any valid licenses, credentials, or reports that required by the endorsement(s) sought.

LIBRARY/MEDIA (PK - 12)

The Library/Media certificate is now standards-based and requires the demonstration of competence in both knowledge and performance areas. Contact the Department for complete details.

Additional Requirements:
A.   A minimum of 18 credits in library and information science;
B.   A minimum of a practicum, or the equivalent, in school library media services and instruction.

SCHOOL COUNSELOR (PK - 12)

The Counselor certificate is now standards-based and requires the demonstration of competence in both knowledge and performance areas. Contact the Department for complete details.

Additional Requirements:
A.   Master's degree with a concentration in school counseling, or the equivalent; and
B.   A supervised internship experience (600 clock hours) in counseling with a minimum of 60 hours of experience in school counseling at both the elementary (PK-6) and middle/secondary (7-12) levels, under the supervision of a licensed school counselor.

SCHOOL PSYCHOLOGIST (PK - 12)

The School Psychologist certificate is now standards-based and requires the demonstration of competence in both knowledge and performance areas. Contact the Department for complete details.

Additional Requirements:
A National Association of School Psychologists (NASP) Specialist Level or Doctoral degree or an American Psychological Association accredited Doctoral degree in School Psychology, or the equivalent.

For the purpose of equivalency, a minimum of 60 graduate semester hours (Specialist Level) or a minimum of 90 graduate semester hours (Doctoral Level) in the knowledge and performance domains of School Psychology is required. Individuals who have completed a minimum of 60 graduate semester hours in clinical, counseling, or industrial/organizational psychology shall follow the American Psychological Association guidelines for re-specialization in obtaining the multiple knowledge and performance domain competencies for the practice of school psychology. In addition, fulfillment of these competencies shall be demonstrated by achieving a score of 660 or higher on the School Psychology examination administered by the Educational Testing Service (ETS) – test code 10400. Note: passage of this examination is not required if the applicant has the NASP or APA accredited doctoral degree in school psychology.

A NASP approved internship, APA accredited internship, or an internship with at least 600 clock hours in a school setting, or other appropriate educational setting with students, under the supervision of a licensed or certified School Psychologist who has a minimum of three years of post-degree experience.

An applicant who is a Nationally Certified School Psychologist (NCSP) shall be considered to have fulfilled all of the Knowledge and Performance Standards and all Additional Requirements for licensure as a School Psychologist in Vermont.

PRINCIPAL

The holder is authorized to serve as a school principal. An educator serving as an Assistant Principal, however named, shall hold a Principal endorsement.

Requirements:
A. Master's Degree OR equivalent with concentration in educational administration;
B. Three or more years of experience as a PK-12 educator;
C. Competence in the following areas: Fundamentals of educational administration/leadership; School law; School finance or school business management; Staff evaluation/development; Curriculum management (i.e., development/supervision/evaluation); and School/community relations; and
D. Recommendation of preparing institution according to Vermont administrative program.
E. Out-of-state candidates must have an individual transcript analysis which includes a resume, out-of-state certificate, transcripts, and three letters attesting to managerial/supervisory skills.

SUPERINTENDENT

The holder is authorized to serve as the chief executive officer of a school district. An educator serving as an Assistant Superintendent , however named, shall hold a Superintendent endorsement.

Requirements:
A. A master's degree;
B. Competence in the following areas: Fundamentals of educational administration/leadership; School law; School finance or school business management; Staff evaluation/development; Curriculum management (i.e., development/supervision/evaluation); and School/community relations;
C. Five or more years of experience including: three or more years of experience as a PK-12 educator, and two or more years of educational administration experience.

STATE OF VIRGINIA

Department of Education
Division of Teacher Education and Licensure
P.O. Box 2120
Richmond, Virginia 23218-2120
Phone: 804-225-2022 / Fax: 804-225-2831
Web Site: **http://www.pen.k12.va.us/VDOE/newvdoe/teached.html**

INITIAL REQUIREMENTS AT A GLANCE:

Also needed will be items A (with original signature), B, C, E, G, N, and O - See page 2. The fee is $50.00 (in-state) and $75.00 (out-of-state). A state administered certification test is NOT required. Scores on the PRAXIS I tests and an appropriate Content Knowledge test of the Praxis II Series test ARE required unless exemption on the basis of 2 years of *verified* teaching experience and holding a out-of-state certificate is applicable. Virginia DOES belong to the Interstate Certification Compact. Courses or compentencies in Special Education ARE required. *Major revisions are pending approval later this year, 2007, and are not reflected in this manual. Please contact the Division for the most current details.*

Recertification Requirements: $25.00 fee. Regular licenses must be renewed every five years. To renew the license, the individual must obtain at least 180 points through a series of 8 professional development options. License holders without a master's degree must earn at least 90 points by completing a three-semester-hour course at an accredited two or four-year college in the content area listed on the license.

ROUTES TO LICENSURE IN VIRGINIA

There are multiple routes to become licensed in Virginia:

I. **Approved Program** - a Virginia state-approved teacher preparation program or an alternative state approved program. (For more information relative to this method of licensure, please contact the Virginia college or university where you wish to enroll.)*

II. **Reciprocity** - Conditions for licensure for out-of-state candidates by reciprocity.

   A. An individual coming into Virginia from any state may qualify for a Virginia teaching license with comparable endorsement areas if the individual has completed a state-approved teacher preparation program through a regionally accredited four-year college or university, or if the individual holds a valid out-of-state teaching license (full credential without deficiencies) that must be in force at the time the application for a Virginia license is made. An individual seeking licensure must establish a file in the Department of Education by submitting a complete application packet, which includes official student transcripts. Professional teacher's assessments prescribed by the Board of Education must be satisfied.

   B. An individual coming into Virginia will qualify for a Virginia teaching license with comparable endorsement areas if the individual holds national certification from the National Board for Professional Teaching Standards (NBPTS) or a nationally recognized certification program approved by the Board of Education.

   C. Licensure by reciprocity is provided for individuals who have obtained a valid out-of-state license (full credential without deficiencies) that is in force at the time the application for a Virginia license is received by the Department of Education. The individual must establish a file in the Department of Education by submitting a complete application packet, which shall include official student transcripts. Unless exempted by the criteria in subsection D of this section, licensure assessments prescribed by the Board of Education shall be required.

   D. Individuals who hold a valid out-of-state license (full credential without deficiencies) and who have completed a minimum of three years of full-time, successful teaching experience in a public or accredited nonpublic school (kindergarten through grade 12) in a state other than Virginia are exempted from the professional teacher's assessment requirements.

III. **Alternative Licensure** - an alternative route to licensure is available through the recommendation of the individual's employing Virginia school division or nonpublic school. A three-year nonrenewable license can be issued through satisfying endorsement course work, experiential learning, or by meeting the provisional-special education requirements.*

*   The web site, http://www.doe.virginia.gov/VDOE/newvdoe/prof_teacher_assessment.pdf , has a

complete description of the assessment requirements in Virginia.

A.   **Satisfying endorsement course work** - an individual who is employed by a Virginia school division or nonpublic school seeking this alternative route must:
   1.   hold a baccalaureate degree from a regionally accredited institution,
   2.   satisfy one or more specific endorsement areas (teaching areas), and
   3.   submit the application packet through the Virginia employing educational agency.

B.   **Experiential Learning** – an individual who is applying for an initial license must meet the following criteria to be eligible to request experiential learning credits in lieu of the coursework for the endorsement (teaching) content area:
   1.   hold a baccalaureate degree from a regionally accredited college or university;
   2.   have at least five years of documented full-time work experience that may include specialized training related to the endorsement sought; and
   3.   have met the qualifying score on the content knowledge assessment prescribed by the Board of Education.
   The experiential learning criteria do not apply to teachers of special education and elementary education (preK-3 and preK-6).

C.   **Provisional (Special Education) License** - an individual employed as a special education teacher in a public school or a nonpublic special education school in Virginia who does not hold the appropriate special education endorsement must:
   1.   Be employed by a Virginia public or nonpublic school as a special educator and have the recommendation of the employing educational agency;
   2.   Hold a baccalaureate degree from a regionally accredited college or university;
   3.   Have an assigned mentor endorsed in special education; and
   4.   Have a planned program of study in the assigned endorsement area, make progress toward meeting the endorsement requirements each of the three years of the license, and have completed coursework in the competencies of foundations for educating students with disabilities and an understanding and application of the legal aspects and regulatory requirements associated with identification, education, and evaluation of students with disabilities. A survey course integrating these competencies would satisfy this requirement. The Provisional License through this alternate route shall not be issued without the completion of these prerequisites.

NOTE: This alternate route to special education is not applicable to individuals employed as speech pathologists.

The following requirements must be satisfied in order to become eligible for the five-year renewable license:
   1.   Professional Teacher's Assessment
   2.   Professional Studies Requirements: Professional studies course work specified below from a regionally accredited four-year institution or an alternative program for licensure.

Early/primary education PreK-3, elementary education PreK-6, and middle education - 18 semester hours:
(a) Human Growth and Development - 3 semester hours
(b) Curriculum and Instructional Procedures - 3 semester hours for the appropriate instructional level (early/primary education, elementary education or middle education)
(c) Classroom and Behavior Management - 3 semester hours
(d) Foundations of Education - 3 semester hours
(e) Reading -
   (i) Early/primary and elementary education: 6 semester hours of language acquisition and reading
   (ii) Middle education: 3 semester hours of reading in the content area and 3 semester hours of language acquisition.

Special education - 18 semester hours:
(a) - (d) from early/primary education;
(e) Language Acquisition and Reading - 6 semester hours

Adult education, PreK-12 endorsements, and secondary grades 6-12 endorsements - 15 semester hours:
> (a) - (d) from early/primary eduction;
> (e) Reading in the Content Area - 3 semester hours

3. One year of successful, full-time teaching experience in the endorsement area in a public or accredited nonpublic school. A fully licensed, experienced teacher must be available in the school building to assist the beginning teacher employed through the alternative route.

IV. **Alternative Route for Career Professions** – an alternative route is available to career switchers who seek teaching endorsements PreK through grade 12 with the exception of special education.

Prerequisite requirements:

A. An application to an approved Career Switcher Program;

B. A baccalaureate degree from a regionally accredited college or university;

C. The completion of requirements for an endorsement in a teaching area or the equivalent through verifiable experience or academic study;

D. At least five years of full-time work experience or its equivalent; and

E. Virginia qualifying scores on the professional teacher's assessments as prescribed by the Board of Education.

TYPES OF LICENSES

I. **Provisional License:** Nonrenewable license valid for a period not to exceed three years issued to an individual who has allowable deficiencies for full licensure as set forth in these regulations. The individual must have a minimum of an undergraduate degree from a regionally accredited college or university (with the exception of those individuals seeking the Technical Professional License).The Provisional License, with the exception of those individuals seeking licensure through a career switcher program, will be issued for three years. Individuals must complete the requirements for the regular, five-year license within the validity period of the Provisional License.

II. **Collegiate Professional License:** Five-year, renewable license available to an individual who has satisfied all requirements for licensure, including an earned undergraduate degree from a regionally accredited college or university and the professional teacher's assessments prescribed by the Board of Education.

III. **Postgraduate Professional License:** Five-year, renewable license available to an individual who has qualified for the Collegiate Professional License and who holds an appropriate earned graduate degree from a regionally accredited college or university.

IV. **Technical Professional License:** Five-year, renewable license available to a person who has graduated from an accredited high school (or possesses a General Education Development Certificate); has exhibited academic proficiency, skills in literacy and communication, technical competency, and occupational experience; and has completed nine semester hours of specialized professional studies credit from a regionally accredited college or university. The nine semester hours of professional studies coursework must include human growth and development (three semester hours), curriculum and instructional procedures (three semester hours), and applications of instructional technology or classroom and behavior management (three semester hours). The Technical Professional License is issued at the recommendation of an employing educational agency. Individuals seeking military science must have the appropriate credentials issued by the United States military. In addition to demonstrating competency in the endorsement area sought, the individual must:

> A. Hold a license issued by the appropriate Virginia board for those program areas requiring a license and a minimum of two years of satisfactory experience at the journeyman level or an equivalent;

> B. Have completed a registered apprenticeship program and two years of satisfactory

experience at the journeyman level or an equivalent level in the trade; or

C. Have four years of work experience at the management or supervisory level or equivalent or have a combination of four years of training and work experience at the management or supervisory level or equivalent.

NOTE: Individuals holding the Technical Professional License who seek the Collegiate Professional or Postgraduate Professional License must meet the professional teacher's assessments requirement.

V. **Pupil Personnel Services License:** Five-year, renewable license available to an individual who has earned an appropriate graduate degree from a regionally accredited college or university with an endorsement for guidance counselor, school psychologist, school social worker, special education speech-language pathologist preK-12 , or vocational evaluator. This license does not require teaching experience.

VI. **Division Superintendent License:** Five-year, renewable license available to an individual who has completed an earned master's degree from a regionally accredited college or university. The individual's name must be listed on the Board of Education's list of eligible division superintendents.

EARLY / PRIMARY EDUCATION
(Grades PK - 3)

A. Possesses a degree in the liberal arts and sciences (or equivalent) and completed course work which covers the appropriate grade level(s); and
B. Professional Teacher's Assessment prescribed by the Board;
C. **Endorsement Requirements:** A minimum of 51 semester hours including (with hours):
    English (including composition, oral communications and literature) - (12); Mathematics (9); Science (including a laboratory course) - (9); History (including American history and world history) - (6); Social Science (including geography and economics) - (6); Arts and Humanities (6)
D. **Professional Studies:** 18 semester hours including:
    Human Growth and Development (3); Curriculum and Instructional Procedures (6); Foundations of Education (3); and Reading and Language Acquisition (6); Classroom and Behavior management (3); Foundations of Education (3); Reading (at appropriate level) - (6); Supervised classroom experience (at least 300 clock hrs. with 150 hrs. in direct teaching activities).

ELEMENTARY EDUCATION
(Grades PK - 6)

A. As in Early / Primary Education (A) and (B) above;
B. **Competencies:** As in Early / Primary Education above
C. **Endorsement Requirements:** A minimum of 57 semester hours including (with hours):
    English (including composition, oral communications and literature) - (12); Mathematics (12); Science (including a laboratory course) - (12); History (including American history and world history) - (9); Social Science (including geography and economics) - (6); Arts and Humanities (6);
D. **Professional Studies:** (Same as for Early / Primary Education)

MIDDLE EDUCATION
(Grades 6 - 8)

A. The candidate must have graduated from an approved teacher preparation discipline-specific program in the middle education 6-8 with one area of concentration from the areas of English, mathematics, science and history and social science; or
B. Possesses a degree in the liberal arts and sciences (or equivalent) and completed a minimum of 21 sem. hrs. of course work in at least one area of concentration that will be listed on the license; and completed minimum requirements for those areas (English, mathematics, science and history and social science) in which the individual is not seeking an area of concentration;

SECONDARY EDUCATION (6 - 12) ENDORSEMENT
PRE-K - 12 ENDORSEMENT; SPECIAL EDUCATION ENDORSEMENT
ADULT EDUCATION ENDORSEMENT

A.   Degree in Liberal arts and sciences (or equivalent);

B.   Professional teacher's assessment prescribed by the Board;

Specific Endorsement requirements; and

D.   Completion of an approved program or, if employed by a Virginia school, through the alternative route to licensure.

E.   **Professional Studies:** A minimum of 15 semester hours including:
Human Growth and Development (birth - adolescence) - (3); Curriculum and Instructional Procedures (6); Foundations of Education (3); Reading as follows: (a) Adult Educ., Pre-K - 12, and Secondary (6-12) - (3); (b) Special Education (language acquisition and reading) - (6); Supervised Classroom Experience (at the appropriate level(s)) - 300 Clock Hrs.

Endorsement(s) in the following areas are contingent upon the satisfaction of specific competencies and course work (indicated in semester hours) as shown below. Contact the DTEL for a complete listing of both requirements and endorsements.

TEACHING ENDORSEMENTS (with semester hours)

Art (Pre-K - 12)	36	Science--Chemistry	32
Computer Science	36	Science--Earth Science	32
Driver education (add-on)	6	Science--Physics	32
English	36	Special Education (Various)	27
English as a Second Language	24	Vocational Education (Various)	39
Foreign language (Pre-K - 12)	30	Adult Education	15
Gifted Education (add-on)	12	Adult English as a second language (add-on)	21
Health & Physical Education (Pre-K - 12)	45	Dance	24
History and Social Science	51	Journalism (add-on)	15
Library Media (NK - 12)	24	Keyboarding (add-on)	6
Mathematics	36	Mathematics - Algebra I (Add-on)	24
Music education (Choral / Instrumental)	42	Theatre Arts (PK - 12)	33
Science--Biology	32	Speech Communications (Add-on)	15

SUPPORT SERVICES CERTIFICATES

School Guidance Counselor:

A.   Master's Degree from an approved counselor education program in school guidance which includes at least 100 clock hours of clinical experiences in the PreK-6 setting and 100 clock hours of clinical experiences in the grades 7-12 setting **OR** a master's degree from an approved college or university and certification from an approved counselor education program that the candidate has acquired the competencies needed for endorsement;

B.   Two years of full-time experience in teaching **OR** two years of successful experience in guidance and counseling;

School Psychologist:

A.   An approved program in school psychology;

B.   60 graduate hours which culminate in at least a master's degree; and

C.   An internship which is documented by the degree-granting institution.
      (OR)

D.   Hold a certificate issued by the National School Psychology Certification Board; and

School Social Worker:

A.   An earned master's of social work from an accredited school of social work with a minimum of 60 graduate hours;

B.   A minimum of 6 graduate semester hours in education;

C.   Completed a supervised practicum or filed experience of a minimum or 400 clock hours in an accredited school discharging the duties of a school social worker **OR** one year of successful full-time supervised experience as a school social worker in an accredited school.

Library/Media (PK - 12):
A. Graduated from an approved preparation program in library media; **OR**
B. Completed 24 semester hours in required areas; and
C. Participated in a clinical experience to give the applicant an opportunity to apply the skills, understandings, and competencies listed above. One year of successful, full-time experience as a school librarian in an accredited public or nonpublic school may be accepted to meet this requirement.

ADMINISTRATIVE PERSONNEL

Virginia offers three options for school-based administrative certification:

A. **Virginia Approved Program**:
1. Hold a master's degree from an accredited college or university;
2. Complete three years of successful full time teaching experience in an accredited nonpublic or public school;
3. Complete an approved administration and supervision program in Virginia which shall ensure that the candidate has met specific Board-defined competencies. The candidate will demonstrate knowledge and understanding of: (a) student growth and development; (b) systems and organizations; © theories, models, and principles of organizational development; (d) the conditions and dynamics of the diverse school community; (e) the purpose of education and its role in a modern society and (f) principles of representative governance that undergird the system of American schools; and
4. Completed a beginning administration and supervision assessment when prescribed the Board reflecting the knowledge and understanding of the stated competencies or completed a full-time internship as a school principal **(OR)** one year of successful, full-time experience as an assistant principal, principal, or instructional supervisor in an accredited school.
B. **Out-of-State Approved Program**:
1. Hold a master's degree from an accredited college or university;
2. Complete three years of successful, full time teaching experience in an accredited nonpublic or public school, and
3. Complete an out-of-state approved program in administration and supervision; and
4. See A4 above (Virginia Approved Program).
C. **Out-of-State Administrative License**:
1. Hold a master's degree from an accredited college or university;
2. Hold a current, valid out-of-state license with endorsements in administration and supervision; and
3. See A4 above.

SUPERINTENDENT

Fees are $100.00 (in-state); or $150.00 (out-of-state). Virginia offers four options for attaining a superintendent's license as well:
A. Option One:
1. Hold an earned doctorate degree in educational administration or educational leadership from an accredited institution; and
2. Complete five years of educational experience in a public and/or accredited nonpublic school, two of which must be teaching experience at the NK - 12 level and two of which must be in administration/supervision at the NK - 12 level.
B. Option Two:
1. Hold an earned master's degree from an accredited institution plus complete 30 graduate hours beyond the master's degree;
2. Complete requirements for administration and supervision Pre-K - 12 endorsement which includes the demonstration of specific Board-defined competencies. The candidate will

demonstrate knowledge and understanding of: (a) student growth and development; (b) systems and organizations; (c) theories, models, and principles of organizational development; (d) the values and ethics of leadership; (e) the purpose of education and its role in a modern society; and (f) principles of representative governance that undergird the system of American schools.

    3.   Have completed five years of educational experience in an accredited school, two of which must be in administration/supervision at the Pre-K - 12 level.

C.   Option Three:
    1.   Hold an earned master's degree from an accredited institution;
    2.   Hold a current, valid out-of-state license with an endorsement as a division/district superintendent; and
    3.   Completed five years of educational experience in a public and/or accredited nonpublic school, two of which must be teaching experience at the PreK - 12 level and two of which must be in administration/supervision.

D.   Option Four:
    1.   Hold a master's degree, or its equivalent from an accredited institution;
    2.   Have held a senior leadership position such as Chief Executive Officer or senior military officer; and
    3.   Be recommended by a school board interested in employing the individual as superintendent.

STATE OF WASHINGTON

Office of Superintendent of Public Instruction
Professional Education & Certification
Old Capitol Building, P.O. Box 47200
Olympia, Washington 98504-7200
Phone: 360-725-6400 / Fax: 360-664-3631
Web Site: **http://www.k12.wa.us/certification/**

INITIAL REQUIREMENTS AT A GLANCE:

Also needed will be items A, B, C, E, J, K, M (WEST-B) - See page 2. Applicants must complete a supplemental questionnaire confirming their moral character and personal fitness. Fingerprint fee: $60.25 (Eff. 10/07). The residency teaching certificate fee is $35.00; the ESA (Educational Staff Associate) and administration certificate is $35.00. As of 9/2002, the state administered Washington Educator Skills Test-Basic (WEST-B) IS required although passing scores on the CBEST or the Praxis I (reading, math, writing) subtests may be accepted in lieu of the WEST-B. The original teacher's certificate is valid for seven (7) years. Washington DOES belong to the NASDTEC Inter-state Contract (Teachers, Support Professionals and Administrators). Washington is a member of the Interstate New Teacher Assessment and Support Consortium (INTASC). A course in child abuse IS required for the Professional Certificate. Study and field experience in Special Education ARE required from in-state programs. Major Administrator revisions occurred in 2004 and Education Staff Associates in 2005.

Renewal Requirements: Professional Certificate - applicant must complete 15 quarter credit hours or 150 clock hours of study since the issuance of the professional certificate: 1 Qtr. Hr. Credit = 10 Clock Hrs.; 1 Sem. Credit Hr. = 15 Clock Hrs. **Residency Certificate** - The residency teacher certificate may be renewed once for two years by teachers who are enrolled in a Professional Certificate Program. For complete details, contact the Certification Office.

NOTE: After August 31, 2000, individuals are able to meet requirements for an endorsement ONLY through the completion of an approved college/university program. Contact the department for additional information about endorsement.

RESIDENCY CERTIFICATE (TEACHER)
(Grades P-3, K-8, 4-9, 5-12, P-12)

Valid for 7 years. May be renewed once for an additional 2 years with verification of enrollment toward a professional certificate. Requirements are as follows:

A.   Bachelor's Degree from a regionally accredited institution;
B.   State approved teacher education program;
D.   Moral character clearance including fingerprinting; and
E.   Passing scores on the three subtests (Reading, Math, Writing) of the Basic Skills test and passing scores on endorsement test(s).

PROFESSIONAL CERTIFICATE (TEACHER)

A.   Completed an approved professional certificate program;
B.   Course or coursework in issues of abuse.
C.   To maintain validity of the Professional Certificate, 150 clock hours of continuing education study and/or equivalent academic credit must be completed every 5 years.
D.   National Board Certification may be used to obtain a Professional Certificate.

LEVEL ENDORSEMENTS

All Levels (P - 12)	**Middle Level (4 - 9)**
Dance	Middle Level: Math & Science
Drama	Middle Level: Humanities
Music - General	
Music - Choral	**Secondary (5 - 12)**
Music - Instrumental	Biology
Visual Arts	Chemistry
Designated World Languages	Earth Science
ESL	Physics
Health / Fitness	Social Studies
Library Media	History
Reading	Agriculture Education
Special Education	Business Education
Bilingual Education (Supporting)	Family and Consumer Sciences
	Mathematics
Early Childhood (B - 3)	Marketing Education
Early Childhood Education	Technology Education
Early Childhood Special Education	Traffic Safety
	English Language Arts
Elementary Education (K - 8)	General Science

LIBRARY MEDIA

A.   Complete a program in Library Media; **AND**
B.   Passing score on the Library Media endorsement test.

EDUCATIONAL STAFF ASSOCIATE CERTIFICATES
School Counselor, School Psychologist and School Social Worker

A.   *Initial Certificate*: Complete all course work (except special project or thesis) for a master's degree with a major in the appropriate service area (Counseling, Psychology, or Social Work) and a state approved college/university preparation program.
B.   *Continuing Certificate*: Complete master's degree in the appropriate service area*; written comprehensive examination; 180 days of experience in a school setting; a Washington college/university course in peer review; and a course in Issues of Abuse.

163

* It is not necessary for a candidate who holds a master's degree or doctorate in another field to obtain the specified master's degree if he or she has completed all course work requirements relevant to the required master's degree.

PRINCIPAL

A. **Residency Principal Certification:** Valid seven years.
 1. Must have completed a state-approved program of preparation for principal, **OR** have served at least three years as a principal, vice principal, or assistant principal under an appropriate out-of-state certificate in another state;
 2. Hold a Master's Degree from a regionally accredited institution;
 3. Must hold or have held a valid regular teaching certificate or Educational Staff Associate certificate; and
 4. Must have demonstrated successful school-based instructional experience.

B. **Professional Principal Certification:** Valid five years, Renewable with 150 clock hours of continuing education every five years:
 1. Meet requirements for Residency Principal Certificate;
 2. Completed Professional Administrator certificate program; and
 3. Completed coursework in issues of abuse.

PROGRAM ADMINISTRATOR

A. **Residency Program Administrator Certification:** Valid 7 years.
 1. Must have completed a state-approved program of preparation for the program administrator or have served at least 3 years as a program administrator in another state under an appropriate out-of-state certificate;
 2. Hold a master's degree from a regionally accredited institution; and
 3. Have completed 24 quarter hrs. (16 sem. hrs) of post baccalaureate, graduate study in education.

B. **Professional Program Administrator Certification:** Valid 5 years, renewable with 150 clock hours of continuing education every 5 years.
 1. Meet requirements for Residency program administrator certificate;
 2. Completed Professional Administrator certificate program; and
 3. Completed coursework in issues of abuse.

SUPERINTENDENT

A. **Initial Superintendent Certification:** Valid seven years.
 1. Completed a state-approved program of preparation for superintendency, **OR** have served as a superintendent, assistant superintendent, or deputy superintendent under an appropriate out-of-state certificate;
 2. Earned a master's degree from a regionally accredited college or university;
 3. Completed a total of 45 Qtr. hours (30 sem. hours) of post-baccalaureate graduate study; and
 4. Hold a valid teacher, ESA or program administrator certificate.

B. **Continuing Superintendent Certification:** Valid five years, Renewable with 150 clock hours of continuing education every five years:
 1. Meet requirements for Initial Superintendent Certificate;
 2. Completed 60 quarter hours (40 sem. hours) of post-baccalaureate graduate work in education, or hold a doctorate in education;
 3. Verify 180 days of full time experience as a superintendent, assistant superintendent or deputy superintendent; and
 4. Completed coursework in issues of abuse.

Department of Education
Office of Professional Preparation
1900 Kanawha Blvd East, Building 6, Room 252
Charleston, West Virginia 25305-0330
Phone: (304) 558-7010 or (800) 982-2378 / Fax: 304-558-0459
Web Site: **http://wvde.state.wv.us/certification/**

INITIAL REQUIREMENTS AT A GLANCE:

Also required will be items A, B (overall GPA of 2.5,), C (or valid teaching certificate from out-of-state), E, G, J, K, N (if taken) and O - See page 2. The fee is $15. There is a $34 fingerprint background fee. The PRAXIS II Principles of Learning and Teaching Exam IS required for ALL candidates. Praxis I - Pre-Professional Skills in Reading, Writing, and Mathematics or waivers based on ACT, SAT Scores or by holding a Master's degree) and content specialization(s) (Praxis II). The professional knowledge test (Praxis II that includes at least a portion of the grade levels indicated on the anticipated license) is also required for the Professional Teaching Certificate. West Virginia DOES belong to the Interstate Certification Compact, the NASDTEC Interstate Contract (Teachers, Administrators, Support Professionals and Vocational Educators), and the Interstate New Teacher Assessment and Support Consortium (INTASC). Courses or competencies in Special Education ARE required. Major revisions occurred in 2007-2008.

Renewal Requirements: As of January 1, 2008, Professional Teaching Certificates can be renewed using one of three different options: 1) six semester hours of coursework with a 3.0 GPA from an accredited institution on higher education; 2) the certificate being renewed reflects an advanced salary classification of MA +30 of higher; or 3) the applicant has reached age 60; **OR** M.A. plus 30 Salary Classification. - Hold a minimum of a master's plus 30 salary classification based on the awarding of a master's degree; **OR** age Sixty. - Has reached 60 years of age and presents a photocopy of the birth certificate; **AND** recommendation of Superintendent. **Exemption** - If the applicant for licensure has completed six semester hours of coursework to qualify for an additional endorsement in an area of critical shortage, s/he is exempt from meeting the instructional technology requirement.

TEACHING CERTIFICATES[1]
Preschool (Birth - PreK); Early Education (PreK - K); Early Childhood (K - 4);
Middle Childhood (5 - 9); Adolescent (9 -12); and Adult

A. **Professional Certificate** - May be issued to an individual who meets prescribed experience and/or academic and professional standards and who has been assessed as competent to assume a role in public education in keeping with the specialization(s) and grade levels designated on this license. A Professional Certificate may be issued in teaching, student support services, or administrative specializations.

B. **Permanent Professional Teaching Certificate** - (No expiration) The applicant for licensure must submit evidence of satisfying the following:
1. Five-Year Certificate. - Hold or be eligible for the Professional Teaching Certificate valid for five years; **AND**
2. Master's Degree - Hold a master's degree related to the public school program; **AND**
3. Experience - Complete five years of educational experience including two within the specialization(s) for which the permanent certificate is requested; **OR**
4. Valid Five-Year Certificate. - Hold a valid Professional Teaching Certificate; **AND**
5. Two Renewals - Renew the Professional Teaching Certificate valid for five years two times based on: (a) six semester hours of appropriate renewal credit reflecting a 3.0 GPA; or (b) a minimum of a M.A. plus 30 salary classification based on the awarding of a master's degree; or (c) age sixty; **OR**

6.   Obtain certification through the NBPTS; **OR**
7.   Valid out-of-state certificate; **AND**
8.   Recommendation of Superintendent - Receive the recommendation of the county superintendent in the county in which the educator teaches or last taught.

C.   **Alternative Teaching Certificate** - May be issued to an individual provided s/he fulfills the general requirements for issuance. An Alternative Teaching Certificate may only be issued in teaching specializations.

D.   **Temporary Certificate** - May be issued to an individual who meets prescribed experience and/or academic and professional standards including the Evaluation Leadership Institute for the Professional Certificate but has not met the testing requirements prescribed for issuance of the Professional Certificate. A Temporary Certificate may be issued in teaching, student support or administrative specializations.

E.   **Career/Technical Education Certificate** - May be issued to an individual who has acquired prescribed career/technical education and/or technical skills through specific wage-earning experience and/or training and who has been assessed as competent to assume a role in public education in keeping with the specialization(s) and grade levels designated in this license. The Career/Technical Education Certificate is equivalent to the Professional Certificate for salary purposes.

F.   **Temporary Career/Technical Education Certificate** - May be issued to an individual who holds a valid out-of-state Career/Technical Education certificate but does not hold the required industry recognized credential and/or has not met the citizenship and/or testing requirements prescribed for issuance of the Career/Technical Education Certificate.

[1] - For complete details on these and all certificates, contact the department.

SCHOOL COUNSELOR AND SCHOOL PSYCHOLOGIST

Professional Student Support Certificate for School Counselor:

A.   **Temporary Professional Student Support Certificate** - issued to eligible applicants for School Counselor.

B.   **Initial Professional Student Support Certificate** - (Valid three years) is issued for School Counselor to an applicant who meets the following criteria: (1) M.A. in Counseling from an accredited institution of higher education; and (2) successful completion of an accredited School Counseling Program.

C.   **Professional Student Support Certificate** - (Valid five years) is issued for School Counselor to an applicant who meets the requirements for a Professional Five-Year Teaching Certificate.

D.   **Permanent Professional Student Support Certificate** - issued for School Counselor to an applicant who meets the requirements for a Permanent Professional Teaching Certificate.

School Psychologist - A Professional Support Certificate is issued to eligible applicants for School Psychologist.

A.   **Temporary Professional Student Support Certificate** - issued to eligible applicants for School Psychologist.

B.   **Initial Professional Student Support Certificate** - issued for School Psychologist to an applicant who completes and approved master's degree in a field related to education from an accredited institution of higher education.

C.   **Professional Student Support Certificate** - (Valid five years) issued for School Psychologist to an applicant who meets the requirements for a Professional Five-Year Teaching Certificate.

D.   **Professional Permanent Student Support Certificate** - issued to an applicant who meets the requirements for a Permanent Professional Teaching Certificate.

ADMINISTRATIVE/SUPERVISORY CERTIFICATES
Principal, Supervisor of Instruction, and Superintendent

A.   **Temporary Administrative Certificate**: (Valid One Year)
        General Criteria - will indicate the specialization(s) and grade levels in which the holder may be assigned within the public schools. Experience gained on the Temporary Administrative Certificate may be used for conversion purposes. The Temporary Administrative

Certificate is issued to an administrator who graduates from an out-of-state institution of higher learning, or who is transferring his/her credential from another state or country so that s/he may complete the requirements for testing if applicable and the Evaluation Leadership Institute.

Conditions for Issuance - The applicant for licensure must submit evidence of satisfying the following:

1. Out-of-State Approved Program - Successful completion of an out-of-state accredited institution of higher education's state approved program with the exception of completion of: (a) the required tests in Pre-professional Skills and/or Content and/or (b) the Evaluation Leadership Institute offered through the West Virginia Center for Professional Development or equivalent training approved by the WVBE; **OR**

2) Out-of-State Certification - For those candidates who hold a valid out-of-state Professional Administrative Certificate in the area for which West Virginia licensure is requested without completion of the Evaluation Leadership Institute offered through the West Virginia Center for Professional Development or equivalent training approved by the WVBE.

B. **Initial Professional Administrative Certificate**: (Valid five years, renewable)

General Criteria - 1) Degree an accredited institution of higher education with a 3.0 GPA and three years of management level experience; 2) the Evaluation Leadership Institute in evaluation skills offered through the West Virginia Center for Professional Development or equivalent training approved by the WVBE. The certificate shall indicate the specialization(s) and grade levels in which the holder can be legally assigned within the public schools.

Conditions for Issuance - The applicant for licensure must submit evidence of satisfying the following:

1. State Approved Program - Successful completion of an institution of higher education's state approved program and the recommendation of the designated official at the college or university through which the program was completed. Out-of-state applicants may present a photocopy of the valid Professional Administrative Certificate or a letter of eligibility from the other state's licensing agency; **OR**

2. Out-of-State Licensure - For those educators who hold a valid out-of-state Administrative Certificate, the applicant needs only to present the official transcripts evidencing graduation from a state-approved teacher education program at a regionally accredited college or university and a copy of his/her valid out-of-state Administrative Certificate to be licensed provide that s/he has completed the Evaluation Leadership Institute. The out-of-state Administrative Certificate must be in the specialization for which West Virginia licensure is available and requested; **OR**

3. Out-of-State Graduate not Licensed - In addition to the general criteria, the educator must satisfy the minimum proficiency level, as adopted by the WVBE, on the content specialization test in educational leadership. Contact the Department for details.

C. **Permanent Professional Administrative Certificate** - (No Expiration) In order to covert the Initial Professional Administrative Certificate to the Permanent Professional Administrative Certificate, the applicant for licensure must submit evidence of satisfying the following: College/University Coursework. - Six semester hours of appropriate renewal credit related to the public school program; **OR**

2. M.A. plus 30 Salary Classification. - Holds a minimum of a M.A. plus 30 salary classification based on the awarding of a master's degree; **AND**

3. Experience. - Five years of educational experience, two years of which must be in any or a combination of the specializations reflected on the Professional Administrative Certificate, and one year of which must be completed in West Virginia; **OR**

4. Obtain certification through the NBPTS; **AND**

5. Recommendation of Superintendent. - If the candidate is currently employed by a county board of education, the candidate must receive the recommendation of the employing county's superintendent. If the educator is not employed by a West Virginia county school system, then s/he must secure a recommendation from his/her most recent education supervisor provided that such employment severance does not exceed one year. If employment in an educational setting is greater than one year, s/he must secure the recommendation from the current employer or community leader.

STATE OF WISCONSIN

Department of Public Instruction
Teacher Education and Licensing
125 South Webster Street, PO Box 7841
Madison, Wisconsin 53707-7841
Phone: 608-266-3390 or 800-441-4563 / Fax: 608-264-9558
Web Site: **http://dpi.wi.gov/tepdl/index.html**

INITIAL REQUIREMENTS AT A GLANCE:

Also needed will be a photo and items A, B, C, E (from Compact state applicants only), J, K, M (for post 8/31/92 graduates), **OR** N - See page 2. The fee is $150.00 for initial out-of-state applicants. All initial in-state applications and licence renewals are $100.00. A state administered certification test is NOT required. Scores on the National Teacher's Examination are NOT required. All initial licenses require Praxis I: PPST scores in Reading, Writing, and Mathematics (or equivalent). The original certificate is valid for 5 years. Wisconsin does NOT belong to the Interstate Certification Compact but has pacts with Iowa, Illinois, Missouri, Kansas, Nebraska, Oklahoma, and South Dakota. A course in Special Education IS required for all teaching certificates. New Licensing rules are in place and effect those applicants completing their education programs after 8/31/2004. See details below.

Renewal Requirements: 5-Year License - All applicants renewing a 5-year license (except substitute teachers and substitute educational interpreters) must have completed continuing education of six semester credits, 180 equivalency clock hours, or a combination of the two. The credits or equivalent must be directly and substantively related to one or more of the licenses held by the applicant or to the applicant's professional competency. Completion of a Professional Development Plan may also be used for renewal. For complete information, contact the Department.

LICENSE TYPES

INITIAL EDUCATOR LICENSE: Valid 5-years; Non renewable, minimum 3 years
An individual who has successfully completed a state-approved educator preparation program after August 31, 2004 and who is issued an Initial Educator License by the Department for the first time in a particular category (Teaching, Pupil Service, Administration). An Initial Educator must develop a Professional Development Plan (PDP) addressing 2 or more Wisconsin standards. A Pre-service portfolio may be used to inform the Initial Educator's development of the PDP. The Initial Educator License may be renewed if the individual has not been employed as an educator for at least 3 yrs. within the 5-year period.

PROFESSIONAL EDUCATOR LICENSE: Valid 5 years; renewable
Requirements: Verification of a Professional Development Plan (PDP) showing growth in 2 or more Wisconsin Educator Standards. A PDP Team must verify completion. Current educators will be grandfathered as professional educators and may renew license using 6 credits or PDP.

MASTER EDUCATOR LICENSE: Voluntary; Valid 10 years; renewable
The Master Educator license is voluntary and offered by completing:
    Completing the Wisconsin Master Educator Assessment Process;
    Completion of a Portfolio, documenting mastery of Wisconsin Educator Standards;
    Demonstration of professional contributions;
    Demonstration of improved student learning;
    Assessed by DPI-trained WMEAP team; and
    A Master's degree

OR
G.   National Board for Professional Teaching Standards Certification

NEW STANDARDS BASED CERTIFICATION REQUIREMENTS

Each defined standard contains three components:
Knowledge (Content) - What the teacher knows
Dispositions (Attitudes)
Performances (Skills) - What the applicant can do

TEACHER CERTIFICATION REQUIREMENTS

To receive a license to teach in Wisconsin, an applicant shall complete an approved program and demonstrate proficient performance in the knowledge, skills and dispositions under all of the following standards:

The teacher understands the central concepts, tools of inquiry, and structures of the discipline(s) he or she teaches and can create learning experiences that make these aspects of subject matter meaningful for students.

The teacher understands how children learn and develop, and can provide learning opportunities that support their intellectual, social, and personal development.

C.   The teacher understands how students differ in their approaches to learning and creates instructional opportunities that are adapted to diverse learners.

D.   The teacher understands and uses a variety of instructional strategies to encourage students 'development of critical thinking, problem solving, and performance skills. 2

E.   The teacher uses an understanding of individual and group motivation and behavior to create a learning environment that encourages positive social interaction, active engagement in learning, and self-motivation.

F.   The teacher uses knowledge of effective verbal, nonverbal, and media communication techniques to foster active inquiry, collaboration, and supportive interaction in the classroom.

G.   The teacher plans instruction based upon knowledge of subject matter, students, the community, and curriculum goals.

H.   The teacher understands and uses formal and informal assessment strategies to evaluate and ensure the continuous intellectual, social, and physical development of the learner.

I.   The teacher is a reflective practitioner who continually evaluates the effects of his/her choices and actions on others (students, parents, and other professionals in the learning community)and who actively seeks out; opportunities to grow professionally.

J.   The teacher fosters relationships with school colleagues, parents, and agencies in the larger community to support students 'learning and well-being.

PUPIL SERVICES CERTIFICATION REQUIREMENTS
Seven Standards for Development and Licensure

To receive a license in a pupil services category in Wisconsin, an applicant shall complete an approved program and demonstrate proficient performance in the knowledge, skills and dispositions under all of the following standards:

The pupil services professional understands the Ten Teacher Standards.
The pupil services professional understands the complexities of learning and knowledge of comprehensive, coordinated practice strategies that support pupil learning, health, safety and development.
The pupil services professional has the ability to use research, research methods and knowledge about issues and trends to improve practice in schools and classrooms.
The pupil services professional understands and represents professional ethics and social behaviors appropriate for school and community.
The pupil services professional understands the organization, development, management and

content of collaborative and mutually supportive pupil services programs within educational settings.

The pupil services professional is able to address comprehensively the wide range of social, emotional, behavioral and physical issues and circumstances which may limit pupils' abilities to achieve positive learning outcomes through development, implementation and evaluation of system-wide interventions and strategies.

The pupil services professional interacts successfully with pupils, parents, professional educators, employers, and community support systems such as juvenile justice, public health, human services and adult education.

ADMINISTRATOR CERTIFICATION REQUIREMENTS
Seven Standards for Administrator Development and Licensure

To receive a license in a school administrator category in Wisconsin, an applicant shall complete an approved program in school administration and demonstrate proficient performance in the knowledge, skills and dispositions under all of the following standards:

The administrator has an understanding of and demonstrates competence in the Ten Teacher Standards.

The administrator leads by facilitating the development, articulation, implementation, and stewardship of a vision of learning that is shared by the school community.

The administrator manages by advocating, nurturing and sustaining a school culture and instructional program conducive to pupil learning and staff professional growth.

The administrator ensures management of the organization, operations, finances, and resources for a safe, efficient, and effective learning environment.

The administrator models collaborating with families and community members, responding to diverse community interests and needs, and mobilizing community resources.

The administrator acts with integrity, fairness, and in an ethical manner.

The administrator understands, responds to, and interacts with the larger political, social, economic, legal, and cultural context that affects schooling.

STATE OF WYOMING

Professional Teaching Standards Board
1920 Thomes Avenue, Suite 400
Cheyenne, Wyoming 82002
Phone: (800) 675-6893 / Phone: (307) 777-6261 / Fax: (307) 777-8718
Email: ptsbtemp@state.wy.us
Web Site: http://ptsb.state.wy.us/certification/applications.cfm

INITIAL REQUIREMENTS AT A GLANCE:

Also needed will be items A, B, C, E, K and O (beginning 9/1/04) - See page 2. The fee is $200 for out-of-state applicants, or $150 for in-state applicants. The fingerprint fee is $50. A state administered certification test is NOT required. Scores on the National Teacher's Examination test are NOT required. The original certificate is valid for five years. Wyoming DOES belong to the NASDTEC Interstate Contract (Teachers, Administrators and Vocational Educators) and maintains direct reciprocity agreements with 19 states. Out-of-state certificates will be recognized if they are current and comparable to a Wyoming certificate. Wyoming requires applicants to demonstrate knowledge of the U.S. Constitution and the Wyoming Constitution either through coursework or an exam. Competencies in Special Education ARE required.

Renewal Requirements: Either 5 post-graduate semester credit hours and/or 75 CEUs every 5 years. Fee: $125.00. Contact the department for complete recertification rules.

Effective 6/1/2007:

Applicants who are issued their 1st five (5) year Wyoming Standard Teaching Certificate on or after June 1, 2007 are "highly qualified" in the area(s) they are endorsed IF their teaching assignment matches their area(s) of endorsement. For these individuals, their standard certificate will serve as evidence of being highly qualified.

Teachers who were issued a certificate prior to June 1, 2007 are required to demonstrate competency in their content area through 1) the HOUSSE rubric OR 2) an approved PRAXIS test.

STANDARD TEACHING CERTIFICATE
(Valid 5 years, Renewable)

A. **Standard Teaching Certificates and Endorsements:**
    1. Pre-School (Age 3 - 5);
    2. Elementary (K - 6);
    3. Middle School (5 - 8);
    4. Secondary (7 - 12); with at least one of the following endorsements:

    Agriculture, Art, Bilingual, Business Education, Classical Language, Computer Science, Drama (Theater), Driver Education, English, English as a Second Language, Exceptional Children Generalist, Home Economics, Industrial Technology, Journalism, Marketing, Mathematics, Modern Foreign Language, Music, Physical Education, Psychology, Science, Social Studies, and Speech.

    5. Grades K - 12, with at least one endorsement.

B. **General Education Requirements:**
    1. Bachelor's Degree from an accredited teacher preparation program;
    2. Recommendation of degree-granting institution verifying program(s), student teaching, grade level(s), subject area(s), and specialization(s);
    3. Coursework in the Constitution of the U.S. and the State of Wyoming;

C. **Professional Education Requirements:** Must include studies in:
    1. Completion of a program that provides a variety of knowledge, skills, and competencies; and
    2. Supervised experiences designed to provide knowledge and competencies required in the teaching profession.

SCHOOL COUNSELOR AND SCHOOL PSYCHOLOGIST ENDORSEMENTS
(Grades K - 12)

School Counselor: The applicant shall satisfy all General and Professional Education requirements and, additionally:
A. Hold a Standard Teaching Certificate;
B. Completion of an approved program meeting all competencies required by Wyoming standards at an advanced level; and
C. Two years successful teaching, school social worker, school psychology, supervisory or administrative experience, **(OR)** three years of comparable experience in a human services setting.

School Psychologist: The applicant shall satisfy all General and Professional Education requirements and, additionally:
A. Completion of an advanced and approved program meeting all competencies required by Wyoming standards; **OR**
B. National Association of School Psychologists certification.

PRINCIPAL ENDORSEMENT
(Grades K - 12)

The applicant shall satisfy all General and Professional Education requirements and, additionally:

171

A. Hold a Standard Teaching Certificate; and
B. Completion of an advanced program in educational administration; and
C. An internship experience in the K - 12 setting; and
D. Three years successful classroom teaching, school social worker, school psychology, supervisory or administrative experience.

SUPERINTENDENT ENDORSEMENT

A. Meet all requirements for the School Principal Endorsement; and
B. Completion of a superintendent program; and
C. Central office, district-wide administrative internship experience in a recognized K - 12 setting; and
D. Successful administrative experience in the K - 12 setting.

INTERSTATE MOBILITY

The *National Association of State Directors of Teacher Education and Certification* (NASDTEC) Interstate Contract (visit http://www.nasdtec.org) facilitates the movement of educators among the states and other jurisdictions that are members of NASDTEC and have signed the Contract. Although there may be conditions applicable to individual jurisdictions, the Contract makes it possible for an educator who completed an approved program or who holds a certificate or license in one jurisdiction to earn a certificate or license in another state or jurisdiction.

If you completed an approved teacher education program or hold a valid teacher's certificate or license in one state and seek certification under the terms of the NASDTEC Interstate Contract, contact the teacher certification/licensure office in the intended receiving state or jurisdiction.

Legend: **T** = Teachers; **S** = Support Personnel; **A** = Administrators; **V** = Vocational Educators

State	Codes	State	Codes	State	Codes
Alabama	T,S,A	Louisiana	T,A,V	Ohio	T*
Alaska	None	Maine	T,S,V	Oklahoma	T,S,A,V
Arizona	T	Maryland	T,S,A,V	Oregon	T*,S*,A*,V*
Arkansas	T,A	Massachusetts	T,S*,A*	Pennsylvania	T*
California	T,A*	Michigan	T*,S*	Puerto Rico	None
Colorado	T,A,S,V*	Minnesota	None	Rhode Island	T,S*,A*,V*
Connecticut	T*,S*,V*	Mississippi	T,A*,S*V*	South Carolina	T,S,A
Delaware	T*,A*,S*	Missouri	T	South Dakota	T,A*,S*,V*
District of Columbia	None	Montana	T,A,V	Tennessee	T,S,A,V
Florida	T*,A*,S*	Nebraska	T*	Texas	T,A,S,V
Georgia	T,S,A,V	Nevada	T,A*	Utah	T,S*,A*,V
Hawaii	T	New Hampshire	T*	Vermont	T*,A*
Idaho	T	New Jersey	T*	Virginia	T,S,A,V
Illinois	T,A,S	New Mexico	T,A*	Washington	T*,S*,A*
Indiana	T,A*,S*	New York	T,S,V	West Virginia	T,S,A,V
Iowa	None	North Carolina	T,S,A,V	Wisconsin	T*
Kansas	T,A,S	North Dakota	T*	Wyoming	T*,S*,A*,V*
Kentucky	T*				

* Certain certification 'route' limitations may apply - contact these states' certification office for details

---

THE NORTHEAST REGIONAL CREDENTIAL

The following states participate in the Northeast Regional Compact (NERC.) All may *issue* and/or *accept* credentials from applicants with a variety of Level One instructional credentials. The current application fee is $125.00. Please check with the individual certification offices to verify any additional requirements, limitations or conditions.

Connecticut	Massachusetts	Rhode Island
Vermont	New Hampshire	Pennsylvania
Maine	New York	District of Columbia

MOINKSA

An agreement between the midwestern states of Missouri, Oklahoma, Iowa, Nebraska, South Dakota, Kansas, and Arkansas. In brief, if you hold a regular teaching license in one of these states, you should be able to accept employment in another participating state expecting that a two-year exchange license/certificate will be issued.

PLEASE NOTE: Final Authority for Issuing a Teaching Certificate Rests with Each of the Individual States

OUR TWENTY-SIXTH YEAR!

This up-to-date reference guide is used in all fifty states and the District of Columbia. Over 4000 Colleges, Schools, Libraries, Business Offices, Placement Offices and Education Departments have this information at their fingertips! *Still the most affordable reference guide of its kind.*

ABSOLUTELY ESSENTIAL FOR EDUCATIONAL INSTITUTIONS, LIBRARIES & CAREER CENTERS!

TEACHER CERTIFICATION REQUIREMENTS – 2008-2009 EDITION

**"HOW AND WHERE TO GET A TEACHING CERTIFICATE
IN ALL FIFTY STATES AND D.C."**

Requirements for elementary, middle, and secondary teachers as well as certification requirements for librarians, counselors, psychologists, principals, and superintendent positions. Each state office is listed with address, phone numbers, web sites and application details.

Your Complete Guide to Certification!
BE PREPARED. DISCOVER WHAT IT TAKES TO CERTIFY.
Certification and re-certification requirements are constantly changing. Are you prepared?

2008-2009 Twenty-Sixth Edition - $35.00 (*$37.45 without Tax Exemption*) - All S&H Included

Standing Order AND Vendor Discounts Are Available

NEW! **Order by Credit Card Using PayPal** (Instructions on Web site shown below)

CALL, FAX, OR USE ORDER FORM BELOW:

ORDER NOW

Attention: _____ Phone: _____

Department: _____ Fax: _____

Institution: _____

Street Address: _____

City, State, Zip: _____ E-Mail: _____

No Copies: _____ Date: _____ P.O. No: _____

Tax Exempt No: _____ Signature: _____

Do Not Write in Space Below

Mail to: Teacher Certification Publications
PO Box 7756
Sebring, Fl. 33872-0113

E-Mail: teachercertification@earthlink.net
Web Site: http://home.earthlink.net/~teachercertification/
Phone: 863-453-4791 / Fax: 863-453-7351